MARY OF OIGNIES

MARY OF OIGNIES

Mother of Salvation

Edited by

Anneke B. Mulder-Bakker

BREPOLS

British Library Cataloguing in Publication Data

Mary of Oignies : mother of salvation. - (Medieval women :
   texts and contexts ; 7)
   1. Mary, of Oignies, 1177-1213 2. Christian saints -
Belgium - Biography - Sources 3. Christian women saints -
Belgium - Biography - Sources 4. Christian communities -
Belgium - History - To 1500 - Sources 5. Belgium - Church
history - Sources
I. Mulder-Bakker, Anneke B.
282'.092

ISBN-13: 9782503517032
ISBN-10: 250351703X

© 2006, Brepols Publishers n.v., Turnhout, Belgium

D/2006/0095/178
ISBN-10: 2-503-51703-X

Printed in the E.U. on acid-free paper

CONTENTS

Part Three: Studies

ACKNOWLEDGEMENTS

Margot King was the very first scholar to draw attention to the 'Desert Mothers' of the Brabant–Liège region from the perspective of women and gender studies. As early as 1981 she was studying the spirituality of these women and started to translate some of their Lives, namely those of Mary of Oignies, Margaret of Ypres, Christina the Astonishing, and Lutgart of Tongeren — every one of them a leading personality among the new devout in the Low Countries of the thirteenth century. She inspired colleagues and friends to translate other Lives and started to publish them in her own company, Peregrina Publishing. We, from the Low Countries, stand in awe that so much has been accomplished across the Atlantic about our 'foremothers'.

Brepols and the board of the series of Medieval Women: Texts and Contexts are very proud that we have been able to follow in her footsteps by re-editing some of the Peregrina editions and completing them with new translations and studies.

As editor of this first volume in this sub-series, it was a privilege and a pleasure to co-operate with Barbara Newman and Constant Mews: the three of us being responsible for these new volumes. I thank them, and also Maryna Mews, the copyeditor, for their ongoing advice and assistance.

ABBREVIATIONS

AASS	*Acta sanctorum* (quoted from the new edition, Brussels–Paris 1868–1925, which has a continuous numbering of all 66 volumes, with month, date, and volume; plus the book and paragraph number of the *Life*).
BUA	Thomas of Cantimpré, *Bonum universale de apibus*, ed. by Georgius Colvenerius (Douai: Bellerus, 1627).
	Der Byen Boeck: De Middelnederlandse ver-talingen van Bonum universale de apibus van Thomas van Cantimpré, ed. by Christina M. Stutvoet-Joanknecht (Amsterdam: VU Uitgevrij, 1990).
CCSL	Corpus Christianorum Series Latina (Turnhout: Brepols, 1954–).
De nat. rerum	Thomas of Cantimpré, *Liber de natura rerum*, editio princeps, ed. by H. Boese (Berlin : De Gruyter, 1973).
DS	*Dictionnaire de spiritualité*, 27 vols (Paris: Beauchesne, 1935–65).
Henriquez	Chrysostomos Henriquez, *Quinque prudentes virgines* (Antwerp: Cnobbaert, 1630).
Hist. fund.	*Historia fundationis venerabilis ecclesiae beati Nicolai Oigniacensis ac ancillae Christi Mariae Oigniacensis*, ed. by Edmond Martène and Ursin Durand in *Veterum scriptorum et monumentorum historicorum*,

dogmaticorum, moralium amplissima collectio, VI (Paris: Montalant, 1729), cols 327–30.

History of the Foundation of the Venerable Church of Blessed Nicholas of Oignies and the Handmaid of Christ Mary of Oignies, trans. by Hugh Feiss OSB.

Hist. Occ.   *The Historia Occidentalis of Jacques de Vitry: A Critical Edition*, ed. by John Frederick Hinnebusch (Fribourg: Fribourg Presse Universitaire, 1972).

Jacques de Vitry, Histoire occidentale, trans. by Gaston Duchet-Suchaux, intro. by Jean Longère (Paris: Cerf, 1997).

LMA   *Lexikon des Mittelalters*, 9 vols (Munich: Lexma, 1980–98).

MB   *Monasticon Belge*, I– (Bruges: Abbaye de Maredsous, 1890–).

Office   'Office liturgique neumé de la bienheureuse Marie d'Oignies à l'abbaye de Villers au xiiiᵉ siècle', ed. by Daniel Missone, *Revue bénédictine*, III (2001), 267–86.

The Liturgical Office of Mary of Oignies by Goswin of Bossut, trans. by Hugh Feiss OSB.

PL   J-P. Migne, *Patrologia cursus completus: Series latina*, 221 vols (Paris: Migne, 1861–64).

RB   *Regula Sancti Benedicti: The Rule of St. Benedict in Latin and English*, ed. by Timothy Fry (Collegeville MN: The Liturgical Press, 1981).

SBO   *Sancti Bernardi Opera*, 8 vols (Rome: Editiones Cistercienses, 1957–77).

VAS   *Vita Aleydis de Scarembecanae* [Alice of Schaarbeek], in Henriquez, pp. 168–98 [Prologue omitted].

Vita Aleydis, in AASS, 11 June, XXIV, 471–77.

VBN   *Vita Beatricis: The Life of Beatrice of Nazareth (1200–1268)* [Beatrice of Tienen], ed. and trans. by

Roger De Ganck (Kalamazoo: Cistercian Pub-lications, 1991).

VCM   Thomas of Cantimpré, *Vita Christinae mirabilis* [Christina the Astonishing], in AASS, 24 July, XXXII, 637–60.

The Life of Christina Mirabilis by Thomas de Cantimpré, trans. by Margot H. King (Toronto: Peregrina, 1986).

VIH   Hugh of Floreffe, *Vita beatae Juettae* [Yvette of Huy], in AASS, 13 January, II, 145–69.

The Life of Yvette of Huy by Hugh of Floreffe, trans. by Jo Ann McNamara (Toronto: Peregrina, 2000).

VIL   *Vita Idae Lewensis* [Ida of Gorsleeuw], in Henriquez, pp. 440–58.

Vita Idae Lewensis, in AASS, 29 October, LXI, 107–24.

VILO   *Vita beatae Idae Lovaniensis* [Ida of Leuven/Louvain], in Henriquez, pp. 289–439.

Vita beatae Idae Lovaniensis, in AASS, 13 April, XI, 156–89.

VIN   *Vita Idae Nivellensis* [Ida of Nivelles], in Henriquez, pp. 197–297 [Incomplete edn].

VJC   *Vita Iulianae Corneliensis* [Juliana of Cornillon], in AASS, 7 April, X, 435–75.

Vita Julianae, ed. and trans. by Jean-Pierre Delville, in *Fête-Dieu (1246–1996) II: Vie de Sainte Julienne de Cornillon* (Louvain-la-Neuve: Université Catholique de Louvain, 1999).

VLA   Thomas of Cantimpré, *Vita S. Lutgardis* [Lutgard of Tongeren/Aywières], in AASS, 16 June, XXIV, 187–209.

The Life of Lutgard of Aywières by Thomas de Cantimpré, trans. by Margot H. King (Toronto: Peregrina, 1987).

VMO   James of Vitry, *Vita Mariae Oigniacensis*, in AASS, 23

June, XXV, 547–72.

The Life of Mary of Oignies by James of Vitry, trans. by Margot H. King.

VMO-ME   'The Lyfe of Seinte Marye of Oegines', ed. by C. Horstmann, in 'Prosalegende: Legende in ms. Douce 114', *Anglia*, 8 (1885), 134–84 [Middle English translation].

VMO-S   Thomas of Cantimpré, *Vita Mariae Oigniacensis, Supplementum*, in AASS, 23 June, XXV, 572–81.

The Supplement to James of Vitry's Life of Mary of Oignies by Thomas of Cantimpré, trans. by Hugh Feiss OSB.

VMY   Thomas of Cantimpré, *Vita Margarete de Ypres*, ed. by G. Meerseman, in 'Les Frères Prêcheurs et le mouvement dévot en Flandres au XIIIᵉ siècle', *Archivum Fratrum Praedicatorum*, 18 (1948), 106–30.

The Life of Margaret of Ypres by Thomas de Cantimpré, trans. by Margot H. King (Toronto: Peregrina, 1990).

Part One: Introduction

GENERAL INTRODUCTION

Anneke B. Mulder-Bakker

M ary of Oignies was born *c.* 1177 into a rich family in Nivelles, a city at the centre of both old monasticism and the new urban spirituality.[1] Her family home was located near the renowned Benedictine abbey where Gertrude of Nivelles, a Merovingian princess from the era of Christianization, was venerated.[2] At that time, Cistercian brothers, who were prototypes for the 'new' monasticism, would also have passed her in the street. Their abbey, established in the time of Bernard of Clairvaux (1146), lay in Villers, about 20 kilometres east of Nivelles. The ascetic spirituality of the monks was a source of inspiration for believers living in the area. As a child, Mary saw the brothers walk by her house and quietly snuck along behind them, 'putting her own feet in the footprints of those lay brothers or monks' (11). Further to the south, Augustinian canons established themselves at Oignies in 1187. The founders of the priory, Giles of Walcourt and his family, lived there in such apostolic spirituality and poverty that their reputation became known even to students in Paris. Mary would retreat to that location in the last years of her life

---

[1] The Latin *Vita Mariae Oigniacensis* was written by James of Vitry [*VMO*] and published in the *Acta sanctorum* [AASS]; a translation of this text by Margot King is included in this collection. In addition, Thomas of Cantimpré wrote a *Supplementum* [*VMO-S*], published in AASS and translated by Hugh Feiss, who also translated the Office of Mary [Office], and previously edited by Misonne, and the *Historia fundationis* [*Hist. fund.*], edited by Martène-Durand. Subsequent references to *VMO* will be indicated in the notes using sigla (see list of abbreviations) followed by book and paragraph number from the AASS edition; this same numbering is used in the translations; quotations from the *VMO* will be indicated with just the paragraph number and will appear in the body of the text.

[2] According to *VMO* 2, 84, there were contacts between the canons of Oignies and Gertrude's abbey.

and there meet James of Vitry, the theologian and future prelate who would write her saint's *Life*. Outside these monastic institutions, beguines were busy forming 'bands of holy women'.[3] According to Thomas of Cantimpré, the second scholar who would write about Mary, there were supposedly one thousand beguines living in and around Nivelles during the thirteenth century.[4] They gave shape to the new spirituality by interpreting it in a non-monastic manner. All of these religious groups attempted, each in their own manner, to realize the ideal of the apostolic life: the *vita apostolica*.

Nivelles itself was a flourishing commercial town with a large number of townsmen living from trade and commerce. Individuals in Mary's circle of family and friends engaging in such activity figure prominently in her life story. One was the merchant who, far from home, suffered terribly from what might well have been a groin hernia. Leaning on a cane, moving with pain and effort, he decided to go back to Mary and ask her for a holy sign — accepting the hair that she pulled from her head to bind up the painful area.[5]

Mary grew up in this world. Through the account of her life that James of Vitry (*c.* 1160/1170–1240)[6] would write after her death in 1213, she would become an icon of the new, non-monastic piety. James used the example of Mary to define and to propagate a new form of secular sainthood. In his eyes, Mary was an exemplary figure, one that he made into an exemplum for others. He wrote his *Life* in *c.* 1215, only a few years after Mary's death. Thomas of Cantimpré added a Supplement to this in *c.* 1230. He placed more emphasis on the thaumaturgical side of Mary, and described the special relationship between Mary and James as well.[7]

---

[3] In *VMO* 1, 3, James speaks of 'multas sanctarum Virginum in diversis locis catervas'.

[4] For a biographical sketch of Thomas, see Hugh Feiss in his introduction to the Supplement in this volume. For beguines in Nivelles: *BUA* 2, 54: 523 (ex. 10). I quote from the edition of the Middle Dutch translation *Der Byen Boeck*, which also has a very good introduction and biographical sketch of Thomas.

[5] *VMO-S* 6.

[6] Recent good biographies of James of Vitry are provided by Jean Longère in *Jacques de Vitry, Histoire occidentale* [*Hist. Occ.*], pp. 7–27; I quote from the *Hist. Occ.* with chapter numbers of the Latin edition along with page numbers from the French translation. Furthermore, see Brenda M. Bolton, 'Faithful to Whom?: Jacques de Vitry and the French Bishops', *Revue Mabillon*, n.s. 9, 70 (1998), 53–72, in particular pp. 53–60; a brief summary of his career is given by Margot King in her introduction to *VMO*, which appears in this volume.

[7] *Hist. fund.* 6 also characterizes Mary as a thaumaturgist: 'In God's name she cured the sick, cleansed lepers, and drove out demons from possessed bodies and, what is more, raised

In James's account, we read that, in her youth, Mary became fascinated with a life devoted to God. He relates the anecdote of the Cistercian brothers who were walking down her street. When grown into adulthood, however, she did not choose the path of a monastic life, as well-bred ladies of previous generations would have done. James does not hint anywhere that she ever wanted to do this. Around 1190 she married John, the son of a rich townsman, and together they designed for themselves a life of prayer, physical labour, and strong asceticism. This led them to abandon their comfortable life for the *vita apostolica*, a life in imitation of the apostles. They decided to live in continence, in a 'spiritual marriage', while serving the poor in a leper colony at Willambroux just outside Nivelles.[8] John's brother Guido was the priest and pastoral leader; the recluse Heldewidis also lived there among other devout men and women. Of course, lepers were living there too, but we do not hear anything about them. Some residents devoted themselves to caring for the lepers, others to teaching and instruction, and still others to prayer and study. We can recognize this lifestyle as an initial phase of a beguinage; the devout experienced their cohabitation as a community of the blessed, a paradise on earth.[9]

Mary and John spent the greatest portion of their adult lives in this community. The liturgical office for Mary's feast day therefore identifies her as Mary 'of Nivelles' and not 'of Oignies' as we tend to do, and sings only about her saintly life in the beguine community. Mary combined personal asceticism with an attention to fellow believers and the dying. She must also have immersed

---

the dead.'

[8] Giles Constable, *The Reformation of the Twelfth Century* (Cambridge: Cambridge University Press, 1996), Chapter 4, emphasizes the great difference between the old notions of the *vita apostolica* in monasteries, in which monks lived (comfortably) without personal possessions in common life, and the new ideas of the apostolic life originating in the twelfth century, in which personal deprivation, personal labour, the virtue of mortification, and apostleship (that is, the performance of pastoral work, preaching, and hearing of confession) is given emphasis. Mary and John adhered to the new ideal.

[9] Office 36: 'Irrigavit Dominus regionem vestram rivulis paradysi'. Compare the *Life of Ida of Nivelles* [*VIN*] 1: 223: 'e diverso tamen nonnullos habet viros in lege Dei timoratos, plurimas virgines Domino devote servientes, quadam etiam piae conversationis inclusas, quae excluso a se toto mundo totas se incluserunt cum Deo, a quo supernae gratiae frequenter pabulo reficientur, ita ut in hac parte idem oppidum quisi quidam paradisus deliciarum esse videatur'. As quoted by Albert d'Haenens, 'Femmes excédentaires et vocation religieuse dans l'ancien diocèse de Liège lors de l'essor urbain (fin du xiiᵉ–début du xiiiᵉ siècle): Le cas d'Ide de Nivelles (1200–1231),' in *Hommages à la Wallonie* [...], ed. by Hervé Hasquin (Brussels: Université libre de Bruxelles, 1981), pp. 217–35 (p. 225).

herself deeply in the Bible and theology, for she was able to articulate her theological insights on her deathbed. She visited places of pilgrimage in the surrounding area, and, as a forerunner of Francis, would have loved to travel around begging and calling people to conversion. But her (clerical?) friends prevented her from doing this.[10]

By living out this life she built up a reputation of being a living saint. With her compelling personality and penetrating eyes, she brought people with whom she came in contact into a state of repentance. In one case, a sceptic met her eyes from some way off and 'suddenly and marvellously he was transformed in attitude [...] he could barely be pulled from the place'.[11] She attracted so many visitors that, at times, she had to flee into the fields. Around 1207, she moved to Oignies. According to James, she made the change out of a desire to be alone with God, which can be interpreted as a turning away from family and fellow townspeople: after all, a true disciple of Christ lives 'as a stranger' far from hearth and home.[12]

The following year, in Oignies, she met James of Vitry, a zealous theologian from Paris. Educated in the circle of Peter the Chanter, James had learned to look beyond the world of the scholastics. He fell under the charm of the pure religiosity in the abbey of St Victor. Becoming vexed about the poorly functioning clergy, he was captivated by the popular preacher Fulk of Neuilly.[13] He saw the need for thorough teaching and preaching, for good pastoral care, and he sought a form of religious practice that was immersed in life. When he heard about the 'ardour of holy religion [...] in the territory of Lotharingia' and perhaps also received word of Mary in Oignies,[14] he decided to bid farewell to the

---

[10] *VMO* 2, 45; 2, 82. Margaret of Ypres begged on behalf of the lepers: *VMY* 22.

[11] *VMO* 1, 39. This is the final long anecdote in Book I; it was obvious to James that she was here displaying her true, saintly nature.

[12] *VMO* 2, 93: 'quae soli Deo vacare cupiebat'; 2, 95: 'Postquam autem de terra sua et de cognatione sua, Domino praecipiente, exivit'.

[13] See John W. Baldwin, *Masters, Princes and Merchants: The Social Views of Peter the Chanter and His Circle*, 2 vols (Princeton: Princeton University Press, 1970). In his *Hist. Occ.* VIII: 88–89, James wrote the following about Peter: 'erat tunc temporis magister Petrus, venerabilis cantor parisiensis, vir potens in opere et in sermone [...] Cepit enim facere et docere, velut "lucerna ardens et lucens"'; on St Victor, a convent for Augustinian canons just like Oignies: *Hist. Occ.* XXIV: 156–59; on Fulk: *Hist. Occ.* VIII: 89–97. I will return to this in the final section.

[14] According to *VMO-S* 1: '[he] heard in Paris the name of [...] Mary of Oignies'; in contrast with *Hist. fund.* 7: James 'came to find out if what he had heard about the devotion

academic world and to convert to evangelical poverty and the apostolic life. Consequently, he came to Oignies and met Mary. A spark must have been immediately ignited between the two. James urged Mary to undertake a more contemplative spirituality removed from the world — according to him, this was the best way in which a saintly woman could choose to live. In her turn, Mary inspired James to preach among the people: he had to develop into an eminent interpreter of Scripture and to turn people away from sin.[15] At her urging, he returned to Paris in order to be ordained as a priest. In 1211, after his ordination, he came back to Oignies, where he held his first sermon in the convent church under Mary's watchful eye.[16]

According to the Supplement written by Thomas of Cantimpré, Mary lived mostly as a recluse in a cell at the convent church.[17] Although she was not officially enclosed, her life as a recluse freed her from normal social relationships and set her apart. James of Vitry observed that 'her manner of life passed beyond the boundaries of human reason and she had been left by herself with some kind of special privilege from God'.[18] Often, she spent the night in church and communed with the saints, whose relics affirmed their actual presence inside the

---

of our earliest days was evident in deeds'; Mary is not explicitly mentioned. See Maria Grazia Calzà, *Dem Weiblichen ist das Verstehen des Göttlichen 'Auf den Leib' geschrieben: Die Begine Maria von Oignies (d. 1213) in der hagiographischen Darstellung Jakobs von Vitry (d. 1240)* (Wurzburg: Ergon, 2000), pp. 35–43. See also Alberto Forni, 'Maestri predicatori, santi moderni e nuova aristocrazia del denaro tra Parigi e Oignies nella prima metà del sec. xiii', in *Culto dei santi, istituzioni e classi sociali in età preindustriale*, ed. by Sofia Boesch Gajano and Lucia Sebastiani (L'Aquila: Japadre, 1984), pp. 457–70.

[15] *VMO-S* 2: Mary urged him 'praedicare populis, revocare animas quas diabolus conabatur auferre'; see also *VMO-S* 26. See Michel Lauwers, 'Entre Béguinisme et Mysticisme: La vie de Marie d'Oignies (d. 1213) de Jacques de Vitry ou la définition d'une sainteté féminine', *Ons Geestelijk Erf*, 66 (1992), 46–69 (pp. 50, 67).

[16] At least, such is reported by Thomas in his *VMO-S* 2. Jean Longère has some doubt about this, partly because Vincent Beauvais indicates that James of Vitry was a priest before 1210, and partly because of James's age; in 1210, he was already forty-five years old: is it possible that he began his church career still later? See *Hist. Occ.* pp. 9–10.

[17] *VMO* 1, 27: 'in cella eius, juxta ecclesiam apud Oignies'; *VMO-S* 13 and 14 mention a window through which she could view the altar.

[18] *VMO* 2, 66: 'praerogativum libertatis'. On the special nature of the reclusive life, see my *Lives of the Anchoresses: The Rise of the Urban Recluse in Medieval Europe* (Philadelphia: University of Pennsylvania Press, 2005).

church building.[19] At the same time, she was included in the circle of women associated with the mother of Prior Giles of Walcourt. The priory must, at least in this initial phase, have been a sort of double monastery, for the Walcourt brothers had established it together with their mother. Later, the female dwellings appear to have been a beguine convent.[20] Furthermore, Mary regularly travelled to pilgrim chapels, especially the chapel of Our Lady of Heigne, on the other side of the Sambre. James was her confessor, her fifth, but only for a short time, as she died early in 1213.

When she felt her death approaching, Mary sang her 'theological testament' for three days. We read, 'She sang about the Holy Trinity, about the Trinity in unity and the unity in Trinity.' She must have sung the same themes as those reportedly sung by Juliana of Cornillon in her liturgy of Corpus Christi. 'She expounded the Holy Scripture [...] and subtly explained many things from the Gospels, the Psalms and the Old and New Testaments which she had never heard interpreted'. Undoubtedly, she would never have heard the Bible 'interpreted' in classes at the university, but she had nevertheless made herself familiar with it. 'She constantly asserted that the blessed Virgin is glorified already in the body' — a doctrine that had, shortly before, been 'seen' by Elisabeth of Schönau and that was evidently shared by Mary. 'She said [...] that the Holy Spirit would be visiting the Church soon and would send holy labourers' — ideas that remind us of Joachim of Fiore.[21] All in all, Mary showed herself to be a proficient theologian, one who was 'well read', to cite the words of James of Vitry, for he states with surprise that Mary knew things 'as if she had seen them written plainly in a book' (101).

It is worth reflecting on this remark a little for it unintentionally gives us a glimpse behind the scenes in James's study. We see how he goes to work on moulding Mary's saintliness. Clearly, she is not regarded as someone who has

---

[19] *VMO* 1, 34; compare 2, 88–89.

[20] *Hist. fund.* 4: Giles 'sold everything which by hereditary right belonged to him in Walcourt and the surrounding area. He took with him his mother and his brothers; his father was already dead', and moved to Oignies; Walter Simons, *Cities of Ladies: Beguine Communities in the Medieval Low Countries, 1200–1565* (Philadelphia: University of Pennsylvania Press, 2001), p. 293.

[21] *VMO* 2, 99. For the liturgy of Juliana, see my *Lives of the Anchoresses*, Chapter 4; on Elisabeth, see Anne L. Clark, *Elisabeth of Schönau: A Twelfth-Century Visionary* (Philadelphia: University of Pennsylvania Press, 1992); for Joachite thought, consult Marjorie Reeves, *The Influence of Prophecy in the Later Middle Ages* (Notre Dame: University of Notre Dame Press, 1993).

read or studied herself, let alone as a person who might display any capacity as a theologian. Nevertheless, James is enough of a historian not to suppress such information when he encounters it. He gives it a slant that suits him.[22]

Thomas of Cantimpré visited the priory of Oignies in 1231 and heard many wondrous tales about Mary, which he wrote down at the request of Prior Giles.[23] The differences in preference and composition between the stories of James and Thomas are striking. Thomas makes Mary into a 'true' thaumaturgical saint, just as he did for Christina the Astonishing at about the same time, and would later do for Lutgard of Tongeren. He more magnanimously attributes to her an active role in pastoral care and allows her to instruct her fellow believers about purgatory. In relating the tale of the above-mentioned pain-ridden Nivelles merchant, Thomas describes how he 'drank in so much grace from just the facial image of her perfection that he experienced completely unclouded self-knowledge and felt the spirit of God miraculously at work in him'. The man confessed his sins (to her?), experienced God's miraculous power through her (by putting a string of her hair in his wound), and allowed himself to be instructed about purgatory.[24] Thomas qualifies Mary as 'prophetissa' and attributes to her the power to discern spirits, 'the greatest of all her miraculous deeds'.[25]

Thomas, too, would study in Paris, and, a generation after James, probably came in contact there with the scholastics discussing the prophetic gifts of religious women, the consequences of decisions taken at the Lateran Council in 1215, and the recently developed ideas about purgatory.[26] If James made Mary into a model of holy life, Thomas made her into a living witness of thaumaturgical holiness. Twenty years after her death, he created her image as a mother of salvation. The above-named merchant 'made his confession and then often returned to the mother of salvation. He grew in virtue, and the grace of God overflowed in him'.[27]

---

[22] See the studies in *Seeing and Knowing: Women and Learning in Medieval Europe 1200–1550*, ed. by Anneke B. Mulder-Bakker (Turnhout: Brepols, 2004). I will return to this subject in the final section.

[23] Giles is, in fact, the witness who reports many of the miracles: *VMO-S* 3, 12–14, 19.

[24] *VMO-S* 4.

[25] 'Prophetissa': *VMO-S* 26; discernment: *VMO-S* 11.

[26] See my *Lives of the Anchoresses*, pp. 93–101; Jacques Le Goff, *La Naissance du Purgatoire* (Paris: Gallimard, 1981); *The Birth of Purgatory*, trans. by Arthur Goldhammer (Chicago: University of Chicago Press, 1984).

[27] *VMO-S* 4.

By the time Thomas wrote these words, James had long left the community of Oignies (1213): he had by then completed a brilliant career in the Universal Church, but had also argued successfully for recognizing the beguines and devout women (*mulieres religiosae*). He did not forget Oignies. When he came back to Liège in 1226 and became suffragan there, he also came to Oignies, and, in 1227, he consecrated five altars. At the same time he consecrated Mary's bones, placed her relics in a shrine, and granted an indulgence to all who came to revere them.[28] At that time, such a liturgical elevation was, in fact, equivalent to a local canonization. It is therefore not surprising that, in the Cistercian abbey in Villers, which maintained very close contacts with devout men and women, an office was written for Mary's feast day in these same years. It was based on liturgical texts about Mary Magdalen. In the opinion of Daniel Misonne, the manuscript's editor, the feast must have been celebrated in the monastery: the manuscript containing a record of it bears the marks of use.[29] Such homage did not, however, develop into an enduring cult.

In his testament, James stipulated that he wanted to be buried in the priory. After studying in Paris, Thomas returned to the Brabant–Liège region and, in following the example of James, in addition to being a learned scholastic, emerged as a renowned preacher and protector of lay spirituality.

Why did Mary of Oignies become an icon of the new spirituality? In what way does she embody anything special? Need we search for this quality in Mary herself and the choices that she made in her life? Should we look to James, the prelate who turned her *Life* into an 'ideological program' that was based on Mary? Or should we look to a combination of the two? We should keep in mind that, on the one hand, there are the *mulieres religiosae* in Brabant–Liège who found their ideas best represented by reform-minded theologians in Paris, followers of Peter the Chanter. On the other hand, there are the theologians who, in practice, discovered in the women what had been missing from the theories in school. Highly educated female theologians (common theologians) emerged as intellectual counterparts to academics (written theologians).[30] And schooled theologians expressed in the language of the Church and in the forms

---

[28] Brenda M. Bolton, '*Vitae Matrum*: A Further Aspect of the *Frauenfrage*', in *Medieval Women*, ed. by Derek Baker, Studies in Church History, Subsidia 1 (Oxford: Blackwell, 1978), pp. 253–73 (p. 271), and her contribution to this volume.

[29] Daniel Misonne in his introduction to the Office, p. 178.

[30] I have introduced and elaborated the concept of 'common theology' in my *Lives of the Anchoresses*, p. 16 and Chapter 7.

of Latin tradition what inspired both the men and the women. They incorporated these ideas into their preaching, into their new pastoral theology, but especially into the saints' Lives that they wrote — about Mary of Oignies, Christina the Astonishing, Yvette of Huy, and Juliana of Cornillon.

Part Two of this volume contains a translation of the *Vita Mariae Oigniacensis* by Margot King, complete with introduction and notes. In addition, Part Two publishes translations of the Supplement and Office by Hugh Feiss, who has also translated the *Historia fundationis*. These texts are similarly provided with introductions and notes. Finally, Part Three comprises two studies, one by Brenda Bolton on the relics and the (lingering) devotion to Mary, and another by Suzan Folkerts about the manuscript tradition of the *Life* in both the Latin and the Dutch vernacular.

Bands of Holy Women

In her living saintliness and exemplary devotion, Mary of Oignies was not alone. In his Prologue, James of Vitry places her in the context of all the devout individuals in the Brabant–Liège region who attempted to live out their devotion to God. He portrays women attempting to lead pious lives while having husbands and children, as individuals who were 'teaching their sons [...] [and] keeping honourable nuptials' (3). Caesarius of Heisterbach, a Cistercian monk who travelled widely throughout the Low Countries, also describes a very distinguished Brabant matron and a 'good woman' living with her, a woman who sent the gift of tears to Abbot Gautier of Villers.[31] They were both married, and yet they were clearly closer to God than even a pious abbot. And there were many others like them. Widows, after the deaths of their husbands, dedicated themselves to God full-time. They 'served the Lord in fasts and prayers, in vigils and manual labour, in tears and entreaties' (3). James also alludes to widows, such as Yvette of Huy, who agreed to be shut up in anchorholds. 'She perceived the sins of many people who had not been absolved through a true confession [...]. As a result of having announced these hidden sins to many people and

---

[31] Caesarius of Heisterbach, *Dialogus miraculorum*, ed. by Joseph Strange (Cologne: Heberle, 1851), II, 20.

inviting them to confess them, she was, after God, the cause of their salvation.'[32] Evidently, this widow, then, was also a mother of salvation.

In addition to married women and widows, there was a third category: virgins who 'clung to their heavenly Bridegroom in poverty and humility and earned a sparse meal with their own hands' (3). Some women were regularly swept away by mystical ecstasies: they were 'rapt outside themselves', sometimes as much as twenty-five times in a single day (7). James sums up the wondrous ecstasies of an entire number of women. He calls to mind such eccentric maidens as Christina the Astonishing, who enacted the pains of hell and purgatory as an example to others, 'so that sometimes she rolled herself in the fire, and sometimes in the winter she remained for lengthy periods in icy water and at other times she was driven to enter the tombs of the dead'. She accompanied souls to purgatory or led them through purgatory into heaven. In the years when James was writing about her, Christina, having become an old woman, was laid to rest: 'she lived in peace and merited grace from the Lord.'[33] In a separate paragraph, he tells how all these women focused a great deal of their devotion on the Eucharist.[34] In brief, a life of fasting and prayer, of manual labour and personal asceticism, the making of confession and worship of the Eucharist, solicitude with their fellow men and women as well as care to protect them from

[32] *VMO* Prologue, 6. James does not identify the woman by name, but we can recognize Yvette in her.

[33] *VMO* Prologue, 8; see *VCM*. It is worth the effort to compare the 'ideology' of James in *VMO* — that is, his literary construction meant to propagate an ideal — with the ideology of Thomas in *VCM*, and to compare both of these with the literary constructions in courtly romance. As for Christina, see the differences in insight between Barbara Newman ['Devout Women and Demoniacs in the World of Thomas of Cantimpré', in *New Trends in Feminine Spirituality: The Holy Women of Liège and their Impact*, ed. by Juliette Dor, Lesley Johnson, and Jocelyn Wogan-Browne (Turnhout: Brepols, 1999), pp. 35–60] and Anneke B. Mulder-Bakker ['The Prime of their Lives: Women and Age, Wisdom and Religious Careers in Northern Europe', in the same collection pp. 215–36 (p. 218).

[34] *VMO* Prologue, 8; see also 2, 72; 2, 91 ('corpus Christi' in the form of a boy).

hellfire,[35] miraculous ecstasies,[36] and weeping, all prove to be the characteristics of the truely devout. Mary possessed these qualities to an exemplary extent.

Many of these women turn out to have been highly educated. Mary always had a psalter within arm's reach, even when she was weaving. Judith Oliver has assembled quite a number of psalters that, according to her, had been owned by beguines. Simons suggests that, in addition to the well-known schools in many beguinages, 'an informal system for lending out manuscripts' must have existed; however, he has not been able to find any evidence of scriptoria. When Dominican clergy came to preach to the regular canons in Cantimpré, their sermons were also attended by beguines. Christina mastered Latin and could interpret the Bible. Mary was also well grounded in the Bible, and, when asked, would explain it to bystanders after a sermon.[37] I will return to this subject in the final section of this introduction.

James called such women '*religiosa*', not religious in the canon-law sense of a nun but in a general sense, such as Makowski defines it: 'according to that definition, devotion, piety, and striving for Christian perfection, a *vita apostolica*, not permanent vows and cloistered spaces, made a woman religious.'[38] In his

[35] See Robert Sweetman, 'Thomas of Cantimpré, *Mulieres Religiosae*, and Purgatorial Piety: Hagiographic *Vitae* and the Beguine "Voice"', in *In a Distinct Voice: Medieval Studies in Honor of Leonard E. Boyle*, ed. by Jacqueline Brown and William P. Stoneman (Notre Dame: Notre Dame University Press, 1997), pp. 606–28.

[36] For James, weeping and the physical display of emotion were signs of true faith. Note Mary's tears: *VMO* 1, 16; 2, 90; the tears of an officiating priest, whom Bolton identifies as James himself: *VMO* 1, 17. At the end of a moving sermon, James himself collapsed in a faint with an effusion of blood, but, quickly recovering, moved the hearts of all who heard him to tears and commitment to Christ. See Bolton, 'Faithful to Whom?', p. 60, note 65.

[37] On the beguines in Cantimpré: *BUA*, pp. 442–43; and on Mary's reading of psalters: *VMO* 1, 25; see also 1, 29 and 2, 102; Judith Oliver, *Gothic Manuscript Illumination in the Diocese of Liège (c. 1250–c. 1300)* (Leuven: Peeters, 1988); Walter Simons, 'Staining the Speech of Things Divine: The Uses of Literacy in Medieval Beguine Communities', in *The Voice of Silence: Women's Literacy in a Men's Church*, ed. by Thérèse de Hemptinne and María Eugenia Góngora (Turnhout: Brepols, 2004), pp. 85–110 (p. 104). *VMO* 2, 68: 'Divinis autem Scripturis prudens discretaque mulier sufficienter instructa erat'; according to James, this is especially to be done by listening to priests and 'circumstantibus etiam de sermone aliqua verba referebat'. See Simons, *Cities of Ladies*, pp. 6–7; my *Lives of the Anchoresses*, pp. 60–62.

[38] Elizabeth Makowski, '*Mulieres Religiosae*, Strictly Speaking: Some Fourteenth-Century Canonical Opinions', *Catholic Historical Review*, 85 (1999), 1–14 (p. 3). James does not use the term, accepted later, of 'beguine'. Thomas does use it; see *VMO-S* 25: 'in humili loco de Oignies inter oves Beghinarum'.

discussions with the pope in 1216 and in later recorded sermons, it can be concluded that James of Vitry preferred to have such women live together in groups as part of a house community in which the women inspired each other in a reciprocal manner.[39] He must have found the life of such a small group of fellow spirits inspiring, as he entered the convent in Oignies himself. However, he also considered that there were practical reasons for women to enter such communities, for instance, in order to avoid too easily becoming playthings for violent men.[40] He did not, however, send them to cloisters.

This is noteworthy, and even more worthy of mention is the fact that James, in his Prologue, never explicitly mentions any monastics. Of course there were many examples of such living at the time. But he does not mention them. Given the programmatic character of his text, this omission must have been made on purpose.[41] Of the more than a dozen holy women known from the Brabant–Liège region in the early thirteenth century, about a half of them were nuns: Lutgard of Tongeren, Ida of Nivelles, Alice of Schaarbeek, Ida of Gorsleeuw, Ida of Louvain, and Catherine of Louvain — all were Cistercian nuns. Informal and independent women devoted to God included Mary of Oignies, Christina the Astonishing of Sint–Truiden, Margaret of Ypres, Yvette of Huy, Elisabeth of Spalbeek, Odilia of Liège, and a generation later, Juliana of Cornillon, and Eve of Saint–Martin, most of whom lived part of their lives as recluses.[42] Why then this exclusive attention to independent religious women in the *Life*? I will come back to this point.

Equally noteworthy is the fact that we depend on clerical authors for information about these women. The women still did not take a pen in hand themselves, or their work has not survived. Female authorship only began to emerge in the second generation: Beatrice of Nazareth, Juliana of Cornillon, and Eve of Saint–Martin, and especially Hadewijch are notable examples.

---

[39] *Lettres de Jacques de Vitry (1160/1170–1240) evêque de Saint-Jean-d'Acre: édition critique*, ed. by R. B. C. Huygens (Leiden: Brill, 1960), p. 74.

[40] James, in his *Second Sermon to the Virgins*; see Brenda M. Bolton, 'Some Thirteenth Century Women in the Low Countries: A Special Case?', *Nederlands Archief voor Kerkgeschiedenis*, 61 (1981), 7–29 (pp. 17–18).

[41] Even in his *Hist. Occ.* a few years later, James hardly deals with any women's convents or nuns, while a large part of the book is devoted to developments in male monasticism.

[42] Most of them are included in Barbara Newman's list of saints' Lives in *Send Me God* [...], trans. by Martinus Cawley, OCSO, with a preface by Barbara Newman (Turnhout: Brepols, 2003), pp. xlviii–xlix.

The religious women in the Brabant–Liège region were not unique.[43] A substantial number of religious women lived outside this area, although they have not attracted similar attention in modern scholarship. I would like to name one (*pars pro toto*), Elizabeth of Thuringia, a woman who, in the later Middle Ages, rivalled all holy mothers of Liège and even blossomed into more of an icon for beguines and hospital sisters than Mary of Oignies or any other Netherlandish woman. She was also known as Elizabeth of Hungary because she came from Hungarian royal stock (1207–31). Married to Landgrave Louis IV of Thuringia–Hesse and mother of three children, she represented *the* role model of the 'secular' saintly wife and mother. Thanks to four of her ladies-in-waiting, who shortly after her death testified before papal inquisitors, we know that Elizabeth 'managed to combine running a royal estate, receiving guests in magnificent dress and accompanying her husband on his travels throughout the country (even when she was pregnant) with personally caring for the poor and the ill, and sleeping on the cold ground as a form of penitentiary devotion'. Her harsh confessor wanted to force her into a 'spiritual marriage' (comparable to what Mary of Oignies actually did), but she refused. She even refused to give up her representative role at court, which she only relinquished after the death of her husband. She then wandered around for a while with her children and her ladies-in-waiting until she established herself in Marburg, where she founded a hospital and devoted herself to the care of the poor and the sick, taking a special interest in the welfare of pregnant women and small children. Emaciated, she died in 1231 at the age of only twenty-four. She was officially canonized in 1235.[44] In the Late Middle Ages, she was far and away the most popular patron saint of hospitals and beguinages, which included many in the Low Countries.

Holy Men

In fact, holy women, those of the female sex, did not represent anything special. They shared the apostolic ideal with men in their region. Modern scholarship has paid even less attention to the latter than to religious women. Just as there

---

[43] In this sense, Bolton ['Some Thirteenth-Century Women'] is correct when she answers 'no' to her question: 'A Special Case?'

[44] Anja Petrakopoulos, 'Sanctity and Motherhood: Elizabeth of Thuringia', in *Sanctity and Motherhood: Holy Mothers in the Middle Ages*, ed. by Anneke B. Mulder-Bakker (New York: Garland, 1995), pp. 259–96.

were many holy women who were not pious nuns, there were, in addition to
monks and Augustinian canons, a substantial number of holy men. They also
enjoyed great popularity in their own time, but have been forgotten in modern
scholarship. Often, especially in the twelfth century, they were hermits, such as
the knight Gerlach of Houthem.[45]

Gerlach (d. 1165), a knight in the retinue of Emperor Frederick Barbarossa,
probably learnt about eremitism in Italy. Back on his own estate in South
Limburg, he established a home for himself in a hollow oak along the traffic
route leading from Cologne to the sea. His intention was not to disappear from
society but to distance himself from his own manner of living, and to convince
his fellow countrymen to convert to the apostolic ideal, just as he had done. He
exemplified penitence and poverty for others, and was always on the go,
summoning people to conversion. Another example is Drogo of Sebourg, the
knight who atoned for his sins by allowing himself to be enclosed in iron bands.
Travelling around as a penitent, he had the habit of quietly listening in the
church building where the local youth were given their lessons. Thus he acquired
his basic religious knowledge and found a suitable way to devote his own life to
God.[46]

As I have demonstrated elsewhere, Gerlach's *Life* was written in 1227. The
author became embroiled in a discussion about Gerlach with an alderman from
Sint–Truiden during a dinner at the local abbey. The alderman poked fun at
Gerlach, his conversion, his ascetic manner of life (he ate bread mixed with ash),
and his so-called virtues.[47] This occurred exactly at the time and in the region in
which we meet the *mulieres religiosae*. The anecdote therefore indicates that the
independent poverty–ideal of laymen and their apostolic zeal was an equally
contentious point of discussion as the religious fervour of women, not only
among the clergy, but also among the citizenry.[48]

---

[45] See Anneke B. Mulder-Bakker, *De Kluizenaar in de Eik: Gerlach van Houthem en zijn
verering* (Hilversum: Verloren, 1995); Herbert Grundmann, 'Zur Vita S. Gerlaci eremitae',
Deutsches Archiv für Erforschung des Mittelalters, 18 (1962), 539–54. In the thirteenth century,
when the Franciscan ideal began to spread, these types of men mostly became mendicants.
Therefore, we are primarily familiar with twelfth-century holy men. There were also male
beguines, known as beghards, whose historical significance still has to be explored.

[46] Life of Drogo of Sebourg, in AASS, 17 April, XI, 437–42.

[47] *Vita Gerlaci* 10, in Mulder-Bakker, *De Kluizenaar*, pp. 164–67.

[48] James remembers this sort of criticism of women in *VMO* Prologue, 4: 'You [ex-bishop
Fulk of Toulouse] have seen and marvelled at those shameless men (indeed you greatly hated

As I concluded in my *Lives of the Anchoresses*,[49] both holy laymen and holy laywomen were devoted messengers of God. Although neither was authorized to preach or hear confession, by living in the midst of humanity they were easily induced to convey God's grace to their fellow human beings. The faithful knew this and flocked to these holy individuals in large numbers. Of the hermit Aybert of Crespin in Flanders–Hainaut (d. 1140), we are told that his cell on an island in the Haine was at times so overrun with believers that it resembled a besieged fortress. The visitors wanted to confess their sins to him, and if they could not press through the crowd they would at times shout out their spiritual anguish *en plein public*.[50] Hagiographers of the thirteenth century are less generous in relating details of this kind about holy women because they no longer fit the Gregorian ideal of the Church. Nevertheless, comparable anecdotes slip out between the lines of their accounts. Mary of Oignies was also beset by many visitors, whereupon she sometimes fled into the fields.

As revealed by the theological testament that Mary sang on her deathbed and by the information that we have about other *mulieres et viri religiosae/i*, an incarnational theology was here taking shape.[51] These people had no interest in abstract reasoning or speculative systems of thought like those occupying most scholastics in Paris; they applied themselves to understanding the Trinity and the significance of the incarnation. Deeply aware of their own human failing,[52] it was

them) who, hostile to all religion, maliciously slandered the religious life of these women.' For that matter, he displays in his *Hist. Occ.* XII that he himself has little idea about the independently living hermits; he only names classical anchorites and monks who had fled the monastery for still greater solitude.

[49] Chapter 7 (pp. 183–84).

[50] For Aybert of Crespin, see Charles Dereine, 'Ermites, reclus et recluses dans l'ancien diocèse de Cambrai entre Scarpe et Haine (1075–1125)', *Revue Bénédictine*, 97 (1987), 289–313 (p. 301–05).

[51] On incarnation theology, see Nicholas Watson, 'Conceptions of the Word: The Mother Tongue and the Incarnation of God', *New Medieval Literatures*, 1 (1997), 85–124, which contains references to older literature; and my *Lives of the Anchoresses*, in which I take a position concerning 'vernacular theology', or, in my terminology, 'common theology'; in addition, see the introduction to *Seeing and Knowing*, ed. by Mulder-Bakker, pp. 1–19. In considering these issues, it is good to realize that religious culture in the Low Countries was essentially different from that in England, where the problem of the 'Lollards' led to extreme reactions from the hierarchy.

[52] In the Lives, a great deal is said about the *poenitentia* of the devoted, generally interpreted in modern scholarship as individual penance for sins that have been personally

vitally important for them to gain insight into the coming of God on earth, Christ's incarnation in the Eucharist, their own redemption, and their future in eternal life. In this light, they meditated on the mysteries of the divinity. This theology was embedded in a strong 'experiential' and visual culture. The faithful experienced salvation by imagining themselves as participants in the events of Christ's life and death, they saw with 'eyes of faith'. They lived out salvation in exempla.

Men and women, clergy and the laity, associated with each other on relatively equal terms. Women gathered sapiential knowledge, as did men.[53] The devout were characterized by practising their faith in the midst of the community. They did not live in the seclusion of a cloister or in the enclosed bulwark of a university. Together with their fellow believers and open-minded clergy, they formed a living community of the faithful, where, in my opinion, the heart of society was beating. We can designate such social structures as 'communities of discourse', informal centres that even included the more charismatically gifted theologians from Paris, who were drawn to the Brabant–Liège region to sit at the feet of the then-living holy women.

Status quaestionis

In his magisterial work *Religiöse Bewegungen im Mittelalter* (1935), the Protestant historian Herbert Grundmann gave an entirely new twist to the study of beguines and religious women, and indeed to the religious ideals of men and

committed (or imagined). *Poenitentia* was, however, the general (canonical) state of lay believers, regardless of their personal situation, and must therefore be understood as insight into the general human state of sin or human failing. This also applies to individual cases. Of Mary, it is stated in *VMO* I, 38: 'Sciebat prudens mulier, primis parentibus post peccatum, et per eos filiis suis, Dominum poenitentiam injunxisse, scilicet, in sudore vultus tui vesceris pane tuo. Unde manibus propriis, quamdiu potuit, laboravit; ut corpus per poenitentiam affligeret, ut indigentibus necessaria ministraret, ut sibi etiam victum et vestitum (utpote quae omnia pro Christo reliquerat) acquireret.'

[53] James of Vitry wrote in a sermon, 'Qui igitur in hac intentione laborant, ut penitentiam a summo sacerdote sibi injunctam faciant, plerumque non minus merentur quam qui tota die in ecclesia cantant, vel de nocte ad matutinas vigilant', quoted by Anneke B. Mulder-Bakker, 'Yvetta of Huy: Mater et Magistra', in *Sanctity and Motherhood*, ed. by eadem, pp. 225–58 (p. 253, note 32).

women.[54] Until then, such research had been dominated by monastics and church historians, people who were primarily interested in the history of their own 'forefathers'. They studied the sources of their own order, the work of their own founder, the new monastic rule that he established, or the pre-history of their own denomination. Women were hardly mentioned by them, unless a scholar, out of local pride, claimed his own city to be the origin of the beguine movement, such as Kurth did for Liège. He found his great opponent in Greven, who sought to locate the origin of this movement in Nivelles, in the circle around Mary of Oignies. As a result, Mary was placed at the centre of this research.

These scholars assumed that the history of the beguines and devout women had to be comparable to that of the monastic male orders and that there must have been a founder and a rule. The possibility that women independent of each other would individually or in groups go to live together in unorganized houses devoted to God (therefore without a founder or rule) was unthinkable. This tendency still has a distorting effect on the study of beguines, although we now know that they did not form any order. For example, Kaspar Elm calls them 'semi-religious', as if the beguines were stuck halfway and never became fully religious.[55] Others still explain the emergence of beguinism as a result of the shortage of 'real' convents, making it necessary for women to 'temporarily' accept life in beguinages. This assumption was not only made by Alcantara Mens in his otherwise brilliant study published in 1947, but more recently by Degler-Spengler, who developed a 'Konversen-these' for the women, and spoke about the 'stopgap solution' furnished by the beguine convent.[56] Only Walter Simons has managed to go beyond this sort of theory. For him beguines were laywomen who did not enjoy any other canonical status than that of the laity: 'In a first

---

[54] Herbert Grundmann, *Religiöse Bewegungen im Mittelalter* (Berlin: Ebering, 1935; 2nd edn, Darmstadt: Wissenschaftliche Buchgesellschaft, 1961); English translation: *Religious Movements in the Middle Ages: The Historical Links Between Heresy, the Mendicant Orders, and the Women's Religious Movement in the Twelfth and Thirteenth Century*, trans. by Steven Rowan (Notre Dame: Notre Dame University Press, 1995).

[55] Kaspar Elm, 'Die Stellung der Frau in Ordenswesen, Semireligiosentum und Häresie zur Zeit der heiligen Elisabeth', in *Sankt Elisabeth, Fürstin, Dienerin, Heilige* (Sigmaringen: Thorbecke, 1981), pp. 7–28.

[56] Alcantara Mens, *Oorsprong en betekenis van de Nederlandse Begijnen- en Begardenbeweging: Vergelijkende studie, xii*–xiii* eeuw* (Antwerp: Standaard Boekhandel, 1947); Brigitte Degler-Spengler, 'Die religiöse Frauenbewegung des Mittelalters. Konversen – Nonnen – Beginen', *Rottenburger Jahrbuch* (1984), 75–88.

period, dating from about 1190 until 1230, beguines gathered informally in loose communities without institutional attachments.' In the ensuing period, beguines began to acquire property as a community, and their community was then often recognized as a formal institution — but by the city and not by the church.[57] Simons also settles the nagging issue of the *Frauenfrage*: were there in effect so many more women than men, and if so, why? During the commercial revolution in Northern Europe (beginning in the twelfth century), many young women moved to the cities because they hoped to find work and the support of like-minded people there. In the beguinages, where they often met family members and friends from their own villages, they were able to find such support groups.[58]

Breaking through older narrow-minded scholarship, Grundmann investigated the shared religious ideals of men and women that had existed in several regions (including the Low Countries, Germany, France, and Italy), and that crossed the boundaries between orders, the distinction between clergy and laity, and indeed even the dividing lines between men and women. His was the first study that gave women their well-earned place in general religious history. Under the ill-starred writing conditions of Germany in the 1930s, the status of the book only began to rise in Europe with the second, strongly enlarged edition of the book in 1961.[59] I still vividly remember how I struggled my way through it while making plans for my master's thesis. This was such different fare from that to which I had been accustomed, and it certainly influenced the direction of my ensuing career.

This does not in any way mean that I then agreed or now agree with all of its fundamental assertions. I have two great objections. By searching for the common denominator of holy men and women in northern and southern

---

[57] Simons, *Cities of Ladies*, pp. 35–36, 48; Martina Wehrli-Johns, 'Das mittelalterliche Beginentum — Religiöse Frauenbewegung oder Sozialidee der Scholastik?', in *Fromme Frauen oder Ketzerinnen?*, ed. by eadem and Claudia Opitz (Freiburg: Herder, 1998), pp. 25–51 (p. 50), sees it somewhat differently: 'Die Entwicklung zum ausgebildeten Beginentum wird man sich vielmehr wie folgt erklären müssen: Auf der Grundlage der neuen Einrichtung der laikalen Büszer "in domibus propriis" schlossen sich zahlreiche alleinstehende Frauen dem "ordo de poenitentia" an.'

[58] Simons, *Cities of Ladies*, and 'The Beguine Movement in the Southern Low Countries: A Reassessment', *Bulletin de l'Institut historique Belge de Rome*, 54 (1989), 63–105. See also Sharon Farmer, 'Down and Out and Female in Thirteenth-Century Paris', *American Historical Review*, 103 (1998), 345–72.

[59] Anglophone historians, who were not capable of reading German, still did not have any knowledge of it, until an English translation appeared, as recently as 1995.

Europe, Grundmann neglected the differences between the two regions. This had adverse consequences for the study of *mulieres religiosae* in the Low Countries. As a matter of course, it was assumed that they were just as powerless and subservient, with as little chance of social agency, as the women in Italy. Mary of Oignies was regarded as an equal to Clare of Assisi, but Clare ended in a cloister under *clausura*, almost without any support from male Franciscans, while Mary, supported by James, became a successful religious leader.

My second objective involves gender. Female scholars in Germany argue that Grundmann's thought-provoking study had the positive effect of making the spirituality of women visible for the first time, but, more negatively, of reducing them to poorly lettered creatures who, on their own or through their confessors, threw their inner feelings onto paper. Grundmann and scholars after him took the words and texts of the women literally: they were emotional heartfelt cries, not well-conceived literary products to be studied as such. Unaware of the gender problem, they did not recognize that the Gregorian Reform and the Lateran Council (1215) had a far-reaching impact, especially on women. It was with these reforms that the clergy began to define their own *corps ecclésiastique* as a separate body: the *sacerdotium*. As Moore concisely summarizes, this and similar activity resulted in 'the creation of a new and cosmopolitan clerical elite, formally defined by ordination but distinguished and united above all by its common Latin culture'.[60] Such a clergy did not tolerate any lay authors making pronouncements about matters of faith, and especially not any women. Women who wanted to do this had to seek out opportunities that did not bring them into difficulty: mystical inspiration from God or the Holy Spirit was one such possibility, against which the clergy could have little to say.[61] Acklin Zimmermann therefore regards their texts neither as emotional cries from the heart nor as specifically mystical outpourings, but rather as theology: 'narrative' theology she calls it. 'Common theology' is the terminology I would use.[62]

---

[60] Robert I. Moore, 'Heresy, Repression, and Social Change in the Age of Gregorian Reform', in *Christendom and its Discontents: Exclusion, Persecution, and Rebellion, 1000–1500*, ed. by Scott L. Waugh and Peter D. Diehl (Cambridge: Cambridge University Press, 1996), pp. 19–46 (p. 39).

[61] See among others Susanne Bürkle, *Literatur im Kloster: Historische Funktion und rhetorische Legitimation frauenmystischer Texte des 14. Jahrhunderts* (Tübingen: Francke, 1999) and studies mentioned there.

[62] Béatrice Acklin Zimmermann, 'Die Nonnenviten als Modell einer narrativen Theologie', in *Deutsche Mystik im abendländischen Zusammenhang*, ed. by Walter Haug and Wolfram

In the decades after Grundmann, his socio-historical approach acquired an increasingly greater following in Europe (as in the group of André Vauchez and Sofia Boesch Gajano in Rome) and North America (Van Engen). Holy men and women were seen less and less as enigmatic figures, persons specially chosen by God and lifted out of history — as they had often been in older studies —— and more as historically comprehensive persons whose inspiration and motives (including those of a religious nature, of course) could be investigated with reference to the social and religious circumstances of their times. In the wake of women and gender studies, the holy mothers of Liège have become the subject of special attention.[63]

Following the brilliant but now outdated research of McDonnell and Mens,[64] and the survey studies of Brenda Bolton, both Vauchez and Lauwers have come out with new theories. Bolton studied the blossoming of female religiosity against the background of monastic developments in the twelfth and thirteenth centuries.[65] She paid special attention to the social, urban context and the issue of the *Frauenfrage*, but still felt that 'the logical outcome ought to have been the creation of a separate female order'.[66] She considered that the institutionalization of female religiosity and ultimate acceptance by the ecclesiastical authorities failed to occur because of unwillingness of the male orders, and perhaps also because of the premature death of Innocent III.

Vauchez, the great expert on the subject of canonization procedures, was the first scholar to address the question why no exemplary devout individuals in the Low Countries were ever canonized: neither Mary, nor any other *mulieres religiosae*, nor any of their male confrères. Comparable virtuosos in Italy were

---

Schneider-Lastin (Tübingen: Niemeyer, 2000), pp. 563–80.

[63] See the informative collected studies in *New Trends*, ed. by Dor and others, and the references it contains.

[64] Ernest W. McDonnell, *The Beguines and Beghards in Medieval Culture, with Special Emphasis on the Belgian Scene* (New Brunswick: Rutgers University Press, 1954); Mens, *Oorsprong en betekenis*.

[65] Brenda M. Bolton, 'Mulieres Sanctae', in *Sanctity and Secularity, The Church and the World*, ed. by Derek Baker, Studies in Church History, 10 (Oxford: Blackwell, 1973), pp. 77–99; see also her 'Some Thirteenth Century Women', and her retractions in 'Thirteenth-Century Religious Women: Further Reflections on the Low Countries "Special Case"', in *New Trends*, ed. by Dor and others, pp. 129–57.

[66] Bolton, 'Mulieres Sanctae', p. 81.

already being honoured during their lives and canonized after their deaths.[67] Netherlandish virtuosos were also regarded as living saints in their lifetimes but usually failed to develop any enduring cults after their deaths, and certainly no requests to canonize them were made to the authorities in Rome. James did not write his *Life* as a piece of evidence intended to spur on such a process. Vauchez argues that James's text, '*ce texte fondateur*', served as a defence for a new genre of religious life and as propaganda for an orthodox feminine way of life against the heretical ideas of the Cathars.[68] Based on a clue provided by James in the Prologue in which the medieval writer explains how he was prompted to write by Fulk, the heresy fighter and former bishop of Toulouse, a great deal of emphasis has subsequently been placed on elements involving the struggle against heresy.[69] However, Vauchez's basic thesis is that this is a new type of hagiography principally intended '*pour faire l'apologie d'un genre de vie religieuse*'. The *Life* is a '*texte fondateur*' because it serves this function.[70]

Lauwers is more concerned with the nature of the new spirituality of which the women provide evidence: their '*sainteté féminine aux allures mystiques*', and the problems that the clergy had with this. He underlines their religious life 'in the world' instead of in a secluded convent, although he continues to view their semi-religious state as a step on the way to a full religious life. He demonstrates how the women were steered in the direction of the contemplative life. For him, the veneration of the Eucharist and the role of pastors and confessors became a focus of attention; the women lived '*une sainteté sous surveillance*'.[71] In Germany,

---

[67] André Vauchez, *La Sainteté en occident aux derniers siècles du moyen âge d'après les procès de canonisation et les documents hagiographiques* (Rome: École française de Rome, 1981); English translation: *Sainthood in the Later Middle Ages*, trans. by Jean Birrell (Cambridge: Cambridge University Press, 1997), pp. 216–18 and passim.

[68] André Vauchez, 'Prosélitisme et action antihérétique en milieu féminin au XIIIᵉsiècle: *La vie de Marie d'Oignies* (d. 1213) par Jacques de Vitry', in *Propagande et Contra-propagande religieuses*, ed. by Jean Marx (Brussels: Éditions de l'Université de Bruxelles, 1987), pp. 95–110.

[69] Iris Geyer, *Maria von Oignies: Eine hochmittelalterliche Mystikerin zwischen Ketzerei und Rechtgläubigkeit* (Frankfurt am Main: Lang, 1992), provides much more information.

[70] Vauchez, 'Prosélitisme', p. 95. Werner Williams-Krapp, 'Literary Genre and Degrees of Saintliness: The Perception of Holiness in Writings by and about Female Mystics', in *The Invention of Saintliness*, ed. by Anneke B. Mulder-Bakker (London: Routledge, 2002), pp. 206–18, argues the same for vernacular Lives in Germany.

[71] Michel Lauwers, 'Expérience béguinale et Récit hagiographique: a propos de la "Vita Mariae Oigniacensis" de Jacques de Vitry (vers 1215)', *Journal des Savants* (1989), 61–103; quotes are from pp. 66, 84; see also his 'Entre béguinisme et mysticisme'; '*Noli me tangere*: Marie

Maria Calzà ventures to subject the *Life* of Mary of Oignies to an entirely different type of research. Influenced by Jungian psychology and adhering to Bynum's thesis that the body is the locus of self-expression, she investigated the '*frauenspezifische Frömmigkeitssprache*' in the text, for which she coined the neologism 'somatophonie'. Unfortunately, the book has not managed to convince me.[72]

In recent years, attention has shifted from the *Vita Mariae* to other writings of James, especially his more than four hundred sermons, including a number of *sermones ad status*, that is, sermons addressed not only to specific categories of believers, clergy and monks, but also to virgins, married couples, and beguines. Although James most likely composed these after he became a cardinal (in 1229), they provide surprising glimpses into his mental world and are, for this reason, worth consulting when interpreting the *Life*.[73]

Book of Life

Why has Mary of Oignies has become an icon of the new spirituality? In what way is there anything special about her? Need we search for this in Mary herself, and in the choices that she made in her life? To be honest, we actually know nothing about Mary's life outside of the interpretations that James and Thomas have given it. There is, consequently, hardly anything that can be said about the 'historical' Mary and her significance. Only now and then can we infer something about Mary herself from the frictions and contradictions evident in James's account. For the rest, we are at the mercy of the prelate, who developed an 'ideological program' that he attached to Mary, as well as a few scattered

Madeleine, Marie d'Oignies et les pénitentes du xiiiᵉ siècle', *Mélanges de l'École française de Rome: Moyen Age*, 104 (1992), 209–68.

[72] Calzà, *Dem Weiblichen*.

[73] To name a few studies that I have consulted: Jessalynn Bird, 'The Religious's Role in a Post-Fourth-Lateran World: Jacques de Vitry's *Sermones ad Status* and *Historia Occidentalis*', in *Medieval Monastic Preaching*, ed. by Carolyn Muessig (Leiden: Brill, 1998), pp. 209–39; *Preacher, Sermons and Audience in the Middle Ages*, ed. by Carolyn Muessig (Leiden: Brill, 2002); and the many editions and introductions by Jean Longère, such as his 'Quatre sermons *ad religiosas* de Jacques de Vitry', in *Les Religieuses en France au xiiiᵉ siècle*, ed. by M. Parisse (Nancy: Presses Universitaires de Nancy, 1985), pp. 215–300; idem, 'Deux sermons de Jacques de Vitry (d. 1240) *Ad servos et ancillas*', in *La Femme au Moyen Âge*, ed. by Michel Rouche and Jean Heuclin (Maubeuge–Paris: Touzot, 1990), pp. 261–96.

interpretations in Thomas's Supplement, the Office, and the *Historia fundationis*. Therefore, I would argue that the convergence of two groups of special personalities, the holy women in the Low Countries and the socially active theologians from Paris, made Mary and the other holy mothers in Liège into what they are.[74]

As James wrote in his *Historia occidentalis* in the 1220s (correctly described by McDonnell as 'a passionate justification of the apostolic life within the ecclesiastical pattern')[75], he was attracted to the moral theology and the harmony of word and deed propagated by Peter the Chanter. Above all, Peter's *Verbum abbreviatum* appears to have influenced James.[76] In Paris, he became a companion of Lothar of Segni (who became Pope Innocent III), as well as Stephen Langton (who later became archbishop of Canterbury), the already-mentioned popular preacher Fulk of Neuilly, as well as two Netherlandish theologians who became dear friends, John of Liro and John of Nivelle, the latter of whom would, just like James, enter the priory of Oignies. Searching and probing, these men attempted to define their position in the Church amidst the intellectual, cultural, and social upheaval of the twelfth and thirteenth centuries.

They did not confine themselves to an intellectual and sophisticated theology in the circle of academics, separate from the common faithful and lacking affective understanding. Peter advocated the salutary effects of a holy apostolic, therefore preaching, manner of life. And Fulk of Neuilly showed how this was to be done. As mentioned above, James wrote lyrically about this popular hero in his *Historia occidentalis*.[77] Fulk was the first to understand that he could never lead his lay followers to eternal life if he, himself, was not thoroughly schooled in the Bible and theology. As a consequence, he carried a wax tablet and stylus to Paris in order to study with Peter the Chanter, and subsequently developed

[74] This is also a principal thesis in my *Lives of the Anchoresses*. In this context, an example from Caesarius of Heisterbach is illustrative. A *mulier religiosa* from Nivelles (who was Mary herself) stated, 'Bonus pastor est Dominus meus Jhesus Christus, boni eciam pastores sunt magister Jacobus [of Vitry], magister Thomas [of Cantimpré], magister Johannes [of Nivelle] et ceteri praedicatores nostri': Caesarius of Heisterbach, *Libri VIII miraculorum*, in *Die Wundergeschichten des Caesarius von Heisterbach*, ed. by Alfons Hilka, 2 vols (Bonn: Hanstein, 1933–37), pp. 128–29; James briefly refers to this same anecdote in *VMO* 2, 70.

[75] McDonnell, *The Beguines and Beghards*, p. 33.

[76] *Hist. Occ.*, especially VIII and IX: 88–100. See note 13, and Calzà, *Dem Weiblichen*, pp. 38–42.

[77] *Hist. Occ.* VIII: 89–97. Fulk even wore armour, just as Gerlach did.

into an inspired popular preacher, endeavouring to '*prêcher de manière simple et accessible ce qu'il avait entendu, à l'adresse de laïcs du commun*'. Learned and ordinary people, high and low — he knew how to move them all. James chuckled that the professors, with their wax tablets and slate pencils, were now filling the benches when Fulk was speaking, in order to learn how things had to be, for this was something new to them. Masters, even good ones, were much too preoccupied with either the satisfaction of their curiosity, '*à seule fin de savoir, ce qui est pure curiosité*', or the parading of their knowledge, '*ce qui est vanité*'.[78] James too struggled with this problem, as he confesses in the *Life* of Mary: 'I was always fearful lest I perhaps fail by giving an imperfect homily. I gathered together many authorities from every source and, when I had collected very many of them, I could talk about almost everything from the top of my head.' Mary had to teach him that this was not an appropriate manner of preaching; that he should choose not to parade his own knowledge but to explain the essential message of God's work in an understandable way. In this respect, she was his 'master' (79).

Mary also revealed to him that (intellectual) understanding was not sufficient in religious life. Salvation had not only to be understood, it also had to be witnessed, represented, and experienced in practice. She herself, anointed by the Holy Spirit, gazed with the eyes of faith, saw through external events and perceived the true meaning. For example, she 'saw' either devils circling the deathbed of a friend (83), or Our Lady (52). She saw the Holy Spirit descending upon a lad who had been baptised; 'she perceived with the eyes of faith the invisible things which God had revealed to her as if they were visible' (71). She felt the approach of saints' feast days, even though she still was not aware of these festivals; she 'celebrated these festive days since they were written in her spiritual consciousness and impressed in her heart as if in a martyrology' (89). She could, therefore, 'read' with the eyes of her heart in the same manner that she could read book learning with the eyes in her head.

On Christmas, she envisioned the baby at the breast of Our Lady. She 'was drawn to him in love as if he had been her own baby. In this way the various feasts took on a new interest according to how he manifested himself and each produced a different state of affective love' (88). In the visual or, more precisely, the experiential culture of the Middle Ages, believers saw salvation 'taking place before their eyes' and felt it experientially. They made it a part of their own world of experience, one involving lived knowledge: *experientia*. This was

---

[78] *Hist. Occ.* VII: 85.

wisdom that encompassed intellectual knowledge and experience so that living and knowing were merged, and reading and experiencing were entangled. It is a phenomenon that is most succinctly expressed by the image of the 'book of life', a metaphor that James regularly uses. He writes, 'When she [Mary] looked more closely into the book of life, she perceived many things in it through the spirit of understanding' (82). She then saw the meaning (of salvation) underlying the history of a person, but also the history of humanity in general. And she subsequently shared it with the people around her, for the sake of their own salvation.

James came to the conclusion that, in this religious world, the common faithful could be models and messengers of salvation and could do just as well in this as clerics and monastics. They were equally capable of serving their fellow men and women as examples and agents of salvation. In his *Historia occidentalis*, he identified lay believers in a similar way as *regulares* belonging to an *ordo* as he did with clergy and monks, although he retreated somewhat from this position later, during his time as cardinal, when he was removed from the sphere of influence of the *mulieres religiosae*. Jessalyn Bird aptly emphasizes the fact that this 'novel emphasis upon one's ability to achieve salvation within one's *ordo*, within the world, rather than being forced to leave it altogether' was nothing less than 'a pastoral revolution'.[79]

James and other well-intentioned socially active pastors were therefore reacting to three things. Firstly, they saw that academic knowledge was not sufficient in this world. Secondly, they recognized that, in the period after the Gregorian Reform and the Lateran Council (1215), the clergy could not substantiate any part of their monopolistic claims. But, thirdly, they were confronted by particularly self-assured women who felt called to provide instruction and pastoral guidance for their fellow believers. These women did not wish to follow the advice of the clergy and to enter a convent. To meet their wishes, reform-minded clergy and laywomen collectively sought forms and theological structures in which the actual activity of women could be made acceptable to the Church and legitimated by it.[80]

---

[79] *Hist. Occ.* 34: 204: 'Non solum hos qui seculo renunciant et transeunt ad religionem regulares iudicamus, sed et omnes Christi fideles, sub evangelica regula domino famulantes et ordinate sub uno summo et supremo abbate viventes, possumus dicere regulares.' Cited by Bird, 'The Religious's Role', p. 224.

[80] Moore, 'Heresy, Repression'; Nicole Bériou, 'The Right of Women to Give Religious Instruction in the Thirteenth Century', in *Women Preachers and Prophets Through Two*

For James, Mary was the embodiment of the new and good Christian.[81] He fell entirely under her spell and identified her as his spiritual mother. He states, 'her external behaviour and appearance manifested the inward state of her mind'. The believers around her 'were spiritually refreshed by her appearance and were stirred to devotion and to tears. Reading the unction of the Spirit in her face as if they were reading from a book, they knew that power came from her' (39). He himself was one of these believers. It is for this reason that he chose her as the case with which to exemplify his new perspective. He turned her, a laywoman, into the living example (*exemplum*) of true religiosity. He made her into both a model of an exemplary manner of life and a proclaimer of a faith (doctrine) that had a salvific effect on fellow believers. He summoned everyone to follow her, both men and women[82] — although it must be added that he certainly warned against adoption of her 'excesses'.[83]

He accordingly divides his *Vita Mariae* into two books. The first book is devoted to Mary's religious practices, elements that can be seen and experienced and that James describes as 'those things that concern the exterior person and externally pertain to the senses'. It is here that Mary's saintly manner of life is portrayed, in which she displays the same qualities as the *mulieres religiosae* in general, albeit to a heroic degree: personal poverty, manual labour, chastity, ascetic behaviour, mystical raptures that are the natural corollary of asceticism, veneration of the Eucharist, and an apostolic attitude towards fellow Christians. Strict obedience to the pastor and confessor was also a part of this, along with great attentiveness to their sermons, of course, and frequent prayer. Her own

---

Millennia of Christianity, ed. by Beverly Mayne Kienzle and Pamela J. Walker (Berkeley: University of California Press, 1998), pp. 134–45, and other studies in this ground-breaking volume.

[81] *VMO* Prologue 9: 'I discovered the fullness of almost all the graces in one precious and surpassingly excellent pearl.'

[82] Vauchez, 'Prosélitisme', and Lauwers, 'Entre Beguinisme et Mysticisme', sees the model of feminine holiness in Mary. This limitation to being a model of saintliness only for women does not appear anywhere in James's text. On one occasion, he explicitly addresses lawyers, therefore men: *VMO* 2, 78. According to *VMO-S* 16, he even sent the *Life* to Cardinal Hugolino of Ostia (Pope Gregory IX) in order to free him from his temptations: 'so take the book about her way of life with you and read it [...] I anticipate that shortly you will sense that you have been relieved of the temptation which keeps you in turmoil'. Manuscript transmission of the *Life* furthermore reveals that it was primarily read in male monasteries, as Folkerts argues in this volume.

[83] *VMO* 1, 12.

holiness radiated out to her fellow worshippers, by means of which her salvation was imparted to them. Book I ends with a visitor's sigh: 'I have received God's power from this holy woman through experience' (39).

The second book, clearly the longer, is concerned with her religious thought, 'the more interior and more subtle things'.[84] This part is composed around the seven gifts of the Spirit from Isaiah II. 2 and Galatians 5. 22. Passing through the lived example of Mary of Oignies, James systematically explains what the gifts of knowledge, counsel, understanding, and wisdom (*scientia, consilium, intellectus,* and *sapientia*) imply, in addition to the fear of the Lord, piety, and perseverance.[85] In the iconography, the seven gifts are often represented as the seven steps to the throne of Solomon, on which Mary, Mother of Heaven and Earth, is seated. Mary herself is seen as the embodiment of the seven gifts. James then makes Mary of Oignies into someone who, following the example of Mary, Mother of God, is in her turn the living incarnation of the seven ways. She lives out the ways of seeing and knowing of which humans, with God's help, can avail themselves.[86] Knowledge is necessary in order to live a virtuous life; counsel allows others to share in these virtues; understanding provides anticipatory insight into heavenly affairs, while wisdom is a rare gift imparted only to the greatest of the faithful, individuals who are permitted a taste of heavenly salvation. James reveals that this can be achieved by means of a person's direct, intimate relationship with God. Of course, he furnishes many examples demonstrating Mary's submission to her confessor–priest. She did precisely what the Church required, but James's description actually demonstrates that Mary, self-willed and opinionated, anointed by the Holy Spirit, in fact travelled her

---

[84] *VMO* I, 41. Compare Geert Grote, the fourteenth-century founder of the Modern Devotion, who visited the charismatic Ruusbroec 'om te siene sine oefeninghe ende wise van buten ende sine leeringhe ende sermone [van binnen]' ('to see his manners and practices from the outside and his teaching and sermons [from the inside]'). Geert Warnar, 'Ruusbroec op bed: Over leefregels en leermeesters in Middelnederlandse teksten', *Tijdschrift voor Nelderlandse Taal- en Letterkunde,* 121 (2005), 117–130 (p. 123).

[85] Isaiah II. 2: 'Spiritus sapientiae et intellectus, spiritus consilii et fortitudinis, spiritus scientiae et pietatis [...] spiritus timoris Domini.' Guibert of Nogent, *De laude Mariae* III, in PL 156, cols 541–42, treats the seven gifts as seven steps to Solomon's throne, on which the Virgin Mary sits.

[86] The Office of Mary's feast day has a similar composition. After 'Hanc educavit spiritus Domini [...] in exemplar praesentium' is sung in a hymn, the two series of nocturnal antiphons (54–66) are followed by the same seven gifts of the Holy Ghost summarized in the *Life.*

own path through life directly to heaven. This is what he portrays to all true believers.

James relates all this using a textual form that strongly deviates from the classic *Life*. It is not without reason that he places his text in the tradition of the *Vitas patrum* of the early Church and the *Dialogues* of Gregory the Great, both documents that consist primarily of exempla. James's *Life* is actually a long string of exempla. It is much less a saint's *Life* intended to promote canonization than a didactic textbook replete with examples, a manner of teaching by graphical illustration or preaching by means of exempla.[87]

An intriguing point of departure for further study relates to the fact that the text, in this way, adopts a form comparable to women's writing. As revealed in recent scholarship on such works as those of Mechthild of Magdeburg, Hadewijch, Beatrice of Nazareth, or Eve of Saint–Martin, such texts often appear, at first sight, to be a random collection of anecdotes. Further examination reveals, however, that each anecdote is in itself an exemplum intended to instruct the reader or listener, and the succession of exempla a treatise of common theology in exemplum form.[88] It appears that Mary and James not only found harmony in their actual religious experience, but they are also closely linked in the written text forms: the *Life* is, in fact, a *Book of Life* for them both.

Research into Mary and her *Life* is far from complete. Indeed, it has merely begun. The source materials published in this collection, together with the introductory essays, are intended to offer the reader a comprehensive companion to Mary for undertaking further study of her and to make it possible for scholars to wander down the new research paths that this volume opens up.

Translated by Robert Olsen

---

[87] *VMO* I, 9: 'ea quae Deus in sanctis modernis in diebus nostris operatur, in publicum posses praedicare'. See Lauwers, 'Expérience béguinale', p. 82.

[88] On this subject, see my *Lives of the Anchoresses*, in which I provide an incentive for such research, or my forthcoming study in *The Book of Life*.

Part Two: Texts

THE LIFE OF MARY OF OIGNIES
BY JAMES OF VITRY

Translated by Margot H. King

INTRODUCTION

This *Life of Mary of Oignies* by Cardinal James of Vitry[1] is, I believe, one of the more important documents in the history of early thirteenth-century spirituality. By means of it, the fame and influence of Mary of Oignies spread throughout Europe and exerted a major influence on Franciscan thought. Whether or not Mary was actually the first beguine will never be known, but it is indisputable that this *Life* is central to an understanding of the beguine movement, a specifically female apostolate which had as its goal a re-creation of the *vita apostolica*[2] within society by those members of the laity who, by reason of their sex, had hitherto been viewed primarily as the recipients of the priestly ministry but never as active agents. The roots of this unprecedented apostolate are shrouded in mystery but what cannot be questioned is that it was primarily as a result of this *Life* and the efforts of its author that the beguine movement became as well known as it did.

---

[1] Hereafter cited as *VMO*. For a complete bibliography and excellent summary of the career and writings of the popular preacher James of Vitry, see Jean Longère, in the French introduction to *Jacques de Vitry, Histoire occidentale* [*Hist. Occ.*], pp. 7–27. See also Walter Simons, 'Jacques de Vitry', in *Dictionary of Literary Biography 208: Literature of the French and Occitan Middle Ages* (Detroit: Bruccoli Clark Layman, 1999), pp. 157–62; John Frederick Hinnebusch in his introduction to the Latin text of the *Hist. Occ.*, pp. x–xiii, 3–15; and Bolton, 'Faithful to Whom?', pp. 53–60.

[2] See M.-D. Chenu, 'Monks, Canons, and Laymen in Search of the Apostolic Life', in *Nature, Man, and Society in the Twelfth Century: Essays on New Theological Perspectives in the Latin West*, trans. by Jerome Taylor and Lester K. Little (Chicago: University of Chicago Press, 1968), pp. 202–38; D. Lapanski, *Evangelical Perfection: An Historical Examination of the Concept in Early Franciscan Sources* (New York: Franciscan Institute, 1981). See now also Constable, *The Reformation of the Twelfth Century*, Chapter 4.

Through the *Life of Mary*, James tried to promote the cause of these holy women to a hierarchy deeply suspicious of all forms of spirituality that did not fit its notions of the divinely ordained concept of female submissiveness. The example of these *mulieres sanctae*, however, made a deep impression on those whose spirituality was not bureaucratic. At its peak, the beguine movement[3] numbered its adherents among the thousands but, despite the efforts of sympathetic churchmen like James of Vitry, it did not receive canonical approbation and continued to operate outside the official Church structure — but within urban structures — until the fourteenth century, when it came under episcopal control. Despite the disregard of subsequent generations of Church historians, its genuine importance can be assessed by the fact that the example of Mary influenced no less a person than St Francis himself who, indeed, had actually begun a pilgrimage to the diocese of Liège in the summer of 1217 to visit these *mulieres sanctae*.[4]

James of Vitry (*c*. 1170–1240) was, above all, a professional churchman. Born into a noble family at Reims, he studied in Paris and, it would appear, came under the influence of the canons of St Victor there. Drawn by the fame of Mary of Oignies, he interrupted his studies and joined the community of Augustinian canons at Oignies in the diocese of Liège.[5] It was she who, in a sense, converted him from an institutional Christian into one who burned with an apostolic zeal. After a brief return to Paris to finish his studies, he was ordained in 1210 and celebrated his first mass in the church of St Nicholas at Oignies in Mary's presence. Although he was her confessor, he confesses that in the spiritual sphere she was master and he disciple. It was she who excited his apostolic enthusiasm and was largely responsible for his success as a preacher.

After Mary's death in 1213 James was commissioned by the papal legate to preach the crusade against the Albigensians in France and in German-speaking Lotharingia. In 1214 he preached the Fifth Crusade in France, again on

---

[3] For beguines, see now Simons, *Cities of Ladies*. The older standard work is McDonnell, *The Beguines and Beghards*.

[4] *Speculum perfectionis seu S. Francisci Assisiensis legenda antiquissima auctore fratre Leone*, 65, ed. by Paul Sabatier (Paris: Fischbacher, 1898), pp. 118–19; André Callebaut, 'Autour de la rencontre à Florence de S. François et du Cardinal Hugolin (en été 1217)', *Archivum Franciscanum historicum*, 19 (1926), 530–58; Alcantara Mens, 'L'Ombrie italienne et l'Ombrie brabançonne: deux courants religieux parallèles d'inspiration commune', *Études Franciscaines*, 17 (1968), 44–47.

[5] See for this also the General Introduction, in particular note 16.

commission. By the end of 1215 he was in Perugia where he was consecrated bishop of Acre in the Holy Land, and that autumn, he took up his duties in the kingdom of Jerusalem. For the next nine years not only did he fulfil his episcopal duties in this see but was also deeply involved in European ecclesiastical and political affairs. After he returned to Italy in 1226, he resigned his office for unknown reasons and returned to Lotharingia. During the summer of 1229 he was made cardinal bishop of Tusculum and spent the remainder of his life as a loyal member of the curia. He died on 1 May 1240.

James's *Life* reflects the deep impression made on him by the charismatic personality of Mary and the other holy women of the diocese of Liège and is a testimony to his personal crusade on their behalf. From his remark that Mary was not yet canonized (*nondum canonizatae*), it must be presumed that he intended it to be used by the Holy See as a document in her canonization process.[6] His failure in this cause may have been the result of his increasing involvement in curial affairs. Thomas of Cantimpré, who wrote a Supplement to the *Life*, laments at James's apparent betrayal of the ideals espoused by his spiritual mother and he rebukes him for having deserted the Liégeois vineyards. Nonetheless, James's crusade on behalf of Mary and the other *mulieres sanctae* was not without lasting fruit, for it was he who provided the channel whereby Francis learned about and was influenced by these Flemish holy women.

The difference between the 1998 edition and the previous one (1990) lies primarily in its notes and in the addition of a bibliography; the translation remains largely untouched. It has been painfully clear to me for some time that the rather superficial — and sometimes fatuous — comments I had made in the first edition (when I did not have access to libraries of the calibre of the Pontifical Institute of Mediaeval Studies and the University of Toronto) simply had to be changed. In the past few years much splendid work has been published on Mary and the *mulieres sanctae* of the diocese of Liège and I would like to acknowledge my indebtedness to, among others, Michel Lauwers, André Vauchez, Walter Simons, Carolyn Muessig, Monica Sandor, Robert Sweetman, and, most recently, Jennifer Carpenter.

I would like to thank Monica Sandor and Judith Oliver for alerting me to errors in the earlier translations, and Kate Galea for not only proof-reading, but also for catching missed biblical citations and, in fact, going through the entire manuscript with a fine-toothed comb. Thanks also are due to the Social Sciences

---

[6] See on this the diverging opinions in the General Introduction and in Bolton's contribution to this volume.

and Humanities Research Council of Canada for granting me the wherewithal by which I was able to spend three months in 1985 in Europe locating manuscripts of the Lives of seven of these *mulieres sanctae* from the diocese of Liège: Mary of Oignies, Christina of Sint-Truiden, Lutgard of Tongeren (Aywières), Alice of Schaarbeek, Ida of Louvain, Ida of Nivelles, and Ida of Gorsleeuw (Léau).

For this new 2006 edition, the revised translation of 1998 is reproduced, and only minor adaptations have been made. Where possible, the editor (Anneke B. Mulder-Bakker) shortened the notes and added references to new publications. The Bollandist division of the *Life* into consecutive chapters and paragraph numbers has been retained, with the Bollandist chapter headings given in italics, alongside the original numbering and headings of each of the two books, divided into thirteen chapters.

PROLOGUE

On the shining sanctity of many women in the diocese of Liège, about just one of whom a Life is written

To Fulk, bishop of Toulouse

1. The Lord instructed his disciples to 'gather up the fragments lest they be lost' (John 6. 12). What does it mean to gather up the fragments after a meal, except to recall to memory the examples[1] of the saints after their death so that the baskets might be filled (cf. John 6. 12; Matthew 14. 20), that is, so that the poor and the little might be refreshed by the examples of the Fathers, 'for the whelps

---

[1] A straightforward translation of exemplum as 'example' is not sufficient. Claude Bremond, Jacques Le Goff, and Jean-Claude Schmitt, *L'Exemplum,* Typologie des sources du Moyen Âge occidental, 40 (Turnhout: Brepols, 1982), pp. 37–38, define the medieval exemplum as 'a brief tale presented as truth and destined to be included in a discourse (usually a sermon) to edify the audience by the utilization of a salutary lesson'. They break down the exemplum into nine elements: 1) its narrative character; 2) its brevity when delivered orally, although in written form it frequently manifests 'une certaine longueur'; 3) its historicity; 4) its subordination to a broader theme; 5) its frequent utilization in a sermon; 6) its persuasive tone and its relation to the rhetorical arts; 7) the relationship between speaker and a particular audience whom the speaker 8) teaches. The exemplum is didactic and derives from pedagogic rhetoric; and 9) its eschatological perspective. Its purpose is not good behaviour nor entertainment nor even the earthly well-being of the listener. Rather, the exemplum is characterized by its emphasis on the last things and by a preoccupation with eternal salvation. Mary, for James, was such an exemplum, a 'living sermon' as Jo Ann McNamara has so happily put it: 'Preaching, except within the community, was generally a task reserved to men. The most direct impact of the saintly woman on the secular public was as a living sermon, a model of the Christian life to be imitated by all', in 'Living Sermons: Consecrated Women and the Conversion of Gaul', in *Peace Weavers*, ed. by John A. Nichols and Lillian Thomas Shank, *Medieval Religious Women*, vol. 2 (Kalamazoo: Cistercian Publications, 1987), pp. 19–37 (p. 32). See also Carolyn Muessig, 'Prophecy and Song: Teaching and Preaching by Medieval Women', in *Women Preachers and Prophets through Two Millennia of Christianity*, ed. by Beverly Mayne Kienzle and Pamela J. Walker (Berkeley: University of California Press, 1998), pp. 146–58. On James's use of exempla, see now also the General Introduction to this volume.

also eat of the crumbs that fall from the table of their masters' (Matthew 15. 27).
It was for this reason that the holy Fathers always had before their eyes the
verdict of the stringent judge concerning the talent that had been entrusted to
them (cf. Matthew 25. 25). They therefore put down in writing the virtues and
the works of the saints who went before them for the use of those coming
afterwards in order to strengthen the faith of the weak, instruct the unlearned,
incite the sluggish, stir up the devout to imitation, and confute the rebellious
and the unfaithful. Although I am passing over countless others, let us look at
the holy Father Jerome. With what toil did he teach the *Lives of the Fathers of
Egypt*,[2] with what diligence did he preserve their memory: with what profit to his
readers did he commit them to writing and gather up wood from different places
so that he might use the material for the fire on the altar of the Lord (cf.
Numbers 15. 32; Jerome 7. 18; Leviticus 6. 12)? With perhaps no less work did the
harpist of the Lord, blessed Gregory the Great, write down the virtues and
examples of the holy Fathers of Italy in one volume of his *Dialogues*:[3] it was as if
he were gathering up the ashes which had been put away in a clean place — that
is, preserved in the pure minds of the faithful — after the sacrifice of many, so
that the feet might be protected, as it were, with shoes by means of the various
examples of the saints: that is to say, were the feet bare when the paschal Lamb
is eaten, they might be harmed by the raw and harsh ropes of teachers. [Reading]
the works of the ancient Fathers [can also be compared to] putting on old
garments because, then [the reader] can be more easily pulled out of the mire like

[2] As Ulla Williams explains in *LMA* VIII: 1765–68, the *Lives of the Desert Fathers*, or in Latin
the *Vitas patrum*, were a compilation of texts that over the centuries grew out of: 1) a book with
long Lives of male saints, such as Athanasius's *Life of Antony* or Jerome's *Life of Paul, the First
Hermit* (about 16 saints' Lives in total), and female saints such as the *Legend of Mary Magdalen*
(about 11 in total); 2) a book with short biographies, taken from the *Historia monachorum* and
other collections; 3) short texts such as exempla, dicts and sayings, and dialogues, called
Apophtegmata in Greek or *Verba seniorum* in Latin. This third part was also handed down as
an independent book in the Middle Ages. Given his preference for exempla and the *Book of
Dialogues* by Gregory, James may in particular have had in mind this third part of the *Vitas
patrum*. The only edition is Heribert Rosweyde, *Vitas patrum* (1613) reprinted in PL 21 and
73–74; partial translation by Benedicta Ward, *The Desert Fathers: Sayings of the Early Christian
Monks* (London: Penguin, 2003); see also William Harmless, *Desert Christians: An Introduction
to the Literature of Early Monasticism* (Oxford: Oxford University Press, 2004), and the General
Introduction.

[3] Gregory the Great, *Dialogues*, trans. by Odo John Zimmerman (Washington: Catholic
University of America Press, 1959).

Jeremiah. In this way, many who are not moved by commands are stirred to action by examples.

2. It was for this reason that when the holy and venerated father, the bishop of Toulouse,[4] was exiled from his own city by the heretics and had come to the countries of Gaul to beg for help against the enemies of the faith, he went as far as the diocese of Liège, drawn as it were by the fragrance and reputation of certain persons, soldiers for God in their true humility. He could not stop admiring the great faith and devotion, in particular of the holy women who venerated the Church of Christ and the sacraments of holy Church with the greatest desire and reverence, but who were almost or completely humiliated and held in contempt in their own regions. He was filled with a great desire that those things that he saw and heard be gathered up, lest they perish.

Therefore, holy father, bishop of Toulouse, or rather of the entire Church of Christ, be aware of this pillar of strength (cf. I Timothy 3. 15). I am speaking to you and have dared to dedicate this little work to you because you, as my teacher, berated me because of my negligence. You know, I repeat, that when you came to our country, it seemed to you that you were in the promised land, for I heard you say how you left Egypt in your own regions and, travelling through the desert, how you found the promised land in the diocese of Liège. When you were in your own regions, you were acquainted with many people

---

[4] Fulk of Toulouse (*c.* 1155–1231), a troubadour of some renown, became a Cistercian at the abbey of Thoronet in Provence in 1195, was elected abbot in 1201, and in 1205, was named bishop of Toulouse. He was an indefatigable and implacable foe of the Albigensian heretics and it was he who fostered St Dominic's mission of preaching the orthodox faith in Languedoc. When Innocent III proclaimed the crusade against the Albigensians on 10 March 1208 he, with the abbot of Cîteaux Arnaud Amaury, provided both spiritual and ecclesiastical support for Simon de Montfort. He created an association called the White Confraternity to combat heresy and usury, burning issues of the thirteenth century. When in 1211 the Toulousans refused to expel Raymond, count of Toulouse, Fulk gave the order that all the clerics leave the city carrying with them the blessed Sacrament. Thus exiled, Fulk roamed about with the armies and in 1212 went to Liège where he preached the crusade and where he observed the 'new' feminine piety exemplified by Mary of Oignies. See R. Lejeune, 'L'évêque de Toulouse: Foulquet de Marseille et la principauté de Liège', in *Mélanges Félix Rousseau: Études sur l'histoire du pays mosan au moyen-âge* (Brussels: La Renaissance du Livre, 1958), pp. 433–48; Brenda M. Bolton, 'Fulk of Toulouse: The Escape that Failed', *Studies in Church History*, 12 (1979), 83–93; John Hine Mundy, *The Repression of Catharism at Toulouse: The Royal Diploma of 1279* (Toronto: Pontifical Institute of Mediaeval Studies, 1985), pp. 18–26.

from our country who had been marked with the cross,[5] who were fervent
against heretics to the faith, wondrously patient in tribulation and overflowing
with the works of mercy. Indeed, as you yourself said to me, you were filled with
wonder by certain women who wept more for a single venial sin than did the
men of your land over a thousand mortal sins. When you came to our regions,
you saw that it was exactly as you had heard. Indeed, you heard so much that
you would hardly have believed it had you not known it by experience and with
the clear-sighted eyes of faith.

3. You saw many bands of holy virgins in different places of the lily gardens
(cf. Song of Songs 6. 1) of the Lord and you rejoiced. They had scorned carnal
enticements for Christ, despised the riches of this world for the love of the
heavenly kingdom, clung to their heavenly Bridegroom in poverty and humility,
and earned a sparse meal with their hands, although their families abounded in
great riches.[6] Forgetful of their people and the home of their father, they
preferred to endure distress and poverty than to abound in riches that had been
wrongly acquired or to remain in danger among worldly pomps. You saw holy
women serving God and you rejoiced. With what zeal did they preserve their
youthful chastity, arming themselves in their honourable resolve by salutary
warnings, so that their only desire was the heavenly Bridegroom. Widows served
the Lord in fasts and prayers, in vigils and in manual labour, in tears and
entreaties. Just as they had previously tried to please their husbands in the flesh,
so now the more did they attempt to please their heavenly Bridegroom in the
spirit. Frequently they recalled to memory the words of the Apostle that the
widow 'that lives in pleasure is dead' (I Timothy 5. 6) and, because holy widows
'share with any of the saints who are in need', they washed the feet of the poor,
'made hospitality their special care' (Romans 12. 13), applied themselves to works

[5] The term *crucesignatus* was used in reference to the Crusades that, in this case clearly refers
to the Albigensian crusade. See Michael Markowski, '*Crucesignatus*: Its Origins and Early
Usage', *Journal of Medieval History*, 19 (1984), 157–65.

[6] Virginity, poverty, labour, and a turning away from family and the world are the very
characteristics that Henrietta Leyser, *Hermits and the New Monasticism: A Study of Religious
Communities in Western Europe, 1000–1150* (London: Macmillan, 1984) has emphasized as the
hallmarks of those whom she calls the 'new hermits'. They are, surely not coincidentally, also
the characteristics of the Desert Fathers and Mothers, especially those called the encratics. The
beguines were thus merely continuing a long ascetic tradition and, as such, Mary could be
called the prototypical thirteenth-century Desert Mother. See on this also the General
Introduction.

of mercy, and promised to bear fruit sixty-fold (cf. Matthew 13. 18).[7] You have seen holy matrons serving the Lord devoutly in marriage and you rejoiced, women teaching their sons in the fear of the Lord, keeping honourable nuptials and 'an undefiled wedding bed' (Hebrews 13. 4), 'giving themselves to prayer for a time and returning afterwards together again in fear of the Lord lest they be tempted by Satan' (I Corinthians 7. 5). Many abstained from licit embraces with the assent of their husbands[8] and, leading a celibate — indeed, an angelic — life, they were so much the more worthy of the crown since they did not burn when put in the fire (cf. I Corinthians 7. 9).

4. You have seen and marvelled at those shameless men (indeed you greatly hated them) who, hostile to all religion, maliciously slandered the religious life of these women and, like mad dogs, railed against customs which were contrary to theirs.[9] And when there was nothing more they could do, they invented new names to use against them, just as the Jews called Christ a Samaritan (John 8. 48) and called Christians Galileans (Acts 2. 7). Do not wonder at this, for the Egyptians hated sheep, malicious men of darkness derided the simplicity of the innocent (cf. Job 12. 4): while these men slandered a life of abstinence, they were eating and drinking. For this reason, when one of St Bernard's holy monks from the abbey called Aulne[10] was in the thick of battle for the Lord and, from his simplicity, was uncertain of what kind these men and women were whom the malicious called new names, he received this answer from the Holy Spirit in prayer: 'They are found firm in faith (cf. Colossians 1. 23) and effective in works.'

---

[7] Except for periods of persecution when martyrs were given the highest place, virgins were said to have borne fruit a hundred-fold, widows sixty-fold, and the married thirty-fold. For James's use of the topos, see Lauwers, 'Entre Béguinisme et Mysticisme', p. 57, and Alberto Forni, 'Giacomo da Vitry, predicatore e "sociologo"', *La Cultura*, 18 (1980), p. 44, cited by Lauwers.

[8] I am grateful to Monica Sandor for having drawn to my attention an error in my original translation. The AASS edition reads 'consensu a liciti amplexibus'. This is clearly a typographical error since all the manuscripts read 'consensu a licitis amplexibus'.

[9] Thomas of Cantimpré refers to these slanders in *VLA* 1, 5: 'May that most vile slanderer blush for shame who said and wrote that those who record the fantastic visions of insignificant women ought to be considered profane. By such slander he wanted to point his finger at the venerable James who wrote the blessed life of the blessed woman Mary of Oignies in an elegant style.' See also *VMO* 1, 10 hereafter.

[10] On 5 December 1147, the Cistercians took over the abbey of Aulne from the Augustinian canons. See *MB* 1: 329–342.

Then that old man united himself to them with such a clinging love that he could not bear it if anyone spoke ill of them in his presence. They bore calumny and persecution with wondrous patience, frequently bringing back to memory the words of Scripture: 'If you had been of the world, the world would love its own' (John 15. 19), and again, 'The servant is not greater than his master; if they have persecuted me, they will persecute you' (John 15. 20).

5. But since it is written 'By their fruits shall you know them' (Matthew 7. 16), it is sufficiently demonstrated that they truly clung to the Lord during the destruction of the city of Liège.[11] Those who could not flee to the churches threw themselves into the river and chose to die rather than to incur harm to their chastity. Some jumped into dung-filled sewers and preferred to be snuffed out in stinking manure than to be despoiled of their virginity. Despite all this, the merciful Bridegroom so deigned to look after his brides that not a single one in such a great multitude was found who suffered either death to her body or harm to her chastity. When one of these holy women was struggling in the river and in great danger, two of the enemy came to her, drew her into their boat and intended to commit vile fornication with her. But what can happen to the chaste among lions, to a lamb among wolves, to a dove among eagles? She preferred to sink again into the river than to be violated. She jumped from the boat into the waves and when the boat sank from the force of her leap, both men were drowned. She, however, managed to reach the shore by the grace of God without harm either to her body or to her soul, since the current was with her.

Marvels piled upon marvels. When a lengthy and intolerable famine prevailed for three years in the kingdom of France and in a large part of the Empire, both in the towns and in the country, men and women were dying everywhere of hunger and those who had been wealthy before were now driven to beg in public and to die of hunger. Despite this, not one among this great multitude of holy women was found in the whole diocese of Liège who was forced either to die of

---

[11] Liège was sacked by armies of Henry I, the Duke of Brabant, on 3–7 May 1212. See Claude Gaier, *Art et organisation militaire dans la principauté de Liège et dans le Comté de Looz au Moyen Age* (Brussels: Palais des Académies, 1968), pp. 254–62.

starvation or to beg publicly,[12] even though they had already given up everything (cf. Matthew 19. 29) for Christ.

But now let us pass down to individual people and individual miracles. I call your holiness as my witness, for you have seen with your own eyes the wondrous workings of God and the distribution of graces (I Corinthians 11. 4) in different people.

6. One woman received such grace from the Lord, as you attested most reliably, that she perceived the sins of many people who had not been absolved through a true confession. As a result of having announced these hidden sins to many people and inviting them to confess them, she was, after God, the cause of their salvation.[13]

You saw other women who were wasting away with such an intimate and wondrous state of love in God that they were faint with desire and who for many years could only rarely rise from their beds. There was no other cause for their sickness except him, since their souls had melted with desire (cf. Song of Songs 5. 6) for him. The more sick they were in body when they were resting

[12] The poverty espoused by the thirteenth-century followers of the *vita apostolica* stood in sharp contrast to the monastic 'poverty' of the period. Up to the eleventh century, the official Church had recognized only two forms of religious life, the priesthood, and religious orders. With the appearance, however, of a heightened lay religious enthusiasm, based on a literal interpretation of the poverty of Christ and his apostles, the Church was faced with a dilemma. It referred to this way of life as *religio stimulata* (feigned religiosity) and, on the basis of I Corinthians 9. 5 ('Have we not power to carry about a woman, a sister, as well as the rest of the apostles and the brethren of the Lord and Cephas?'), was scandalized because women belonged to it. Public begging of course, was the most obvious manifestation of this suspect apostolate. Innocent III (*c.* 1160–1216) finally permitted apostolic poverty as long as its practitioners recognized the validity of the hierarchy and the sacraments. The Franciscans, for whom poverty was absolutely fundamental, were the first new order to emerge from this movement. Although James of Vitry petitioned for the beguines in Rome, they were never able to gain official approbation and were therefore easily suspect, especially if they indulged in the potentially scandalous practice of public begging. For background, see the magisterial studies of Giles Constable, *Three Studies in Medieval Religious and Social Thought* (Cambridge: Cambridge University Press, 1995) and his *The Reformation of the Twelfth Century*; and for an incisive discussion of the ecclesiastical politics underlying James's portrayal of Mary and the *mulieres sanctae* of Liège, see Lauwers, 'Expérience béguinale'.

[13] This could either be Lutgard of Tongeren or Christina of Sint-Truiden both of whom called many to confession of their sins: *VCM* 27, and especially, 4. 44; *VLA* 2. Yvette of Huy is perhaps even more likely: Mulder-Bakker, *Lives of the Anchoresses*, pp. 51–77.

delightfully in the Lord, the more they were comforted in spirit.[14] They cried aloud in their heart[s], although from modesty they pretended it was otherwise: 'Stay me with flowers, compass me about with apples, for I languish with love' (Song of Songs 2. 5).

When the soul of one of these women wondrously and perceptibly melted from the magnitude of love, her bodily cheeks became sunken and wasted away. Indeed from the honeycomb of the many spiritual sweetnesses in her heart, a savour of honey overflowed perceptibly in her mouth, drawing forth sweet tears and maintaining her mind in devotion. She obtained the grace of so many tears that, as often as God was in her heart through thought, a stream of tears flowed from her eyes through devotion, so that the traces of her tears appeared on her cheeks from her habitual weeping. Nevertheless these tears did not leave her head depleted but, rather, they restored her mind with a certain fullness and they wondrously invigorated her body and gladdened the whole city of God with the holy stream of the river (Psalm 45. 5).[15]

7. Others were so rapt outside themselves with such a spirit of inebriation, that they rested in that holy silence throughout almost an entire day, 'while the King was on his couch' (Song of Songs 1. 12); they neither spoke nor were they sensible of anything external to them. The peace of God so overcame and overwhelmed their faculties that not even a loud noise could awaken them nor did they feel any bodily hurt no matter how strongly it was applied.[16]

I saw another who, for almost thirty years, was kept with such zeal by the Bridegroom in the cloister[17] that even if a thousand men had tried to draw her out with their hands, no one could entice her out of her cloister. Many times she

---

[14] James uses the words *spiritus* and *cogitatio* here. Thomas of Cantimpré defines spirit as 'the rational mind' (*mens rationalis*) and it is there that the eye of the soul resides; to it pertains the image (*ymago*) and knowledge (*cognitio*) of God': *De nat. rerum* 2. 7, 1. This seems to be James's meaning, too.

[15] Here James is clearly referring to Mary. See below, *VMO* 1, 18 where she describes, in almost exactly the same words, how her head feels after so many tears.

[16] Literally, 'there was neither voice nor sense in them'.

[17] Compare James's *claustrum* with 'the cloister of the heart' (*claustrum pectoris*) as found in *VBN* 6. On this, see Gerhard Bauer, *Claustrum animae: Untersuchungen zur Geschichte der Metapher vom Herzen als Kloster* (Munich: Fink, 1973).

tried to withdraw while the others were trying to entice her out, but it was in vain for they were quickly overstrained.[18]

I saw another who was rapt outside herself more than twenty-five times in one day and who once, when I was present, was (as I believe) rapt more than seven times. She would remain immobile in whatever posture she was placed until she returned to herself, but she never fell, no matter how far she was bent, for her familiar spirit was holding her up.[19]

Sometimes her hand would hang down immobile in the air in the same position in which it was placed. When she returned to herself, she was filled with such joy that once on a feast day when she was occupied with the direction her thoughts were leading her, she was driven to show her inner joy by a bodily tic

[18] There are similarities between the women described in James's Prologue and the descriptions of the 'freezing' of post-encephalitic patients by Oliver Sacks. Describing one woman, Sacks says, 'Movement would become difficult during a crisis, and her voice would be abnormally soft, and her thoughts seemed to "stick"; she would always experience a "feeling of resistance", a force which opposed movement, speech and thought, during the attack. She would also feel intensely wakeful in each attack, and find it impossible to sleep; as the crises neared their termination, she would start to yawn and become intensely drowsy; the attack would finally end quite suddenly, with restoration of normal movement, speech, and thought (this sudden restoration of normal consciousness Miss D. — a crossword addict — would call "resipiscence")': Oliver Sacks, *Awakenings* (London: Duckworth, 1976; London: Picador, 1982), p. 39. Compare this to *VLA* 2, 10 and the story of a nun possessed by a devil whose 'hands and limbs contracted with an overpowering rigidity and her mouth was closed so firmly that it could not be opened at all, even with a knife'. After Lutgard and Simon of Aulne had prayed for her, however, her limbs 'returned to their original position and, taking food, she was comforted'.

[19] Compare Sacks: 'Mrs Y. will suddenly be arrested like a film in a "freeze-frame". These still-states may last a second or an hour, and cannot be broken by any voluntary action from Mrs Y. herself (indeed such action is impossible and unthinkable at such times. They may cease spontaneously, or with the merest touch or noise from outside, and then Mrs Y. moves immediately again into free-flowing motion/speech/thought)' (pp. 101–02).

and by jumping up and down[20] in the way David had jumped before the ark: 'My heart and my body exult in the true God' (Psalm 83. 3).

8. When some of these women received 'the bread which comes down from heaven' (John 6. 50), they took it not only as refreshment in the heart but also received it in their mouth as a perceptible consolation, 'sweeter than honey and the honeycomb' (Psalm 18. 11).

While the meat of the true Lamb filled them, a wondrous savour overflowed from the palate of the heart to the palate of the body. Some of them ran with such desire after the fragrance (cf. Song of Songs 1. 3) of such a great sacrament that in no way could they endure to be deprived of it; and unless their souls were frequently invigorated by the delights of this meal, they obtained no consolation or rest but utterly wasted away in languor. Let the heretic infidels be ashamed who receive the delights of this food neither in the heart nor with faith. [21]

I knew one of these holy women who, when she violently desired to be refreshed by the meat of the true Lamb, the true Lamb himself could not endure that she languish for a long time but gave himself to her and, thus refreshed, she recovered.[22]

I saw another[23] in whom God worked so wondrously that after she had lain dead for a long time — but before her body was buried in the ground — her soul returned to her body and she lived again. She obtained from the Lord that

---

[20] *Plausu corporali* (lit. a corporeal clapping) refers to something rather more than hand-clapping and it now seems likely to me that it corresponds to what Sacks calls 'tic-disease': Miss A., for instance, would 'have a sudden, spontaneous urge to run, and would be impelled forward in a frenzy of little, stamping steps, which were accompanied by shrill screams, tick-like movements of the arms, and [unlike Mary!] a terrified expression' (p. 146). 'Mrs Y. became excited with the act of clapping, and after about fifteen claps, suddenly switched to an alternation of clapping and slapping her thighs, and then to an alternation of clapping and touching her hands behind her head' (p. 92).

[21] The high esteem in which the Eucharist was held by these women has been frequently emphasized. See especially Caroline W. Bynum *Holy Feast and Holy Fast: The Religious Significance of Food to Medieval Women* (Berkeley: University of California Press, 1987). See now also Miri Rubin, *Corpus Christi: The Eucharist in Late Medieval Culture* (Cambridge: Cambridge University Press, 1991) and Mulder-Bakker, *Lives of the Anchoresses*, pp. 93–117.

[22] Perhaps this was Ida of Leuven. See *VILO* 1, 8.

[23] This was Christina of Sint-Truiden, whose *Life* Thomas of Cantimpré wrote. See *VCM*, now also Barbara Newman, 'Possessed by the Spirit: Devout Women, Demoniacs, and the Apostolic Life in the Thirteenth Century', *Speculum*, 73 (1998), 733–70, and her 'Devout Women and Demoniacs'.

she would endure purgatory, living in this world in her body. It was for this reason that she was afflicted for a long time by the Lord, so that sometimes she rolled herself in the fire, and sometimes in the winter she remained for lengthy periods in icy water and at other times she was driven to enter the tombs of the dead. But after she had performed penance in so many ways, she lived in peace and merited grace from the Lord and many times, rapt in spirit, she led the souls of the dead as far as purgatory, or through purgatory as far as the kingdom of heaven, without any harm to herself.

9. But what need is there to narrate the diverse and wondrous varieties of graces in diverse peoples (cf. I Corinthians 12. 4) when I discovered the fullness of almost all the graces in one precious and surpassingly excellent pearl (cf. Matthew 13. 45)? She shone wondrously among the others like a jewel among other stones; she was like the sun among the stars. It was her reputation less than the reality of the actual fact that especially led you to our country and in your first encounter with her you yourself had wondrous experience of her virtue. You saw the many marvels of her life when she had eaten almost nothing at all for forty days and was awaiting the approach of her death with desire and merriment of mind.[24] With what a disposition of love you asked me, as her intimate friend, to write down her life before she went to the Lord and to entrust to memory many things about her virtues. Indeed you asked me to write not only her life but [the lives] of other holy women in whom the Lord worked wondrously in the country around Liège. Although you said that it was very fitting for you and many others to preach in public against the heretics in your province by means of those contemporary saints in whom God works in our days, yet I did not agree to entrust to writing the virtues and deeds of those who are still alive because they could in no way endure it.

10. But lest I appear to be utterly disobedient to your holiness, I have undertaken the present work aided by your prayers, compelled by your desire, incited by its utility to the many people who will read it. By so doing, I [hope that I] might, with the Apostle, collect twigs with which I might heat myself and others, although I do not doubt that I too will be bitten by the serpent (cf. Acts 28. 3). Paul, however, was not harmed by the viper nor do I greatly fear that I will incur any harm from the bites of detractors. Although 'the sensual man does not perceive these things which are of the Spirit of God' (I Corinthians 2. 14), yet

---

[24] See *VMO* 2, 104.

I will not give up the plan already initiated on account of the sensual envy of many persons since it will be very useful to many others. There are many animal men who do not have the Spirit of God, although they are considered to be prudent among themselves. They do not want to see what they cannot understand by human reasoning.[25] They deride and despise those things that they do not understand. The Apostle spoke against them when he said 'Extinguish not the spirit; despise not prophecies' (I Thessalonians 5. 19, 20). They extinguish the spirit the more it is in them, and they despise prophecies because they scorn spiritual people, thinking them to be either insane or idiots, and they consider prophecies and the revelations of the saints to be fantasies or illusions of sleep. 'The hand of the Lord is not shortened' (Isaiah 59. 1) and there has been no time since the beginning when the Holy Spirit did not work wondrously in his saints (cf. II Thessalonians 1. 10), either openly or secretly. For the oil which descends from the head to the beard, from the beard to the skirt of the garment and from there to the fringe (cf. Psalm 132. 2) is [how the Holy Spirit] will descend to his saints in the last days.

11. We will therefore report in large part what we have seen and know from experience for the honour of God and his servant and for the consolation of the friends of this handmaid of Christ. We will, however, tell only a few things among many, for it is impossible to gather together all the miracles from her life during the many years in which she served the Lord devoutly and faithfully. Scarcely would a day or night pass when she did not have a visitation from God or his angels or from those saints in heaven about whom she almost constantly spoke.

In order that the reader may find more easily what he is looking for among such a variety of things, I have given titles to what follows by means of separate chapter headings. With the help of these chapter headings, the reader, as it were, will be able to recall to his understanding of what follows with keys, so that his spiritual mind will be cleared of all confusion and, as it were, be illumined by flashing stars.

---

[25] Compare *VIH* Prologue, 7: 'animalis homo non percepit ea quae sunt Spiritus Dei'.

BOOK I

Her religious life, and her complete conversion to God

Chapters

Chapter I

Youth, marriage, continence, persecution, and compunction

1. Her childhood

11. There was in the diocese of Liège, in a town called Nivelles, a certain young woman whose name was Mary, as gracious in life as in name. Her parents were not of common stock[26] but even though they abounded in riches and many temporal goods, yet, even from her early childhood, her spirit[27] was never attracted by transitory goods. Cast in this way upon the Lord (cf. I Peter 5. 7) almost from the womb, she never or rarely mixed with those who were playing as is the custom of small girls nor 'did she make herself partaker with them that walked in lightness' (Tobit 3. 17). Rather she kept her soul from the concupiscence and vanity of them all and foreshadowed in her youth what, through a divine sign, she would be in the future in her old age.[28] Wherefore, when she was still young, she would frequently kneel before her bed at night and offer up certain prayers that she had learned to the Lord as the first fruits of her life (cf. Exodus 22. 29).

Thus mercy and righteousness grew in her from her infancy and she loved[29] the religious life as if with a natural affection.[30] For example, it once happened that when some Cistercian brothers were passing in front of her father's house, she glanced up at them and she so admired their religious habit that she followed them stealthily. And when she could do no more, she put her own feet in the footprints of those lay brothers or monks from her great desire.

And when her parents, as is the custom of worldly people, wished to adorn her in delicate and refined clothing, she was saddened and rejected them as if what she had read had impressed itself naturally in her spiritual consciousness,[31]

---

[26] 'Non mediocribus orta parentibus': AASS inserts a *non* absent from the manuscript used by the editors, but it is clear from *VMO* 2, 58 ('a certain knight whose name was Ywain of Zoania who was related to her, noble by birth') that the emendation is correct.

[27] 'Numquam tamen ejus animum bona transitoria ab annis puerilibus allexerunt': *animus* is a very difficult word to translate. One possibility is 'rational consciousness' since it is a parallel to reason which, patristically and medievally speaking, is an active and 'masculine' faculty and contrasts to the passive, 'feminine' soul (*anima*). Here, I choose to translate it as 'inclination', since this word is frequently used in reference to the will and seems to have active overtones.

[28] This is merely a rhetorical device for, in fact, Mary died at the age of thirty-six.

[29] *Diligebat*: in these Lives, *diligo* usually means to love in the natural order, as distinct from divine love. Here, James adds the rider, 'quasi naturali affectione'.

[30] *Naturali affectione*: here not affectivity but the more obvious 'affection'.

[31] 'Acsi naturaliter ejus animo impressum legeretur': while this indicates that, unlike many medieval women, Mary was literate, it also refers to the memory which, according to Mary Carruthers, was conceived of as 'a mental picture' or phantasm which is impressed, like a seal in wax upon the brain; and reading, primarily a visual act whereby 'whatever enters the mind changes into "a see-able" form for storing in memory', in *The Book of Memory: A Study of*

that is to say those things which Peter the apostle had said concerning women: 'Do not dress up for show: doing up your hair, wearing gold bracelets and fine clothes' (I Peter 3. 3), and what Paul the apostle had said: 'Without braided hair or gold and jewellery or expensive clothes' (I Timothy 2. 9). When her parents saw this kind of behaviour, they mocked their little girl and said, 'What kind of person is our daughter going to be?'

II. Her marriage

12. Her parents were indignant when they saw these auspicious deeds and when she was fourteen years old they joined her in marriage to a certain youth.[32] Living apart from her parents, she was now set on fire with such an ecstasy[33] of ardour and punished her body with such warfare that she enslaved it to such a degree that it frequently happened that after she had toiled for a large part of the night with her own hands,[34] she would pray for a lengthy period after she had

---

Memory in Medieval Culture (Cambridge: Cambridge University Press, 1990), pp. 17–18. See, for instance, *VMO* 2, 89 where James describes Mary's foreknowledge of Church feasts 'since they were written in her spiritual consciousness and impressed in her heart as if in a Martyrology'.

[32] This young man whose name was John (*VMO* 1, 13) was the brother of Master Guido, chaplain of the church of Willambroux, concerning whom see notes 106, 107, and 129.

[33] The literal meaning of '*excessus*' is 'to step out of oneself' and usually refers to the state in which one contemplates God, its end being the knowledge of the transcendent divinity. The meaning of '*exstasis*' is slightly different. According to Bernard, it is the state in which 'the soul is cut off from awareness of life though not from life itself': *On the Song of Songs*, 52. 4, in *SBO* I: 92, and trans. by Kilian Walsh and Irene M. Edmonds (Kalamazoo: Cistercian Publications, 1979), p. 52. '*Exitus*' refers to the departure from the shadows of powerlessness and passibility; '*egressus*', like '*alienatio*', to the state in which the soul is distanced from the world; and '*transitus*' to the transformation of the soul beyond the normal bounds of consciousness. See Robert Javelet, 'Extase chez les spirituels du XIIᵉ siècle' in *DS* IV: 2113–30.

[34] James devotes *VMO* 1, 38 to Mary's work with her hands. Although manual labour had been an integral part of the way of life of the Desert Fathers and Mothers and in the Rule of St Benedict, by the later Middle Ages it was little regarded by monastics and was one of the characteristics emphasized by those who wished to restore an apostolic and desert fervour to their lives. See Leyser, *Hermits and the New Monasticism*, p. 56, who quotes the statutes of Fulgentius: 'When the principle of our way of life had been confirmed and the path of the regular life entered upon, we could not discover a more rightful or devout path of salvation than that we should gain nourishment and clothing by the labours of our hands and remain content with these': *Monachorum Afflighemensium et imprimis B. Fulgentii primi coenobii abbatis statutum de decimis rerum omnium in eleemosynas expendendis*, ed. by H. P. Vanderspeeten, *Analecta bollandiana*, 4 (1885), 254, trans. by Leyser. In the *VMO*, it acquires a deeper

finished her work. As often as was licit for her, she passed a very short part of the night in sleep on planks that she had concealed at the foot of her bed. And because she clearly did not have power over her own body, she secretly wore a very rough cord under her clothing that she bound with great force.

I do not say these things to commend the excess but so that I might show her fervour. In these and in many other things wherein the privilege of grace operated, let the discreet reader pay attention that what is a privilege for a few does not make a common law. Let us imitate her virtues but we cannot imitate the works of her virtues without individual privilege. Although the body be forced to serve the spirit (cf. Romans 7. 25) and although we ought 'to carry the wounds of the Lord Jesus Christ in our body' (Galatians 6. 17), yet we know that 'the honour of the King loves justice' (Psalm 98. 4) and sacrifice from the robbery of the poor is not pleasing to the Lord (cf. Isaiah 61. 8). Necessary things are not to be taken from the poverty of the flesh, although vices are to be checked. Therefore, admire rather than imitate what we have read about the things certain saints have done through the familiar counsel of the Holy Spirit.

III. The conversion of her husband and how they, renouncing everything, lived chastely

13. And after she had lived in marriage with her husband, John, in this fashion for a short time, the Lord looked on the humility of his handmaid and hearkened to the tears of the suppliant, and John, who previously had had Mary as his spouse, was inspired to entrust her to the protection of God. The Lord entrusted a chaste handmaid to a chaste man: he left her a faithful provider so that she might be comforted by the presence of a protector and thereby serve the Lord more freely. And John, who formerly had acted with a certain natural sweetness of spirit, did not oppose the holy plan of his wife (as is the custom of other men), but he suffered with her and bore with her labours good-naturedly enough. He was visited by the Lord and he not only promised to live a celibate and truly angelic life in continence, but also promised to imitate his companion in her holy plan and in her holy ascetic life by giving up everything to the poor for Christ.[35]

significance as the prime weapon against the temptation of 'acedia'. See also below, notes 56 and 58.

[35] See now Dyan Elliott, *Spiritual Marriage: Sexual Abstinence in Medieval Wedlock* (Princeton: Princeton University Press, 1993).

14. The further he [John] was separated from her in carnal love, so much the more closely was he joined to her by the knot of spiritual matrimony through natural love.[36] For this reason the Lord later appeared to his handmaid[37] in a vision and promised that he would repay her in heaven in reparation for the marriage and for her partner who, through love of chastity, had withdrawn himself from carnal commerce on earth.

Let the unhappy men blush and tremble who befoul themselves outside marriage with illicit comminglings, when these two blessed young people abstained from licit embraces for the Lord and overcame the intensity of fervid adolescence with the fervour of an ascetic life. They extinguished fire with fire and deserved triumphal crowns. The Lord gave them a place in his house, within his walls, and a name better than sons and daughters while, like the blessed martyrs, they pierced their flesh with the nails of the fear of the Lord. They did not burn in the fire but immolated their self-will even while they were close to an abundance of sexual delights. Although near a river, they thirsted and in the midst of banquets, they hungered. Indeed, they utterly degraded themselves for the Lord, when they, for a time, laboured in a place called Willambroux near Nivelles for the sake of the Lord.[38]

IV. The contempt and persecution by her relatives

15. Demons looked at them and regarded them with malice. Worldly people, as well as their own relatives, looked at them and gnashed their teeth against the persons whom they had honoured before when they were wealthy. The persons made poor for Christ's sake were now condemned and mocked. They were accounted vile and degraded for the Lord's sake and 'the reproaches of their accusers fell' (Psalm 68. 10) on them for the sake of the Lord.

[36] Such are the difficulties of translating words like these: *'affectu carnali'* (carnal affectivity); *'dilectionem'* (the natural love spoken of in note 29).

[37] *'Ancillae suae'*: this is a hagiographical commonplace. See Michael Goodich, *'Ancilla Dei*: The Servant as Saint in the Late Middle Ages', in *Women of the Medieval World: Essays in Honor of John N. Mundy*, ed. by Julius Kirshner and Suzanne F. Wemple (Oxford: Blackwell, 1985), pp. 119–36.

[38] For Willambroux and the *leprosarium* where Mary and John served the poor, see Jules Tarlier and Alphonse Wauters, *La Belgique ancienne et moderne: géographie et histoire des communes belges*, 4 vols (Brussels: [n. pub], 1873–87), I, 158, see also Simons, *Cities of Ladies*, App. I, 81, 99, p. 293. On thirteenth-century attitudes towards lepers, see *Voluntate Dei leprosus: les lépreux entre conversion et exclusion au XIIème siècle*, ed. by Nicole Bériou and François-Olivier Touati (Spoleto: Centro italiano di studi sull'alto medioevo, 1991).

Do not fear, O handmaid of Christ, to put aside worldly joy and honour, to approach the persecutions of the cross with your Christ, your Bridegroom. It is good for you 'to be abject in the house of the Lord, better than to dwell in the tabernacles of sinners' (Psalm 83. 11). You have lost the favour of relatives, but you have found the favour of Christ. Indeed, you did not lose the favour of relatives since they loved only your goods and never loved you. For as flies follow honey and wolves follow carrion, so did this crowd follow its prey that is not a man.

'You are good, Lord, to those who hope in you' (Lamentations 3. 25). You are true to those who wait on you. Your handmaid condemned the kingdom of the world and all its adornments for your love. You indeed gave back to her a hundred-fold[39] in this world and life eternal in the future world. Let us then consider your precious friend whom you embellished with so many gems of the virtues like a solid gold vase that is ornamented with every precious stone. With how many miracles have you decorated her, she who has been degraded and mocked by worldly people!

v. Her compunction and tears

16. Your cross and your Passion marked the beginning of her conversion to you, the first fruits of love.[40] She 'heard you hearing and was afraid' (Hebrews 3. 2); she 'considered your works' (Ecclesiastes 7. 14) and feared.[41] One day, already chosen by you, she was visited by you and she considered the benefits that you had generously shown forth in the flesh to humanity. She found such grace of compunction therein that a great abundance of tears[42] was pressed out

---

[39] Although Mary was married, she was neither a widow nor a wife bound by the obligations of the marital bed. It is presumably for this reason that James bestows on her the rank of a virgin. See above note 6.

[40] *Dilectionis*: her human love.

[41] The beginning of Mary's conversion in Book I is the fear that arose from her meditation upon the Passion. This is parallelled in Book II, where *the 'timor Domini'* is the first gift of the Holy Spirit, see *VMO* 2, 42.

[42] Within the monastic tradition, compunction was highly esteemed. Its roots go back to the Egyptian and Syrian deserts and it was considered to be an infused gift of God. True compunction as an interior grace occasioned an awareness of one's unworthiness before God and remembrance of sin, accompanied by tears. See Sandra McEntire, *The Doctrine of Compunction in Medieval England: Holy Tears* (Lewiston NY: Edwin Mellen Press, 1990), p. 38; P. Adnès, 'Larmes', in *DS* IX: 287–303; J. de Guibert, 'La componction du coeur', *Revue d'ascétique et de mystique*, 59 (1934), 225–40. Much valuable work has been done on the subject

by the wine-press of your cross in the Passion, and her tears flowed so copiously on the floor, that the ground in the church became muddy with her footprints. Wherefore, for a long time after this visitation she could neither gaze at an image of the cross, nor speak, nor hear other people speaking about the Passion of Christ, without falling into ecstasy through a defect of the heart. Therefore she sometimes moderated her sorrow and restrained the flood of her tears and, disregarding Christ's humanity, would raise her consciousness to his divinity and majesty so that she might therein find consolation in his impassibility. But when she tried to restrain the intensity of the flowing river, then a greater intensity of tears wondrously sprang forth. When she directed her attention to how great he was who had endured such degradation for us, her sorrow was renewed and new tears were revived in her soul through her sweet compunction.

17. One day, just before Good Friday, when the Passion of Christ was approaching, she began to offer herself as a sacrifice with the Lord in even greater showers of tears and with sighs and gasps. One of the priests of the church softly but firmly exhorted her to pray in silence and to restrain her tears. She was always timid and, with the simplicity of a dove, tried to obey in all things but, conscious of the impossibility of this thing, she slipped out of the church unknown to him and hid herself in a secret place which was removed from everyone. There she tearfully implored the Lord that he show this priest that it is not in man's power to restrain the intensity of tears when the waters flow with the vehemence of the blowing spirit (cf. Psalm 147. 18; Exodus 14. 21).

Then, when the priest celebrated mass that day, 'the Lord opened and none shut' (Isaiah 22. 22) and 'he sent forth waters and they overturned the earth' (Job 12. 15). His spirit was drowned in such a flood of tears that he almost suffocated, and as much as he tried to repress its intensity, by that much the more was he drenched with his tears and the book and the altar cloths were dripping as well. What could he do, he who had been so thoughtless, he who had rebuked the handmaid of Christ? To his chagrin, he learned through experience what he previously had not wanted to know because of [a lack of] humility and compassion. After much sobbing and stammering in a faltering and disordered fashion, he barely escaped disaster. Someone who saw this and who knew the

from an Eastern Orthodox perspective, notably Irénée Hausherr, *Penthos: The Doctrine of Compunction in the Christian East* (Kalamazoo: Cistercian Publications, 1982). For a modern approach to this ancient tradition, see Maggie Ross, *The Fountain and the Furnace: The Way of Tears and Fire* (New York: Paulist Press, 1987).

priest personally has borne witness to this. Long after mass had ended, the handmaid of Christ returned and, speaking in a wondrous manner as if she had been present, reproachfully told the priest what had happened. 'Now', she said, 'You have learned from experience that it is not in man's power to restrain the intensity of the spirit when the south wind blows'.

18. Both day and night her eyes continuously brought forth outpourings of the waters that fell not only on her cheeks but also on the church floor, and lest her tears make the ground all muddy, she caught them in the veil with which she covered her head. She used up so many veils in this manner that she often had to change her wet veil for a dry one. While suffering in disposition, after long fasts, after many vigils, after great floods of tears, I asked whether she felt any injury or pain on her enfeebled head (as was often the case). These tears, she said, are my refreshment, they are my bread day and night. They do not afflict the head, but nourish the mind; they twist without pain, but refresh the soul with a kind of serenity; they do not empty the braid, but fill the soul to the full, and soothe it with a kind of smooth ointment; they are not extracted through violence, but are delivered freely by the Lord.

Chapter II

Confession, satisfaction, fasting

VI. Her confession

19. Now, after her compunction, let us look briefly at her confession. I call God as my witness that I was never able to perceive a single mortal sin in all her life or in anything that she said. If sometimes it seemed to her that she had committed a little venial sin, she would present herself to the priest with such sorrow of heart, with such timidity and shame, and with such contrition that she was often compelled to shout aloud from her intense anxiety of heart, like a woman in the throes of childbirth. Although she guarded herself against small and venial sins, it often happened that after a fortnight she could not detect even one disordered thought in her heart.[43] Since it is a habit of good minds to recognize a sin where there is none, she often flew to the feet of priests and made

---

[43] For the medievals, thought (or memory) was located in the heart. See Carruthers, *The Book of Memory*, pp. 48–49.

her confession and never stopped accusing herself. We could barely restrain from smiling when she remembered something she had idly said in her youth, for example some words she had uttered in her childhood.

20. After she had purged herself of childish things, she took great pains to guard her soul with much fear, her senses with much diligence, and her heart with much purity, and she always had before her eyes [the words of Scripture], 'he who fails in little things falls little by little' (Sirach 19. 1). We never or rarely were able to notice in her any idle word, any disordered mannerism, any dishonourable habit of body, or any immoderate look. She did not manifest any indecorous or disordered movement of the body, even though she often could scarcely contain herself from the immense joy of her heart. Sometimes she was so exhilarated that the jubilation of her heart was forced to show itself — with perhaps a tiny bit of excess — on her face and in her bodily movements, and sometimes she would burst forth into modest smilings from the serenity of her heart. Sometimes she would even receive some of her friends who had come to her with a small shamefaced embrace or, from the intensity of her devotion, she would kiss the hands and feet of certain priests. Yet when she had returned to herself after a kind of mental inebriation, she would count up all her actions very strictly and weigh them carefully at vespers to see if she had been excessive in any small way and, making her confession with an admirable contrition of heart, she would punish herself and frequently would tremble with fear where there was [no occasion for] fear. It was only for this that we sometimes reprimanded her, but we did this because we were looking for some consolation for our own sloth, since she would confess the small sins that we mentioned above more frequently than we would have wished.

VII. Her penance and satisfaction

21. Now after her confession we will add how much and how wondrously she offered her body in sacrifice to the Lord and with what great love and wondrous delight[44] she was tortured in body by embracing the cross of Christ. Let us first look at that first lesson of the school of Jesus Christ, that first text of the teaching of the evangelist: 'Who wishes to come after me, let him renounce himself and take up his cross and follow me' (Luke 9. 23). She frequently turned these words over in her heart and took pains to follow Christ in these three steps. Not only

---

[44] 'Quantaque dilectione et mirabilis delectione': dilection (natural love) and delectation (delight). A neat pun.

did she refuse the goods of others but, by renouncing all things (even her own), she never coveted them. Not only did she afflict her body but she utterly gave up her own will and denied herself through obedience by subjecting herself to the will of another. She took up the cross by chastising her body through abstinence and imitated Christ by casting herself down through humility.

22. Thus since her spirit had partaken of food, she considered all delights of the flesh to be foolish. One day she brought back to her memory a time when she had been forced to eat meat and had to drink a little watered wine because she had had a very serious illness. Then from a kind of horror at her previous delight, she did not have rest in her spirit and by wondrously torturing her flesh, she afflicted herself until she had made recompense for those delights she had had before. From the fervour of her spirit and as if inebriated, she began to loathe her flesh when she compared it with the sweetness of the paschal Lamb and she needlessly cut out a large piece of her flesh with a knife[45] which she then buried in the earth from a sense of reticence. She had been so inflamed by an overwhelming fire of love that she had risen above the pain of her wound and, in this ecstasy of mind, she had seen one of the seraphim standing close by her. After she had died, the women who were washing her corpse were amazed when they found the places of the wounds, but those who had known of this event through confession understood what the scars were. Why do those who show amazement at the worms which swarmed from the wounds of Simeon and at the fire with which Antony burnt his feet not astonished at such fortitude in the frail sex of a woman who, wounded by charity and invigorated by the wounds of Christ, neglected the wounds of her own body?[46]

VIII. Her fasting
23. The handmaid of Christ excelled in such a great grace of fasting that during those days when she had to come to dinner for the refreshment of her

---

[45] On self-mutilation, see Giles Constable, *Attitudes Towards Self-Inflicted Suffering in the Middle Ages* (Brookline, MA: Hellenic College Press, 1982), and Jane Tibbetts Schulenburg, 'The Heroics of Virginity: Brides of Christ and Sacrificial Mutilation', in *Women in the Middle Ages and the Renaissance: Literary and Historical Perspectives*, ed. by Mary Beth Rose (Syracuse: Syracuse University Press, 1986), pp. 29–72.

[46] Giving the examples of Simeon Stylites, who sat upon a pillar for thirty-six years and the Egyptian hermit Antonius, two famous Desert Fathers, James practises what he promised in the Prologue: setting Mary, as a modern example, in the long tradition of the *Vitas patrum*. See note 2.

body, it was as though she were taking medicine. She would eat only once a day and then only a little; in the summer she ate at vespers and during the winter at the first hour of the night. She did not drink wine nor did she eat meat. She never or very rarely partook of fish and when she did, she ate only the smallest ones but she was sustained on fruits from trees, herbs or beans. For a long time she ate such hard black bread that even the dogs could barely chew it and her mouth bled from the gashes and wounds caused by its extreme roughness and hardness.[47] The memory of Christ, however, rendered the blood sweet to her and her wounds were soothed by the wounds of Christ and the harshness of the extremely hard bread was made soft by the sweetness of the heavenly bread.

One day while she was refreshing her body with food, she saw the ancient enemy wasting away with malice and when there was nothing more he could do, he insulted her saying, 'Behold, O glutton, you are filling yourself up to excess', for she was constricted[48] and all dried up from her long fasts and sometimes it was difficult for her to eat. She suffered pain from a cold and constricted stomach and she would become bloated by only a little food that she would then spit out. Knowing the tricks and wiles of the enemy, she was disturbed, for he would willingly have enfeebled her through excessive abstinence had he known how fearful she was. The more the venomous serpent was tormented by it, however, the more she jeered at him by trying to eat. Whether in eating or in fasting, she did everything for the glory of God (cf. I Corinthians 10. 31).

24. She fasted continuously on bread and water from the Feast of the Holy Cross[49] until Easter for three years, and yet she sustained no hurt to the health of her body or to the work of her hands. When she was in her cell below the church,[50] she would refresh her tiny body on a little bread and she only drank water at vespers or during the night. During her abstemious supper, some of the holy angels would stay by her from the beginning of the blessing before meals

---

[47] See Bynum, *Holy Feast and Holy Fast*.

[48] *Confecta*: she was probably constipated.

[49] From 14 September until Easter, about six months.

[50] At no point in the *Life* does James ever explicitly describe Mary as an anchoress, but the location of her cell indicates that this was the kind of life she led. The anchoress's cell was normally located adjacent to the church with a window that looked on to the altar so that the anchoress could participate in the liturgical services. For a discussion of Mary's cell, see Lauwers, 'Entre Béguinisme et Mysticisme', pp. 48–49. For the general anchoretic background, see Mulder-Bakker, *Lives of the Anchoresses*.

until the thanksgiving and would ascend and descend before her as if on a bright ladder. She had such great consolation from their presence and such an exultation of spirit that her spiritual refreshment surpassed all sweetness of taste.

St John the Evangelist, whom she loved with a wondrous love, sometimes came to her table while she was eating and when she was with him in this way, her love caused her to lose her sensible appetite so that she could scarcely eat any food. The Lord recompensed her in her mind for the corporeal delights she had given up for the sake of Christ, for it is written 'Man does not live on bread alone' (Matthew 4. 4; Luke 4. 4). This food gave her such strength that she sometimes fasted for eight days — and sometimes even for eleven days — that is, from the Ascension of the Lord until Pentecost and she neither ate nor drank anything at all but, in a wondrous manner, she felt absolutely no pain in her head nor did she set aside manual labour because of this. She was not less effective in work on the last day of a fast than she had been on the first. Even had she wished to eat on those days, she could not until her sensible appetite returned to her that, as I said, had been absorbed in the spirit. As long as her soul was so full and copiously overflowing with spiritual food, it did not allow her to accept any refreshment from corporeal food.

25. Sometimes she would gently rest with the Lord in a sweet and blessed silence for thirty-five days and she never ate any corporeal food and could utter no word except this alone: 'I want the Body of Our Lord Jesus Christ'. When she had received it, she would remain with the Lord in silence for whole days at a time. On those days she had the feeling that her spirit was separated, as it were, from her body or as if it were lying in a vessel of clay or, again, as if her body were enveloped in garments of clay and her spirit clothed in them, so abstracted was she from sensible things and rapt above herself in some kind of ecstasy. Nevertheless after five weeks she returned to herself and opened her mouth and received corporeal food and she spoke to those who had been standing around her and who had been struck with wonder.[51]

Long after this, it happened that she could in no way endure the smell of meats or of any fried food or even the smell of wine except in the ablution after

---

[51] For this rather exterior description of Mary's ecstasy, see Karin Glente, 'Mystikerinnen aus männlicher und weiblicher Sicht: Ein Vergleich zwischen Thomas von Cantimpré und Katharina von Unterlinden', in *Religiöse Frauenbewegung und mystische Frömmigkeit im Mittelalter*, ed. by Peter Dinzelbacher and Dieter R. Bauer (Cologne: Böhlau, 1988), pp. 251–64.

she had taken wine at the sacrament of the Body of Christ. Then she was able to endure both the smell and the taste without any difficulty. When she was passing through various towns, she used to go to the bishop of the town or to someone else so that she could receive a strengthening of her faith through the sacrament and the smells did not bother her that previously she had not been able to endure.

Chapter III

The perseverance of her prayer and also her efficiency in driving out demons

IX. Her prayers

26. To the extent that she had weakened her body by fasting, so much the more freely did she make her spirit fat by prayers. As she weakened her body by fasting, her soul was the more comforted in the Lord. She obtained so much and such special grace of praying from the Lord that for days and nights she never or rarely relaxed her unconquered spirit from prayer. She prayed without interruption by crying to the Lord with a silent heart or by expressing her love through the office of the mouth of the heart. Aromatic smoke continually ascended to the sight of the Lord from the altar of her heart (cf. Song of Songs 3. 6), for while she worked with her hands and put her hand to the test and her fingers clasped the spindle, she had her psalter placed before her from which she would sweetly belch forth psalms to the Lord. Through such things and through this kind of wondrous experience, it was as if she had joined her heart to the Lord with keys lest it wander astray. And when she prayed in a special way for anyone to the Lord, he replied to her in the spirit. Her spirit was fastened to the Lord with the fat of devotion and she sweetly grew sleek in prayer when the Lord granted her what she had asked for. She often knew from the elevation or dejection of her spirit whether he had heard her or not.

27. Once when she was offering prayers to the Lord for the soul of a certain dead man, it was said to her, 'Do not pour out your prayers for him because he has been condemned by God. He has been transfixed by a mortal wound and has miserably died in a tournament and has been sold into the eternal fires.'

One day when she was in her cell adjacent to the church at Oignies, she saw a multitude of hands before her as if in supplication. Amazed and not knowing what this vision was, she was struck by some little fear and fled to the church. On another occasion when she was in her cell, she once again saw these same hands and was terrified, but when she again fled to the church, she was held back and detained by the hands. Then she ran to the church as though it were a tabernacle so that she might have counsel from the Lord. She begged the Lord that he tell her what it was those hands wanted of her. The Lord replied that the tortured souls of the dead in purgatory were asking for the prayers of her intercession that would soothe their sufferings as if with a precious ointment. Then, because of the sweetness of contemplation, she interrupted her usual prayers for a time and could neither open her mouth nor think of anything except God.

28. Almost every year she used to go on pilgrimage to the church of blessed Mary of Heigne[52] where she received great consolation from the blessed Virgin. The church was about two leagues distant from her home and once when the winter was bitterly cold, she walked with bare feet to the church and the ice did not wound her feet. And once when she went with only one handmaid as a companion and they did not know the way because the path was very tortuous and dark, some kind of light preceded her and showed the way and she never went astray. On that day she had eaten absolutely nothing and had kept vigil in the church all night. On the following day she returned home and did not eat until vespers, but she went her way without any difficulty and holy angels held her up on her right and left side. The Lord entrusted his angels that 'they keep her in all her ways' (Luke 4. 11) and they carried her in their hands 'lest perhaps she strike her foot against a stone' (Luke 4. 11). And sometimes on the same path when a fierce rainstorm was threatening and she did not have rain clothes that could protect her from the flood of waters, she would glance up and see what seemed to be stars obediently holding back the rain and in this way she remained utterly untouched during the rainy season.[53]

29. Sometimes when her holocaust in prayer had been made even richer than usual (cf. Psalm 19. 4) and when her soul was, as it were, filled with fat and oil, she could not cease from her prayers. It was for this reason that she would salute the blessed Virgin by genuflecting eleven hundred times both day and night, and

[52] This is probably the same church of blessed Mary as Thomas writes of in *VMO-S* 9. The chapel and priory of Heigne, located two leagues from Oignies towards Charleroy, attracted many pilgrims in the thirteenth century. See *MB* I: 303–04.

[53] Thomas has the same, or a similar, miracle in *VMO-S* 8.

this wondrous unheard-of devotion continued for forty days.[54] First, she would genuflect without stopping because of the intensity of her spirit; then she would read the entire psalter and recite each individual psalm while standing upright and would offer up the angelic salutation of the blessed Virgin on bended knees; and, thirdly, when she genuflected, she would be blown even more vehemently by the south wind (cf. Luke 12. 55). She would then beat herself with a discipline three hundred times and would offer herself up to God and the Holy Virgin as a sacrifice by a long martyrdom. At the last three strokes, a copious flood of blood would pour forth which thus would become the seasoning[55] for the other strokes. Finally, she would consummate the sacrifice in simplicity with fifty more genuflections. She accomplished this not with human power but with angelic help sustaining and raising her.

The power of her prayers was so great that not only did other people experience succour from them, but demons as well were tortured by them, whom she drove with ropes and who were compelled to come to her, forced there by the fire of her prayers. Sometimes they gnashed their teeth at her; at other times they howled and complained about her; and sometimes it almost seemed that they were pleading with her. When anyone of her close friends was troubled by any temptation, the precious pearl of Christ was moved with a spirit of compassion and did not cease until she had overthrown the author of evil by the weight of her prayers and had snatched the poor and needy from the hands of the strong ones.

30. Once, the noonday devil (cf. Psalm 90. 6), who walks in the shadows, tempted one of her special friends, the more dangerously because the more subtly.[56] That cunning enemy transfigured himself into an angel of light with an

---

[54] The practice of multiple genuflections accompanying the recitation of the Hail Mary was a common devotion among the Dominicans. See Émile Bertaud, 'Génuflexions et métanies', in *DS* V: 224–25 and Henri-Dominique Simonin, 'Frères prêcheurs: La dévotion au rosaire', in *DS* V: 1431–32. On the rosary, see now Anne Winston-Allen, *Stories of the Rose: The Making of the Rosary in the Middle Ages* (University Park, PA: Pennsylvania State University Press, 1997).

[55] '*Ad condimentum*': an awkward translation but it would seem that James is saying that she wanted to 'put salt on her wounds' to make up for the sweetness she had received at other times. *VMO-ME*: 'with the thre laste strokes, to sauer with the tother [...]'

[56] On the noonday devil, see especially Rudolph Arbesmann who says that Jerome had identified it 'with Satan who, in the disguise of an angel of light, seeks to corrupt the Christian dogma. Satan's instruments are the heretics who claim to possess the light of truth and,

outward appearance of righteousness and privately appeared to her friend in his dreams, reprimanding him for some vices and knavishly warning him about some good things that he should do. The serpent first gave him an antidote so that he might the more secretly slip in the poison: he smoothly exercised his honeyed tongue so that afterwards he might pierce him with his teeth and the poisonous snake draw him to the last end. In the same way he presented himself as though he were constant in truthfulness and, like a sophist, that traitor strove to obscure his falsehood by deceitfully hiding the evil in an amalgam of blameless things.[57]

His [i.e. the serpent's] machinations finally had the result that this brother would have fallen into miserable confusion had not the handmaid of Christ perceived the pretence of the cunning sophist through a revelation of the Holy Spirit. And when she said that it was not a revelation from God but rather a deception of the spirit, he argued with her from his own spirit and not from the Holy Spirit and replied, 'Since that spirit has done me so much good and has foretold so many true things which are going to happen, he certainly does not wish to deceive me.' Then, fleeing for succour to her usual battalion of prayers, she watered the feet of the Lord with tearful wailing and vehemently beat on

---

distorting the meaning of many passages in holy Scripture, by this deceptive method spread their false doctrines', in 'The *daemonium meridianum* and Greek and Latin Patristic Exegesis', *Traditio*, 14 (1958), 17–31 (p. 25). The Desert and Church Fathers saw a connection between this noonday devil and 'acedia', that 'boredom with the ascetical life which haunts the cloister especially at noonday' (ibid., p. 19). For the medieval understanding of 'acedia', see, above all, Siegfried Wenzel, *The Sin of Sloth: Acedia in Medieval Thought and Literature* (Chapel Hill: University of North Carolina Press, 1967). In the Middle Ages, the term, while retaining its old meaning, was extended to include slackness in the performance of religious duties, somnolence, sadness, and mental agony: Siegfried Wenzel, 'Acedia 700–1200', *Traditio*, 22 (1966), 73–102. James's noonday devil who here tempts by an appeal to scrupulosity recalls the devil described by Bernard of Clairvaux whose task is 'to lay ambushes for the perfect, those persons of tried virtue who have survived all other temptations: pleasures, applause, honors. What further weapons has the tempter with which to fight openly against men of this kind? But what he does not dare openly he will attempt in disguise; and when he is aware that a man will abominate what he sees to be patently evil, he tries to seduce him by means of a counterfeit good'. See *On the Song of Songs*, 33. 13, in *SBO* I: 242; trans. by Walsh and Edmonds, pp. 155–56.

[57] On the serpent, see *Le Serpent et ses Symboles* [...], ed. by Maryse Choisy, Alliance mondiale des religions, 9 (Méolans-Revel: Éditions DésIris, 1994). See also *The Exempla or Illustrative Stories from the 'Sermones Vulgares of Jacques de Vitry'*, ed. by Thomas Frederick Crane (London: Nutt, 1890; repr. New York: Lenox Hill, 1971), pp. 65–66, and Thomas of Cantimpré, 'Liber VIII de serpentibus', in *BUA* 8: 276–91.

heaven with her prayers. She did not rest until one night that unrighteous one appeared with a mighty groan and was seen standing ignominiously in full view before her while she was praying in her cell. Then she looked carefully at him who possessed a certain false splendour and said, 'Who are you and what is your name?' Looking at her with a lofty expression and with savage eyes, he said, 'Damnable woman, I am the one whom you compelled to come to you through your prayers, for you have taken away my friend through violence. My name is Sleep[58] for I appear to many in sleep as Lucifer — especially to monks and religious. Through my encouragement they obey me and fall into self-exaltation because they account themselves worthy to be visited with angelic and divine words of comfort. In accordance with my will, you have taken my friend from me whom I had led astray from any good plan.' In this way the eggs of the asp were broken and the deceitful counsels of the evil one manifestly revealed, as the outcome of the event made clear.

31. There was a certain young woman in a monastery of the Cistercian order[59] who served God in the habit of religion along with the other nuns. The ancient serpent looked at her with even more malice than usual because, despite her fragile sex and youth, he saw that she was undertaking a plan of arduous living. When he found out that she was a simple virgin, timorous and humble, he cast her into despair, faint-heartedness, and disordered fear, and he attacked the innocent little virgin by visiting her with blasphemies and unclean thoughts. Unaccustomed to such things, she was terrified and at the very moment that the thought occurred to her, she imagined that she had lost her faith, even though she resisted it with great sorrow for a long time and sorrowed greatly. She, however, was not able to endure it since she did not open the wound of her heart to anyone to receive a medicine and she therefore fell into despair because of her faint-heartedness. The enemy had so depressed her mind that she could not say the Lord's Prayer or the Creed, nor did she even want to confess her sins. If, at times, she was forced to confess by coaxings or threats, she could not be induced

---

[58] See note 56 above. One of the characteristics of *acedia* is somnolence. Wenzel, 'Acedia', p. 86, note 48, refers to the *Glossa ordinaria* 'which, in commenting on "Dormitavit anima mea prae taedio" (Psalm 118. 28), explains "Dormitatio est quae dicitur acedia"' (Antwerp, 1617). Wenzel notes that the sources for this gloss go back to Cassiodorus and Cassian.

[59] This can be either La Cambre near Brussels which was founded in 1200 or Aywières, the site of Lutgard's convent. On this example, see Lauwers, 'Entre Béguinisme et Mysticisme', pp. 65–66.

to request indulgence from the Lord. She could not bring herself to be present at the sacraments of the Church nor did she want to receive the Body of Christ. She was in such distress that she frequently tried to kill herself and spurned the word of God and cautionary warnings concerning her salvation. She finally came to hate all good in herself and the devil vomited forth many words of blasphemy through her mouth. Her righteous sisters poured out many prayers to the clement Lord, but they could not extricate his dove from the jaws of the devil nor were they able immediately to expel this kind of demon by fasting and prayer (cf. Mark 9. 26). It was not because the clement Bridegroom spurned the righteous prayers of his holy virgins but because he left that kind of demonic atrocity to be overcome by the spirituality of his handmaid who might therefore pierce the cheeks of the leviathan and powerfully draw out his prey from his mouth through the efficacy of her prayers.

32. When therefore this young woman was led to the handmaid of Christ, she received her kindly both in her cell and in her heart through the spirit of charity, because she was overflowing with the spirit of compassion and the honey of spiritual sweetness. After she had poured out many prayers for her to the Lord, that good-for-nothing who thought that he was holding her firmly did not want to let her go. Then she offered herself even more intensely in sacrifice to the Lord and fasted for forty days with tears and prayers. Eating nothing, she abstained from all food and only interrupted her fast two or three times a week so that she might refresh herself.

At the end of her fast, this most hideous spirit left the virgin and, restrained with bonds, was forced to come in sorrow and confusion to the handmaid of Christ. He suffered such wretched punishment from an angel of Christ that it seemed that he was vomiting forth all his bowels and wretchedly carrying all his entrails around his neck, for although the Lord works invisibly in the spirit, sometimes he visibly displays external signs (cf. Hebrews 11. 3). Then, groaning and pleading with her to have pity on him, he begged the friend of Christ to impose a penance on him, for he said that he had been compelled to come to her and had to do whatever she imposed upon him.

Then she who never took herself for granted nor wanted to do anything without counsel, called an intimate master whom she trusted. He advised her to send him into the desert where he could not harm anyone until Judgement Day, but then another man, who was not in public office but who knew them both quite well, arrived unexpectedly. When he found out what had happened, he (who was more fervent through the intensity of a powerful spirit) said, 'By no means! If this is done, the traitor will escape. Instruct him to descend immediately into the depths of hell.' So she instructed him and he plunged to the depths with a howl and, in the spirit, she heard the immense uproar that the infernal spirits made when they saw their mighty and powerful prince approaching. The handmaid of Christ was greatly astonished and gave thanks to the Lord and that very same hour the aforesaid virgin was freed and after she had made her confession, she received the Body of Christ and gave thanks to God and returned home.

Once when she was resting in bed after many vigils and prayers, the devil appeared to her in different guises and, gnashing his teeth against her, he cursed her. 'You are resting in your evil', the unrighteous one said. 'May you have quiet with us in hell. I am not the less tormented by your rest as I am tortured by your toil and your prayers.' She, however, smiled and, making the sign of the cross, forced him to withdraw.

Chapter IV

Her vigils, her clothing, the manual labour she undertook, her external appearance

X. Her vigils and sleep

33. This strong and prudent woman considered that to waste precious leisure time was grievous and intolerable, for days pass and they do not come back, they slip away and do not return. Therefore the harm caused by lost time is irretrievable and, unlike other material things that we possess, days that are thus lost cannot be restored. Thus, insofar as it was permitted to her, she took the greatest care lest any hour of the day or night be lost through idleness. She rarely slept at night for she knew that sleep which was mercifully left to us by the Lord has no merit except for the refreshment of our human weakness, since we earn nothing when we sleep for we do not have the use of our free will. She therefore abstained from sleep as much as she was able and served the Lord in nocturnal vigils, the more devoutly because the more freely, and without the noise of people clustering around her. The resoluteness of her abstinence weakened and desiccated her body and, inwardly burning with the fire of love, drove out all somnolence from her. The sweet songs of those angelic spirits with whom she often spent her sleepless nights banished all sleep from her eyes without any harm to her body. Thus removed from human fellowship, an army of the blessed spirits was present for companionship during her nocturnal vigils, whose intonation — coming as if from numerous troops — wondrously soothed her ears with a certain sweet harmony and shook off all torpor, refreshed her head, sprinkled her mind with a wonderful sweetness, stirred up devotion, and inflamed her desire to give praise and thanks. She frequently repeated the 'Sanctus, Sanctus, Sanctus', and incited others to follow her example.

34. May wretched and foolish virgins take heed and lament, they who light the fire of lust with their lascivious songs and make embers burn with their breath and thus alienated from the song of the angels, perish in their vanity. Their laughter is turned to tears, their joy into eternal sorrow, their song into wailing. The Lord has promised them 'a cord for a girdle, a filthy stench for a sweet odour, baldness for curly hair' (Isaiah 3. 24). In truth, our Mary trampled underfoot such choirs of vanity and all the pomps of Satan for the love of Christ and thus deserved to be present among the joyous choirs of the holy angels most happily and most sweetly.

During her nocturnal watches she guarded the precious relics of the saints that profusely furnished and adorned the church in Oignies.[60] These relics celebrated the festive night with her, gladdening her spirit with a wondrous solace as if in approval of her guardianship. Indeed, during her last illness, they consoled her with a loving compassion and they promised her their patronage before God, and rewards for her toil and guardianship.

She had in her cell a bed covered with only a scrap of straw, but she rarely rested on it since she more often used to sit in the church and, leaning her head against the wall, would refresh herself with a little sleep and then return to the sweet labour of her vigils.

35. Even the time she spent sleeping did not pass by without fruit, for even while she slept, her heart was awake and she who had clung to Christ while awake, kept him in her heart and dreamed only of Christ. Just as people who are thirsty dream while asleep that they are drinking from water fountains, and just as those who are hungry imagine that a banquet has been placed before them, just so did she have the One whom she desired always before her eyes in her dreams. For 'where love is, there is the eye', 'where the treasure is, there also is

---

[60] On the relics in the church of Oignies, see also *VMO* 2, 91; and *History of the Foundation of the Venerable Church of Blessed Nicholas of Oignies and the Handmaid of Christ Mary of Oignies*, trans. by Hugh Feiss [hereafter *History of the Foundation*], 7. See also the study of Brenda Bolton in this volume.

````` 

the heart' (Matthew 6. 21). In the same way Christ said of himself 'Where I am, there also shall my minister be' (John 12. 26). Often the Lord warned her in her dreams in the same way that he had warned Joseph and other saints, and he visited his handmaid with many revelations lest her sleep pass unprofitably, just as the Lord promised through the prophet, 'Your old men shall dream dreams and your young men shall see visions' (Joel 2. 28).

Sometimes she was permitted to rest in her cell and sometimes when a very important solemn feast was approaching, she could not find rest unless she were below the church in the presence of Christ. And then she had to remain there for days and nights, for often it was not in her power nor in her free will to remain resting in her cell or in the church. A familiar angel was assigned to watch over her[61] whom she had to obey as if he were her own abbot.[62] Sometimes when she was exceedingly afflicted because of her vigils, he warned her that she should rest, and after she had rested a little, he would rouse her and lead her back to the church.

**36.** Once, from the Feast of St Martin to Quadragesima Sunday, when [her angel] was furiously spurring her on in this way and strengthening her with resolution, from the Feast of St Martin to Quadragesima Sunday, her soul so clung to the floor of the church that no matter whether she was sitting or lying down, she could not bear to have even a little stick placed between her and the bare ground. While she was sleeping, she used the bare earth or the rod that stretched across the pedestal of the altar instead of a pillow. I remember that during that winter it became so bitterly cold and the world so icy that while the priest was celebrating mass, the wine in the holy chalice actually froze all of a sudden. Nevertheless she did not feel the cold nor did her head ache even a little, since it was being mercifully supported by the hand of a holy angel.

Woe to you who sleep and lasciviously lie between your sheets and in your ivory beds and who use soft fabrics. You will die and be buried in your voluptuousness. You spend your days in good fortune but in an instant you could fall to the lowest part of hell 'where maggots will be the pallet beneath you and worms your coverlet' (Isaiah 14. 11). Mark this: because she served the Lord devotedly, the earth served the servant girl of Christ lest she be bruised by its hardness; the winter spared her lest she be tormented by cold; the holy angels ministered to her lest she be harmed in any way. All the lands of the world will

[61] *RB* 7, 28.

[62] *RB* 2, 6, 17; 3, 5; 4, 61; 5, 2; 71, 1, 4, and passim.
`````

fight against you, insensate people that you are, for the sake of the Lord because his creation will be armed for vengeance against his enemies. Those who devote themselves zealously to work against the creator will burn in torment.

XI. Her clothing and appearance

37. She who was clothed in the fleece of the spotless Lamb, she who was inwardly adorned with wedding garments, had 'put on Christ' (Romans 13. 14) from within and did not worry about her outward adornment. Yet she wore ordinary clothes because she was not at all pleased by affected filth nor meticulous cleanliness. She fled both ornamentation and filth equally because the one smelled of delights and the other of vainglory. She knew that the blessed John the Baptist had been commended by the Lord for the harshness of his clothing and that Truth had spoken these words: 'Those who are clothed in soft garments are in the houses of the king' (Matthew 11. 8). She did not wear a linen shirt against her skin but a rough hair shirt that is called 'estamine' in the vernacular.[63] For a covering, she had a white woollen tunic and a cloak of the same simple colour without the addition of any fur[64] or any puffery. She knew that after the fall of our first parents, the Lord did not cover their nakedness with precious but unnatural clothing or with coloured fabrics.

She was content with the simplicity of these clothes and because of the inward heat with which she was burning, did not fear the external cold at all. Sometimes she did not even need material fire to ward off the winter cold. One winter when it was even more bitterly cold than usual and the icy waters had frozen over, while she was praying her outer body became hot in a wondrous fashion, in accordance with the glowing heat generated in the spirit. Sometimes her aromatic sweat even made her clothing smell sweet. Frequently when she offered her prayers to God from the thurible of her heart, the odour of her garments was like the odour of incense.

What do you say to this, you extravagant and ostentatious women, you who adorn your cadavers in many different fashions and put trains on your gowns,[65] you who manifest degenerate bestiality while you array yourselves as though you

---

[63] Papebroeck notes that *estamine* is a French word and means either a light hair shirt or one which was very finely woven from goat's wool, flax or hemp.

[64] Papebroeck notes that *'foderatura'* is *voedering* [or *voering*] in the Germanic languages, meaning 'the fur or cloths with which clothing is stuffed'.

[65] '*Caudatis vestris vestibus*': *caudatis* is 'having a tail'. My thanks to Kate Galea for help with this passage.

were temples? Your garments will be eaten by worms (cf. Proverbs 25. 20) and
they will stink. In contrast, the clothes of this holy woman have been kept as
relics because they smell sweetly. They are precious garments because no matter
how thin they were, she was never conquered by cold. They have been sanctified
because of the cold and, precisely because of this sanctification, they have been
kept carefully after her death by the devout and are honoured with a pious love.

XII. Her manual labour

38. The prudent woman knew that after the sin of our first parents, the Lord
enjoined penance through them to their sons, that is to say, 'You will eat your
bread by the sweat of your brow' (Genesis 3. 19). This is the reason why she
worked with her own hands as long as she could so that she might mortify her
body with penance so that she might furnish the necessities of life for the poor
and acquire food and clothing for herself — in other words, for all those things
which she had given up for Christ.

The Lord bestowed upon her such strength in labour that she far outstripped
her companions and she was able to obtain for herself and for her companion the
fruit of her hands, giving diligent heed to the words of the Apostle, 'Whoever
will not work will not eat' (II Thessalonians 3. 10). She accounted as sweet all
exertion and labour when she considered that the only begotten Son of the high
King of heaven was nourished by Joseph's manual labour and by the work of the
Virgin, the poor little woman,[66] he 'who opens his hand and fills with blessing
every living creature' (Psalm 144. 16). In quiet and silence she followed the
injunction of the Apostle and she ate the bread which she had won by 'the
labour of her hands' (I Thessalonians 4. 11), for her 'strength was in silence and
hope' (Isaiah 30. 15). She so loved quiet and silence that she fled noisy crowds
and once barely said a word from the Feast of the Holy Cross until Easter. The
Holy Spirit revealed to her that the Lord had accepted this kind of silence and,
because of it especially, that she had obtained from the Lord that she would fly
up to heaven without going to purgatory. When one considers how pleasing
silence is to the Lord, it is clear how much vice there is in loquaciousness, for 'a

---

[66] '*Virginis pauperculae quaestuarie*': in Book II, James uses the term *paupercula* to refer to
Mary herself (*VMO* 2, 45 and 46). Beatrice of Nazareth is described as *Christi paupercula* (*VBN*
1, 37) and Ida of Louvain as *venerabilis Christi paupercula* (*VILO* 1, 7). Caroline Walker Bynum
has said of this topos that it 'is often used [...] as an ironic and assertive statement of female
ability', in '"And Woman his Humanity": Female Imagery in the Religious Writing of the
Later Middle Ages', now in her *Fragmentation and Redemption: Essays on Gender and the
Human Body in Medieval Religion* (New York: Zone Books, 1992), pp. 151–80.

man full of tongue shall not be established in the earth' (Psalm 139. 12). Indeed every day she multiplied all the talents entrusted to her (cf. Matthew 25. 14–23) and, since she had left behind every sensible thing under her feet, each day she mounted from virtue to virtue on Jacob's ladder and was situated in the highest position, having been placed, as it were, on the highest step. Thus was her sensual being so absorbed by the overpowering spirit and so totally occupied with Christ, she could do nothing without 'the food that does not perish' (John 6. 27). Wherefore, like someone who has retired from active duty and is freed from all manual labour, she lingered with the Lord in the liberation with which Christ had endowed his handmaid.

XIII. The appearance and composition of her face and other limbs

39. Her external behaviour and appearance manifested the inward state of her mind. The serenity of her expression could not hide the joy of her heart, but nevertheless with an astounding moderation, she tempered the mirth of her heart by a serious expression and hid the merriment of her mind a little with the simplicity of a modest face. And since the Apostle said 'women shall pray with their heads veiled' (I Corinthians 11. 6), the white veil that covered her head hung before her eyes. She walked humbly with a slow and mature gait, her head bent and her face looking to the ground (cf. *RB* 7. 63). Thus was the holy grace of that Spirit reflected in her face from the fullness of her heart so that many were spiritually refreshed by her appearance and were stirred to devotion and to tears. Reading the unction of the Spirit in her face as if they were reading from a book, they knew that power came from her.[67]

It happened one day that a certain amiable man who was on intimate terms with religious personages and a friend of Guido who had had once been cantor of the church of La Cambre went out of his way to visit her. One of his companions who had perhaps not known from experience until then the degree to which intimacy with good people and visits to them can contribute to pious minds, said to this devout man as if mocking his pious labour, 'What in God's name are you looking for, lord cantor? Why have you made such a useless

---

[67] Mary has so thoroughly assimilated the Word of God that it is as if she is the Book itself and teaches in the same way as does holy Scripture. The power referred to is the power of God. On *virtus*, see André Vauchez: 'the supernatural dynamism that had imbued [the saints] in their lifetimes', in his *The Laity in the Middle Ages: Religious Beliefs and Devotional Practices*, trans. by Magery J. Schneider, ed. by Daniel E. Bornstein (Notre Dame: University of Notre Dame Press, 1993), p. 6.

detour? Why do you want to chase after flies or butterflies and catch them like a child?' As the cantor was gentle and patient, he did not give up his proposed trip because of this, but devoutly proceeded towards the handmaid of Christ because he had received not a little comfort from her presence on another occasion. While they were speaking, his companion (who, in the manner of worldly men, had put little stock in his words) was occupied somewhere else in idle conversation, but when he became bored with waiting, he came to the cantor and urged him to hurry. Perhaps it happened when he looked into the face of the handmaid of Christ, but suddenly and marvellously his spirit was transformed and he dissolved into a great flood of tears so that for a long time afterwards he could scarcely be moved from the place and from her presence. Although the cantor wanted to hide himself out of a sense of propriety, he waited and because he knew what had happened, he rejoiced and he, in turn, laughed at his friend and said, 'Let's go! Why are we standing here? Perhaps you want to chase butterflies!' The man, however, could barely be pulled away from that place and, after many sighs and tears, said, 'Forgive me! I did not know at all what I was saying before. Now, however, I have received God's power from this holy woman through experience.'

40. Once it happened that her little body could no longer endure the fervour of her spirit and she fell into a great sickness. Then the good Father subdued his beloved daughter with the whip of discipline so that her limbs were twisted in an amazing fashion. Sometimes it happened that her pain caused her arms to move in circles and she was forced to beat her breast with her hands. When, after a little time, the force of the illness abated, she returned to herself and gave great thanks to God who 'lays the rod on every son whom he acknowledges' (Hebrews 12. 6) since the words of the Apostle were clearly fulfilled in her when he said, 'When I am weak, then I am the stronger' (cf. II Corinthians 12. 10). After the Lord had put his chosen one 'to the test' through this infirmity as if she had been 'gold in a furnace' (Wisdom 3. 6; Proverbs 27. 21), she was so completely purified and refined that the Lord gave her so much perseverance in fasting, vigils and other labours that even strong men could barely have endured a third part of her toil. Despite her strength, however, it sometimes happened that when one of her friends was labouring in any trouble or was falling prey to any temptation, then she became ill with the ill person and burned with the same vehement sorrow as the person who had been caused to stumble. She often felt these illnesses in each of her limbs and when this new kind of miracle occurred, she would immediately call a priest to make the sign of the cross over the afflicted place, and it was as though the illness took fright at the power of the holy cross and fled to another place. When the priest repeatedly made the sign of the cross, the intermittent and fleeting sickness dared no longer endure the weight of the cross, but completely left the body of the handmaid in a wondrous and unheard of kind of veneration of the cross. Truly she gazed with the eye of faith at the bronze serpent (Numbers 21. 9) and, freed by God from the bites of the serpent's poison, she gave forth many thanks to the holy cross.

41. The expression on her face enabled many people not only to obtain the grace of devotion from looking at her but, after having spoken with her, they also obtained a honey-tasting sweetness (both spiritually in the heart and sensibly in the mouth) which overflowed to others. Let hard men and those who have come late to believing hear and grumble. Those who have experience in divine consolations such as these easily agree when they hear these words, 'Thy lips, my spouse, are a dropping honeycomb, honey and milk are under thy tongue' (Song of Songs 4. 11).

One day when a certain great personage[68] who considered himself little in his own eyes had come from very distant parts to visit her and was speaking to her out of his abundant humility and intense charity, he received so much consolation from looking at her that for an entire day no material taste of the food he ate could dispel that taste of honey from his mouth. I am intentionally not telling the name of this holy man because when people speak his praises, he is wondrously tortured by praises and, as it were, is 'proved like gold in the furnace' (Wisdom 3. 6; Proverbs 27. 21). As a result of this experience, it happened that the righteous consoler of souls [i.e. Mary] greatly lightened her servant's bitterness that he was suffering on account of his exile.

Why are you covered with embarrassment? Why are you angry at me? Who called you by name? Although I said that this man was an exile, are not there many bishops of Toulouse besides you who lived before and could come after you? Why ought I to be silent about the praises of the handmaid of Christ because of your embarrassment? What is it to you? What do you have that you cannot accept? It does not concern your glory but the glory of Christ for 'he who plants is nothing nor is he who waters but it is God that gives increase' (I Corinthians 3. 7). Therefore stop grumbling against me. These things of which

---

[68] This is, of course, Fulk of Toulouse, exiled from his see in 1211, whom James sets at the beginning of the *Life* (*VMO* Prologue, 1) as the patron, here at the end of the first book, and once more in *VMO* 2, 104, when he visits Mary on her deathbed.

I speak are not yours but the Lord's, given by God and humbly received by you, and they belong to the handmaid of Christ who lightened with her merits the hardships of your pilgrimage.

But now we are making an end to this first little book in which we have spoken of those things that concern the exterior person and externally pertain to the senses. Having, as it were, reached the middle room, let us rest a little before passing on to more interior and more subtle things.

BOOK II

On Mary's interior life and her holy death

Chapters

Chapter V

**The fear of the Lord, the absence of even minor avoidance, her choosing
avoidable sins, her striving for poverty and humility**

I. The different virtues of the King's daughter and the seven gifts of the Holy Spirit

42. In addition to the above, we will now speak about the greatness of the
inner glory of the King's daughter, and of how she was encircled with a great
variety of virtues, and of how the Father interiorly adorned her. Many daughters
in our days have amassed wealth, but we believe that only she has surpassed them

all. Her Father made for her a damask tunic of many colours on which was depicted every kind of virtue and decorated with all the flowers of the gardens of the Lord. But since we are incapable of counting each individual star of this shining firmament, or all the flowers in this paradisal meadow,[69] or all the different kinds of virtues she possessed, we will therefore limit ourselves to the original sources from which all her good deeds flowed — that is to say, to the seven gifts of the Holy Spirit.

The Lord filled her with the spirit of wisdom and understanding, counsel and fortitude, knowledge and righteousness, and fear of the Lord. The spirit of wisdom rendered the daughter of the King 'flowing with delights' (Song of Songs 8. 5) and fervent in charity. The spirit of understanding rendered her contemplative of the higher things. The spirit of counsel gave her foresight. The spirit of fortitude rendered her patient and long-suffering. The spirit of knowledge made her discerning. The spirit of righteousness made her inner parts overflow with mercy and the spirit of the fear of the Lord rendered her cautious and humble.

II. The spirit of the fear of the Lord

43. We will first look at the spirit of the fear of the Lord not only because 'it is the beginning of wisdom' (Proverbs 1. 7), but because it is also the guardian of all graces. Although 'perfect charity banished all fear' (I John 4. 18) from the King's daughter, that is to say it banished the pain and anxiety of fear, yet she was filled with fear from the abundance of her love, and she took such care in all her works and all her words and thoughts that she did not neglect even the smallest thing. She frequently took heed of what is written 'Who disregards the little things falls little by little' (cf. Sirach 19. 1), for she 'feared all her works' (Job 9. 28) and 'always had the Lord in her sight' (Psalm 15. 8; Acts 2. 25), and she 'always thought on him in all her ways' (Proverbs 3. 6) lest she displease him in anything. For she knew that even though one can avoid great things, yet one may still be buried in the sand — Absalom died after having been hung by many individual strands of hair (cf. II Kings 18. 9–17). Many venial sins, whether enjoyed or neglected, lead to eternal death if disregarded. Therefore chaste fear was in her heart like a breast belt to control her thoughts, in her mouth like a bridle to restrain her tongue, and in her works like a goad to prevent her from becoming indolent through sloth: she was ruled in all things by fear lest she exceed the mean. This fear swept duplicity from her heart like a broom and

[69] The adjective *amoenus* almost always refers to paradise.

cleansed her mouth of falsity and her works from all vanity. She was 'an enclosed garden' and 'a covered fountain' (Song of Songs 4. 12), and received nothing lightly except Christ and those things that belong to Christ. Christ was for her a meditation in the heart, a word in the mouth, an example in her works. I do not remember that I ever heard a worldly statement from her lips, for she could barely speak a single sentence without repeatedly interspersing it with a Christ-like seasoning.

44. Holy fear of the Lord thus so occupied her mind that while she lived in Willambroux near Nivelles, she often gathered those plants which are not sown and others which grow by themselves and made soup from them, lest she accidentally eat something taken from a beast — that is to say, lest she eat those alms which robbers and usurers are in the habit of giving to the houses of lepers. She abstained not only from illicit things but also from many licit things as well, lest through unrestrained spiritual laxity she slip into illicit deeds.

45. She conceived such a great love for poverty through the spirit of fear that she hardly even wanted to possess the bare necessities of life. Thus one day she made plans to flee so that, unknown and despised among strangers, she might beg from door to door: that naked she might follow the naked Christ[70] and, like Joseph (cf. Genesis 39. 15, 18), leave behind the mantle of all worldly goods; like the Samaritan woman, leave behind the water pitcher (John 4. 28); like John, leave behind fine linen (Mark 14. 52).[71] She frequently heeded and recollected the poverty of Christ who, when he was born, did not have a place in the inn (Luke 2. 7); who did not have a place to lay his head (Matthew 8. 20); and who did not have money with which he might pay the tribute. Thus she wanted to be fed with alms and she wanted to be received in strangers' houses. She burned with such a desire for poverty that she took with her a little bag in which to put alms and a little cup from which she might drink water or into which she might put food if it were given to her while she was begging. When she was clothed in old

[70] This is the medieval motto of the new piety in the twelfth century. See Réginald Grégoire, 'L'Adage ascétique *nudus nudum Christum sequi'*, *Studi storici in onore di Ottorino Bertolini*, ed. by Ottavio Banti and others (Pisa: Pacini, 1972), pp. 395–409.

[71] Papebroeck suggests that this is the young man who ran to the garden when Christ was captured: 'And a certain young man followed him, having a linen cloth cast about his naked body. And they laid hold on him. But he, casting off the linen cloth, fled from them naked' [Mark 14. 51–52]; and that Ambrose, Jerome, Epiphanius, John Chrysostom, and others considered that the youth was John the Evangelist.

rags in this way, she was only barely discouraged by the copious tears of her friends. When the poor little woman of Christ had said her farewell and wanted to take to the road clothed like this and with her little bag and her cup,[72] her friends who loved her in Christ sorrowed so much and shed so many tears that she could not endure it and she was filled with compassion. Although she wanted to flee and to beg, she was restrained by two things: she chose to remain because her absence would have seemed intolerable to her brothers and sisters.[73] Also she did what was permitted for her to do. After these events, she persevered in such a love of poverty that at times she even cut off pieces from napkins or from the cloths on which she ate her bread and, keeping a bit of them for herself, gave the rest to the poor.

46. 'Woe to you that join house to house and lay field to field, even to the end of the place' (Isaiah 5. 8) for you 'cannot be satisfied with money nor shall you reap any fruit from them' (Ecclesiastes 5. 9). You who 'lay up to yourselves treasure on earth where the rust and moth consume and where thieves break through and steal' (Matthew 6. 19) are always gathering together and are always needy and in want. What did the poor little woman of Christ lack, she who always fled wealth and always had enough to give to others? She always loved poverty so extravagantly that the Lord provided her with the necessities of life. She not only spurned wealth through a spirit of fear but, in a spirit of poverty, she also considered herself small in her own eyes. She cast herself down with such humility that she accounted herself as nothing and whenever she had done anything well, she felt as if she were useless. She said this not only with her mouth but she also felt it in her heart. Considering herself to be inferior to everyone, she never presumed anything in herself and accounted everyone superior to her. When the Lord did something good to her, she imputed it to the merit of others and never sought her own glory, but referred everything to him from whom all good comes. She judged herself unworthy of the goods she had received and she condemned no one, neither the weak man nor the sinner, and despised only herself. She was indifferent alike to blame or to praise and, surrounded on the right and the left by the shield of truth (cf. Psalm 90. 5),

[72] On the cup relic venerated as Mary's cup, see Bolton's contribution to this volume.

[73] Although James says that Mary was restrained from begging for two reasons, he only specifically mentions the first one. The second, unquestionably, was her dutiful obedience to the Church teachings on mendicancy: 'She did what was permitted to her to do.' On poverty and the apostolic life, see above, note 12.

shadows were to her the same as light and she was not depressed by reproof or raised up by praise.

47. From her abundant humility, she always strove to hide in herself, but when, because of the jubilation in her heart and the fullness of grace, she could not remain secreted within herself, she would flee to neighbouring fields and thickets.[74] By thus avoiding the eyes of the curious, she was able to keep her 'secret to herself' (Isaiah 24. 16) and keep it in the ark of a pure conscience (cf. I Timothy 3. 9). Nevertheless, the prayers of her friends sometimes compelled her to console the faint-hearted, or God sent her especially to someone, or she was spurred to action out of feelings of compassion. Then she would tell a few of her many friends what she felt humbly and modestly. O how many times did she say to her friends, 'What are you asking me? I am not worthy to feel these things you are asking me about?' How many times did she reply to God, almost as if she were grumbling, 'Why are you bothering me Lord? Send whom you must send. I am not worthy to go to declare your counsels to another.' Nevertheless, she could not resist the stirring of the Holy Spirit because through it she could be of service for the help of others. How often she forewarned her intimate friends of dangers! How often she detected the hidden traps of the evil spirits to help her friends! How often she strengthened the faint-hearted and those wavering in faith by wondrous divine revelations! How often she warned others not to perform some things that they were privately planning to do! How often she lightened the burdens those who were falling into sin and almost in despair by divine consolations!

48. Why therefore do you blush, O timid one? Why, O avaricious one, do you deprive the needy of so many good things? Why do you depart from your neighbour's dwelling because of your excessive humility? Is it really possible that God showed you so many and such great things for your own benefit, you who do not need revelations of this kind since you, as it were, cling inseparably to God? Did he not rather reveal such things for the benefit of those who believe in you and need your help? Alas, how often and how greatly have you kept to yourself those things that could have strengthened the sick, incited the listless, illumined the unlearned? In this way the Lord could have been shown forth through his wondrous saints. Why do you conceal your talent? Why do you not

---

[74] Compare *VMO* 2, 65 and Christina the Astonishing, in *VCM* 1, 9, and 4, 46, who also hid away in the fields and the trees.

show your Christ to the world? He is not diminished in you if you share him with others. When 'the King led you into the wine cellar' (Song of Songs 1. 3), is it not possible that you sometimes cried out in your inebriation, 'O Lord why are you hiding yourself? Why do you not show what you are? For if the world knew you, it would sin no more but would immediately 'run after the fragrance of your ointment' (Song of Songs 1. 3).

But blessed be God who, through his liberality, curbed your avariciousness and revealed your hiding place whether you liked it or not. Had it not been that you had to breathe, you would have burst from [the pressure] of the fermenting must of a fervent spirit. When you could not any longer endure the burning fire without being consumed, then finally the truth was drawn out of a pure and inebriated heart. Then you belched forth[75] many and wondrous readings from a wondrous and unheard of fullness and, had we been able to understand, you read to us from the book of life (cf. Revelations 20. 12), suddenly changing from a disciple into a master.[76]

You were like a robust person who had been befuddled with wine and roused from a drunken stupor[77], but when you returned to yourself, you would be silent

[75] The image of words uttered in ecstasy being compared to burps caused by an excess of gas strikes this modern reader as quite extraordinary. Note, however, that Bernard of Clairvaux uses the same image of belching to great effect in his *On the Song of Songs*, 67. 3–4, in *SBO* I: 190; trans. by Walsh, pp. 7–8: 'The Bride thinks it no robbery to take to herself the words of the Prophet: "My heart has belched a goodly theme", since she is filled with the same spirit. "My beloved is mine, and I am his." There is no conclusion here, no prayer. What is there? It is a belch. Why should you look to find connected prayers or solemn declarations in a belch? What rules or regulations do you impose upon yours? They do not admit of your control, or wait for you to compose them, nor do they consult your leisure or convenience. They burst forth from within, without your will or knowledge, torn from you rather than uttered.' Thomas of Cantimpré's use of the same image in *BUA* 2, 49: 2, greatly scandalized Robert Lerner who considered passages such as these to be pantheistic expressions of an earthly union with God rather than 'the deification of the soul in heaven': Robert Lerner, 'The Image of Mixed Liquids in Late Medieval Mystical Thought', *Church History*, 40 (1971), 397-411 (p. 398). I am indebted to Dr E. Rozanne Elder for the reference to Bernard's Sermon.

[76] Note that James, a man of his time, makes it clear that Mary becomes 'master' and he 'disciple' only when she is rapt in ecstasy and the words she speaks are not her own. In all things that pertain to Church law, Mary is a 'dutiful daughter'. See notes 12 and 128.

[77] Thomas describes both Christina and Lutgard in their befuddlement after ecstasy; both seem drunk and both consider themselves foolish: *VCM* 26; *VLA* I, 16. See Aimé Solignac, 'Ivresse spirituelle: au Moyen Age', in *DS* VII: 2312–38 and Jean Leclercq, 'Jours d'ivresse', *La Vie spirituelle*, 76 (1947), pp. 574–91.

as if you had forgotten what you had said. If you remembered something, then from a sense of diffidence you would become confused and would think yourself garrulous and stupid and, astonished at what had happened, you would ask forgiveness from God.

49. Once when we asked her whether she ever had any excited sense of vainglory from human praise or from divine revelations, she said: 'In view of the true glory which I desire, all human praise can be counted as nothing — indeed it is nothing.' She was so rooted in truth and so firmly established in the Lord that she was filled with genuine goods and fattened and refreshed with spiritual food. Like a person who has been sated by all kinds of delicate meats and for that reason spits out insipid and stale meat, in the same way she did not tolerate the vanity of human praise but spat it out with horror in her heart when she compared it to the goods of eternity. Indeed, just as Christ cannot be sweet to the person to whom the world is sweet, so the sweetness of Christ so overcame her entire mind that nothing tasted sweet to her except Christ.

Chapter VI

Her piety towards the Lord, her assistance displayed to the dying and to the souls in purgatory and in danger; diseases cured

III. The spirit of piety

50. She guarded herself from all kinds of evil, not only through the spirit of fear but also through a disposition to all good. She did not think that bodily exercise had much effect on piety for, as the Apostle says, 'bodily exercise is profitable for little, but godliness is profitable to all things having promise of the life that now is and of that which is to come' (I Timothy 4. 8). She regularly kindled the fire of charity in the lamp of her heart with the oil of mercy lest perhaps, like the foolish virgins, she be found without oil and be sent away from the wedding feast of eternal joy (cf. Matthew 25. 2–13). From the abundant piety of her heart she therefore busied herself as far as she was able in the external works of mercy. But in these works of mercy, she occupied herself above all in assisting the sick and being present at deathbeds for contrition,[78] or at burials

---

[78] Although James does not specify how Mary assisted at deathbeds for contrition, I am irresistibly reminded of Christina's behaviour at the deathbed of Count Louis when she heard his confession. Thomas, however, goes to some length to emphasize that this was not a

where she very often received many things concerning the heavenly secrets through a revelation of God. One day when she was in her cell and the sister of a brother of Oignies was labouring in her last agonies and the prayers for the death were already being said because she was thought to be near death, she perceived a multitude of howling demons around the bed of the ailing sister. Then, it was as if she had forgotten her usual gravity and innate reserve and she ran to the bed of the sick woman and set herself against the unclean spirits, not only fighting against them with her prayers but even driving them away with her mantle as though they were flies.[79] When those impious ones resisted her in a terrible fashion and wanted to lay claim to the soul of the sister as theirs, she could bear it no longer and cried out to her Christ, incessantly calling upon the death of the crucified one and his blood which he had poured out for sinners. Then they howled and prepared themselves for the feast and attacked the soul with many calumnies, but she received confidence from the Holy Spirit — for where the spirit of God is, so there is liberty (2 Corinthians 3. 17) — and she

sacramental confession and that she did this 'not for absolution which she had no power to give, but rather that she be moved by this atonement to pray for him' (*VCM* 44). In 1228 the General Chapter of the Cistercian Order forbade abbesses to hear confessions, thus indicating that women had previously, indeed, been involved in this kind of non-canonical activity. See Amedée Teetaert, *La Confession aux laïques dans l'église latine depuis le VIIIe jusqu'au XIVe siècle: étude de théologie positive* (Paris: Gabalda, 1926); Jean Leclercq, 'Medieval Feminine Monasticism: Reality Versus Romantic Images', in *Benedictines*, ed. by E. Rozanne Elder (Kalamazoo: Cistercian Publications, 1981), pp. 53-70 (p. 61), and A. Murray, 'Confession as a Historical Source in the Thirteenth Century', in *The Writing of History in the Middle Ages: Essays Presented to Richard William Southern*, ed. by R. H. Davis and J. M. Wallace-Hadrill (Oxford: Clarendon Press, 1981), pp. 275-322.

[79] See *The Nine Ways of Prayer of St. Dominic*: 'A curious thing about [the ninth way of prayer] was that he seemed to be brushing away ashes and flies from before his face, and because of this he often defended himself with the sign of the cross', and Tugwell's comment: 'This very curious detail seems to refer to some kind of demonic molestation, in view of the explicit connection between the gesture of brushing away flies and Dominic's making the sign of the cross. The Middle Ages certainly knew about Beelzebub as "the Lord of the Flies", but they do not seem to have taken the flies to be anything more than ordinary flies attracted by the bloody sacrifices associated with the horrible cult of Beelzebub': *The Nine Ways of Prayer of St. Dominic*, trans. by Simon Tugwell (Dublin: Dominican Publications, 1978), p. 46. See also *VLA* I, 12: 'from that day forth [i.e. after Christ and Lutgard had exchanged hearts] in the same way as a nurse watches over an infant in its cradle with a fan lest the importunate flies disquiet it, so did Christ hold close to the entrance of her heart like a watch-man so that no temptation of the flesh nor the smallest unclean thought might discompose her mind even for a moment.'

replied, 'Lord I stand surety for this soul for although she has sinned, she has confessed. Although she cannot speak, if perhaps any sin remains in her through neglect or ignorance, you have still left her some time for contrition.'

51. Her brothers noted the sound of her voice and the way in which she behaved against the demons and they poured forth devout prayers to the Lord for the soul of their sister. Finally, the demons were overcome and put to flight and, after the holy angels had come, she gave praise to God. Then she came to herself again and rested and then picked up the mantle which she had cast aside during her battle and fled. After the modest one had returned to her cell, she closed the door and hid herself. Not long after this — at the feast of Peter and Paul — she devoutly prayed to the Lord for that soul and because she was concerned about the state of the woman for whom she had stood surety, blessed Peter showed her that soul being violently afflicted in the pains of purgatory. Blessed Peter revealed to her the pains and the reasons why she suffered them. She was tortured with violent heat because she had loved the pleasures of the world with an excessive ardour. Sometimes she was tortured with great cold because she had been slow to do every good thing, but especially because she had been very negligent in correcting her sons and her own family. She also was miserably tormented with thirst because when she was alive, she had wasted far too much time drinking.[80] She suffered as well the greatest discomfort from nakedness because she had possessed far too many clothes. Since the righteous handmaid of Christ entirely overflowed with a profound loving-kindness towards those who were being tortured in purgatory and, not content with her own prayers, she obtained many intercessions from the prayers and masses of other people.

52. On another occasion, a certain religious widow was labouring in the agonies of her last hours at Willambroux near Nivelles. She had served God for

---

[80] Heat, cold, thirst, and nakedness are characteristics commonly found in descriptions of purgatory. On purgatory in general, see Barbara Newman, 'On the Threshold of the Dead: Purgatory, Hell, and Religious Women', in her *From Virile Woman to WomanChrist: Studies in Medieval Religion and Literature* (Philadelphia: University of Pennsylvania Press, 1995), pp. 108–36; Brian McGuire, 'Purgatory, the Communion of Saints, and Medieval Change', *Viator*, 20 (1989), 61–84; Le Goff, *The Birth of Purgatory*, and Adriaan Bredero, 'Le Moyen Âge et le Purgatoire', *Revue d'histoire ecclésiastique*, 78 (1983), 429–52. See also Robert Sweetman, 'Visions of Purgatory and their Role in the *Bonum Universale de Apibus* of Thomas of Cantimpré', *Ons Geestelijk Erf*, 67 (1993), 20–33.

a long time in holy widowhood and had kept her daughters unspotted for the heavenly Bridegroom in holy virginity. Then she [i.e. Mary] saw the blessed Virgin standing by the holy widow and, as it were, fanning her with a fan to moderate the heat of the fever that was miserably tormenting her. When her soul wanted to go out of her body, a crowd of demons that had been lying in ambush would not withdraw despite her insistent prayers until a heavenly key-bearer drove them away in a confused rout with the banner of the crucifix. When the widow died, the handmaid of Christ saw the blessed Virgin with a multitude of heavenly maidens around the body and it was as if they were divided into two choirs and they were chanting psalms and praising God. When the priest had discharged the Office of the Dead in proper fashion then, as it seemed to her, the highest priest completed the office with a multitude of the saints and, in a wondrous way, the Church triumphant gave the responses to the Church militant.

When the body had been taken away to be buried, the handmaid of Christ saw the soul that had not yet been entirely purged in the world made perfect in purgatory for those things that it still lacked. The woman's husband had been a merchant and, in the manner of merchants, had acquired some goods by fraud. She herself had received in her inn some of the cortege of the dukes of Louvain and they spent a great deal of their unjustly acquired goods in her house. Because of these things she had not yet done perfect restitution and she herself said that she had still to be confined in purgatory. When her daughter, the devout virgin Margaret of Willambroux, and her sisters were told of this, they had many prayers said for her and, as far as possible, made restitution for her. Not long afterwards, the soul of the widow appeared to the handmaid of Christ, more transparent than glass, whiter than snow, and brighter than the sun. Having been offered hospitality, she ascended to heaven and was now rejoicing in the eternal banquet and giving thanks. It seemed to her [i.e. Mary] as if [that woman] was holding the book of life in her hands and was reading the deeds of the highest Teacher to learned men.

53. When a certain holy and blessed old man was close to death, she was present at his sick bed and assisted him. This man, John of Dinant[81], also known as 'the gardener', had persevered from his youth in innocence and virginity and had left all for Christ and had acquired many souls for the Lord by his example

---

[81] Both John of Dinant and Richard of Menehen-Capella (mentioned later in this story) flourished in 1195.

and holy admonitions. She saw a multitude of angels assisting and rejoicing with the old man and, smelling a marvellously sweet fragrance, she could not contain herself for the immensity of joy she felt because she had greatly loved him and had considered him almost like a father. Then it was revealed to her by the Holy Spirit that that old man had flown to the Lord, freed from all pains of purgatory, he who had done such penance while he lived in the flesh and who had patiently endured so much calumny and persecution for Christ and had lived in such justice and fear. It was for this reason that whenever she passed his grave in Oignies, she humbly bowed, and afterwards when she was labouring in her last illness, the souls of the old man and of Brother Richard of Manechan (another friend of hers who had died) were sent to visit her and they gave her spiritual consolation. The handmaid of Christ was especially filled with compassion towards the sick and she spent many sleepless nights praying for them.

54. When the mother of the brothers at Oignies was labouring in a very grievous and lengthy sickness, she often assisted her and consoled her. This woman was almost a hundred years old[82] and, now close to death, was finding it extremely difficult to breathe. One night when [Mary] was standing by her bed and this holy woman could scarcely take a breath without a great pain in her heart, [Mary] remained by her side, although she thereby did violence to herself. When she could endure it no longer, the Lord saw the humility of his handmaid and put into her mouth a taste like a precious aromatic wine and for almost three days she was sensible of a very sweet fragrance which seemed like burning incense and no odour of any food could expel this aromatic fragrance.

55. The Lord bestowed consolation and patience on many people not only through her presence but he often rendered bodily healing through her merits as well. Some boys who had broken their limbs were carried to her and when she laid her hands on them, they were healed.

A certain boy who lived in Oignies was dangerously ill and was continually bleeding from the ear. Although no medical art could effect a cure, he was perfectly restored to health by the medicine of her prayers and by the laying on of hands. Then his mother brought him to the church and gave thanks to God for the prayers of his handmaid.

---

[82] Given her extreme age, this woman must have been the mother of Master Giles. See notes 106 and 127. Thomas mentions her in *VMO-S* 10.

Another woman was restored to health by her touch from a very seriously infected abscess of the throat, called *squinancia*. Similarly, a cleric who fell ill in Oignies, whose name was Lambert, was cured from the same illness by her touch. Another was Guerric, a priest of Nivelles whose doctors despaired of saving him after he had laboured in a very grievous illness. When there was no one who could promise him health, he came to the handmaid of Christ and with many prayers, begged her to lay her hand on him. That very night the blessed Virgin appeared to him in his sleep and, after she had departed, he was restored to health.

Another priest, Master Guido of Nivelles, a humble and devout man and her spiritual father, was perfectly cured after the handmaid of Christ had put her hand on a vicious swelling in his throat. And there was another concerning whose sickness everyone had despaired but after many doctors had attended him and it seemed that nothing could avail except to await his death, he received health by the touch of her hair.

56. But why do we linger over small details when so many great and marvellous things still remain? Although it is a mark of piety to relieve bodily sickness, it is far and incomparably better to give healing for the benefit of souls, for there is no sacrifice more pleasing to God than zeal for souls. She always remained happy, cheerful and joyous in heart except when some peril of dark sorrow or the fall of souls disturbed her mind. In this alone (I am speaking of her peacefulness of soul) she had no moderation. Anxiously she wept, desolately she grieved; she could not eat her meals and drove sleep away from her eyes, and she cried out like a woman in childbirth. You would have thought that she was wounded with immense sorrow when troops of demons, roaring and gnashing their teeth, rushed on the holy virgins who were devoutly serving God in the village of Manne.[83] When she saw that these impious and envious demons who had obtained their will were dancing[84] for joy at the banishment of the holy women, she could barely restrain herself from wailing from her sorrow of heart.

[83] This is apparently an informal house community, for it is not listed in the Repertory of beguine communities, in Simons, *Cities of Ladies*.

[84] The word used here, *tripudiare*, is an ironic reference to the ecstatic dance of the mystic after a vision of the Lord.

57. Another time she saw a great army of evil spirits returning from the devastation of Liège,[85] bloody as if after battle, coming with a proud and pompous uproar and who were threatening even more evil deeds with elated countenances.

Not long after this vision, messengers came to Oignies with the announcement that the city of Liège was destroyed, the churches plundered, the women brutally attacked, and the citizens killed. Indeed, they reported that the enemy had seized and carried off the goods of the entire city.

As it happened, there was present at that time in Oignies a holy man of an honest way of life and of good reputation among evil men, the light, teacher and spiritual father of the whole diocese whose name was Master John of Nivelle.[86] When he heard these most evil reports, he was cast down in mind and he grieved inconsolably for the holy virgins whom he had gained for the Lord by his preaching and example. He was especially worried lest perhaps they had been overcome by violent force (as certain men had lyingly reported), although, like a concerned father, he doubted this. He did not greatly mourn over the loss of temporal goods — since he counted such things as dung — but, sick at heart, this holy man who was exceptionally and outstandingly adorned with the gem of all virtues mourned instead over the violence done to the churches and the destruction of souls. The father, the patron of churches, wept for his son and the friend of the Bridegroom, wept for his daughters, for the chaste virgins whom he had pledged to present to the chaste Bridegroom. The handmaid of Christ, however, was not greatly troubled when she heard these rumours and her friends marvelled since they knew with what affection she loved these chaste virgins who served Christ devoutly in the city of Liège, but she had been forewarned and forearmed by the Lord and the holy father knew that unless his daughter had been forewarned, she would have been overcome by an excess of grief.

When, in the manner of clerics, the brothers of Oignies were greatly afraid because it was said that the enemy was invading their region, she remained unperturbed at the news and without fear, for the holy angels had already consoled her and had announced 'on earth peace to men of good will' (Luke 2. 14). She felt a great calm and quiet around the house at Oignies almost as if, in

---

[85] The plunder of Liège by the soldiers of Henry I of Brabant on 3–7 May 1212 is mentioned in the Prologue, *VMO* 1, 5.

[86] John of Nivelle was a canon of St John in Liège whose name is frequently mentioned in documents after 1199. He died on 16 March 1233. See *BUA* 2, 31; Simons, *Cities of Ladies*, pp. 126–27.

the spirit, the peace and purity of the aforementioned holy virgins had been guaranteed to her as certain. Yet it seemed to her that the earth trembled and complained because men set themselves against their Creator with such a monstrous sin.

58. Once it happened that a certain relative of hers, a knight named Ywain of Zoania, noble in birth, strenuous in arms and given over to worldly vanities, was divinely inspired and, aided by the admonitions and prayers of the holy woman, left the world behind him and was converted to God. Then the evil and unruly demon was wondrously confused and appeared to the handmaid of Christ, raging at her with a threatening countenance like a monstrously large dog, and he whined and said, 'O wanton! You are our enemy and adversary! Through you I have just received the greatest harm, for you have taken away from me one of my most special helpers!'

After this same soldier had persevered for a little time in his good purpose, it happened one day that he was eating in the home of an innkeeper from whom he had borrowed money when he had lived in the world. This man was a rich burgher of Nivelles and Ywain had lived in his house in an extravagant and worldly fashion and, as soldiers do, had squandered large amounts of money. It was not easy for him to break the ties of intimate friendship with this man to whom he was still bound through his debts. As his host was serving him with many delicate dishes and they were eating sumptuously, the iniquitous enemy had collected together a company so that he might capture the fortified city (Jeremiah 1. 18) and was waiting for a suitable time to tempt him. The crafty tempter brought before his eyes the fleshpots of Egypt (Exodus 16. 3) and brought back to his memory the glory he had had in the world, the gourds and garlic of Egypt.

59. Then his determination began to waver and it seemed that 'Satan sifted him like wheat' (Luke 22. 31), but the merciful lover of men who 'does not permit anyone to be tempted beyond his strength' (I Corinthians 10. 13) and who 'does not extinguish the smoking flax nor break into small pieces the bruised reed' (Isaiah 42. 3; Matthew 12. 20), announced in the spirit to his handmaid how this knight was not avoiding the company of worldly men and for these reasons was wavering with an infirm mind. While he was still sitting at the table and deliberating many things within himself with a wandering mind, a messenger of the handmaid of Christ had been waiting furtively at the door. As soon as he could speak he told him that he should come immediately to his lady.

When he came to the place just outside Nivelles where the pearl of Christ was living, he discovered that she was sick with sadness and anxiety of heart and was bathing with a flood of tears the feet of the crucified one and embracing it. He was struck with wonder at this sight and his determination began to falter. When he asked her why she was weeping, she said 'I weep for good reason. I sorrow for you; my soul is disturbed because of the misery that you began in the spirit. You are consuming meat and proposing to be miserably consumed. You "have put your hand to the plough" (Luke 9. 62) and have looked behind you like Lot's wife (cf. Genesis 19. 26). You are ungrateful and unmindful of the benefits and superabundant mercies of him who liberated you from the fire of this world while others have perished.' Then he returned to himself and was filled with healing compunction at the miracle of such a revelation and he said, 'Forgive me holy mother and pray for me, miserable creature that I am. I promise you[87] and God that I will remain unmoved by these other things in the service of him who called me through you.' And although he was involved in the world to some degree (for he was still entangled in worldly business and was frequently compelled to go to the courts of the powerful), those who once had been his friends — both his relatives and his intimate acquaintances — mourned over him as if he were dead and pointed at him with their fingers as though he were a freak. Some laughed at him and others softened him up with flattery, while still others tried to drive him to exasperation and to break him with calumnies and scorn.

60. Some of the devil's attendants distracted the noble man who was not used to such injuries to cap or hood,[88] but he put before them all a shield of wondrous patience, although at times he was a little confounded in the manner of humans. When he returned home, he was like a sheep snatched from the jaws of wolves and ran to the solace of his spiritual mother after such great danger. She was divinely inspired in a wondrous manner and reported the injuries and insulting calumnies that had been spoken about the soldier of Christ and, with a prophetic spirit, told him the hour when he had been a little perturbed. 'Ah!' she said, 'It was at the very hour when you needed help that I was offering prayers for you to the merciful Lord so that he would grant you the grace of despising the

---

[87] *Vos*: note that as a sign of her moral superiority, James uses the second person plural form 'you' not the more familiar 'thou'.

[88] This is obviously an idiom, but I have no idea what it means unless it refers to injuries to those who wore a scholar's (or cleric's) cap or monk's hood.

prosperity of the world through imitation of him and of not fearing its adversity.' He was comforted by this miracle and by the solace of the handmaid of Christ so that neither wind nor rain could cause his house to fall that was founded on hard rock (Matthew 7. 25). Frequently he was pushed and almost fell but, with the merits of his handmaid, the Lord supported his hand lest he slip.

61. Sometimes when she was at Willambroux she saw demons preparing hidden traps with devious tricks so that they could capture some of her friends and, through their fall, cause great scandal to the simple. When the enemy had drawn his bow 'to shoot in the dark the upright of heart' (Psalm 10. 3), she was not content with tears or prayers but she would begin to fast, for she knew that this kind of demon was not easily driven out except by fasting and prayer (cf. Mark 9. 28). After she had humbled her soul through a forty-day fast, the Lord could endure her suffering no longer and he had compassion on his handmaid. He showed her that he had liberated her friend through her merits and he revealed to her into what a great pit of sin her intimate friend might have fallen had her fasts and prayers not overcome the enemy.

It would be woeful indeed for us who have lost such consolation in this misery and so much help in our temptations and tribulations, were it not that recompense is made for us in heaven for that which we have lost in this exile. Although the insistency of her prayers was helpful medicine against various and manifold sicknesses of the soul, yet because of a singular grace she excelled in helping those who were tempted by the spirit of blasphemy[89] and despair. Among all others, that spirit is the most evil of all temptations and she was most powerful in helping those who were tempted in this way.

62. It happened that a monk of the Cistercian order had a great zeal for innocence and purity but had so little knowledge, that through fervour of spirit, he tried to achieve something like the state of our first parents. After he had laboured long and hard to no avail and had tormented himself by abstinence and vigils and prayers and tears but still could not recover the first state of innocence, he fell into depression and melancholy. He wanted to eat but did not want to feel any pleasure of the senses while he was eating. Not only did he attempt to repress the first stirrings of sensual pleasure but tried to extinguish them

---

[89] See *VMO-S* 15–17 for the story of how Hugh, bishop of Ostia (later Pope Gregory IX) was miraculously cured from the spirit of blasphemy by Mary's finger. On this relic see Bolton's contribution to this volume.

altogether. He was trying to keep his life in perfect purity without committing even a venial sin. He was, in fact, aspiring to the impossible. It thus happened that at the prompting of the noonday devil (Psalm 91. 6) he was utterly unable to achieve the state he desired no matter how hard he tried and because of his extreme sadness he fell into a well of despair.[90] He no longer hoped to attain salvation because he considered those venial sins (which we cannot avoid in this life) to be mortal sins and therefore thought that he was living in a state of corruption. He did not want to receive the Body of Christ, even on those days when it was prescribed by the order. See how the ancient one, under the guise of good, draws a simple soul to great misfortune and to such a miserable fall. Once a soul has renounced free will and thrust aside the yoke of obedience, it becomes sick and even flees medicine.

63. But so that I tell a fable in a non-fabulous way let me interject what is not false, without fiction. This same monk who had tried to arrive at the state of our first parents, is very much like a frog who, when it sees an immensely strong and large ox wants to become like it and to become as large as he is. He then begins to blow himself up with great effort, but to no effect — for unless he burst, he cannot equal the ox's size. Thus did the brother want to raise himself above himself but, through despair, miserably fell beneath himself. When the abbot, a holy man and a friend of all good, found out about the sickness of his soul, he and many others poured out prayers for the monk, but despite these efforts, the enemy who had tortured the monk ceaselessly and had bound him in a powerful snare prevailed. Then the abbot, who was a friend of the holy woman and who knew her power[91] since he had sometimes felt it through experience, had the monk brought to the handmaid of the Lord. While the monk was saying the Confiteor just before the Introit of the mass, she supplicated the Lord with tearful sighs for the monk in a wondrous fashion. While she was most insistently pouring out prayers for him, something like little black stones were seen falling from the mouth of the monk at each word of the Confiteor. When, through a vision, she perceived that the stubbornness of despair and the blackness of sorrow and sadness were leaving the monk, she gave thanks to the Lord who 'does not wish the death of sinners but rather that they be converted and live' (cf. Ezekiel 33. 11). After mass it was as if the monk had come back to himself from

---

[90] On the noonday devil and *acedia*, see above notes 34, 56, 58.

[91] *Virtutem*: see above, note 67.

a distant place and he received the Body of Christ and he took the medicine of salvation and recovered perfectly.

Chapter VII

Through the spirit of wisdom, Mary is permitted to penetrate divine matters with discernment, and to keep peace with men

IV. The spirit of knowledge

64. Since she fled evil through a spirit of fear and did good through a spirit of piety — for circumspection is the necessary protection of discretion — the Father of light whose unction teaches us about all things, illumined his daughter with the spirit of knowledge so that she knew when and in what manner something should be done or avoided, and thus she seasoned every sacrifice with the salt of knowledge. For evil things are close to good and often while we are avoiding one vice, we fall into a contrary one. When one flees lavishness, sometimes one falls into avarice, or when one avoids the sumptuousness of worldly clothing one revels vaingloriously in sordid attire. Often vices seem to have the appearance of virtues and thereby deceive more perversely those who wish to follow virtue because they are hidden under a veil of virtue. For cruelty flourishes under the pretext of justice and careless sloth is thought to be mildness. Often what happens to the body through negligence is believed to have happened through indulgence. She, however, never bent either to the right or the left but trod the middle and blessed path with a wondrous moderation. For she rendered to God what belongs to him (Mathew 22. 21; Mark 12. 17; Luke 20. 25) and kept the peace of her neighbours as much as she could. She was peaceful not only with men of peace but also with those who hated peace. Living prudently among men of a depraved nation, she became 'all things to all men' (1 Corinthians 12. 6) so that she might win over all people to God. In this way her two blood brothers and certain others, although they had previously been immersed in worldly things, divinely inspired and aided by her prudent admonition, left everything and entered the Cistercian order.

65. Another time when she was sweetly and smoothly made one spirit with the Lord, she clung to the Lord with the paste of fear; we reported to her that some people had come to see her from distant places and had to return home quickly. Although the Lord had adjured us through [the example] of 'the roes and the harts' not to 'stir up nor awaken the beloved until she please' (Song of Songs 2. 7), sometimes we confidently roused her because she never wished to be awakened but always desired to lie with the Lord in the noonday (Song of Songs 1. 6). Sometimes when she heard a stranger arrive, she did violence to herself lest perhaps she cause scandal to anyone. She tore her spirit with such great sorrow from that sweetly joyful contemplation and from the embraces of the Bridegroom that sometimes it seemed that her entrails had burst and she vomited and spat out pure blood in great profusion. She, however, preferred to be afflicted by this kind of martyrdom than to disturb the peace of the brothers or, even more so, the peace of the pilgrims. Sometimes she knew about someone's arrival beforehand through a revelation of the Holy Spirit even when they were a long way distant. She would then flee to a field or a nearby forest, and although we tried to search for her, it was only with difficulty that we could find the hidden one, even after a whole day of searching.[92] Nevertheless sometimes for the sake of someone in need, she would be forced to interrupt her sleep [of contemplation], but she did this only because she had been incited by the Holy Spirit who would say to her, 'Go! But do not go from idle curiosity but rather because someone is waiting for you from necessity.'

Although she kept the peace with regard to her neighbours with marvellous discretion — and not just those who were good but also those who were unruly — yet she was very headstrong with regard to herself and abased herself to an extreme degree and afflicted herself — as it sometimes seemed to us — beyond measure. But she was so discreet with regard to herself that she would not presume to do anything for herself unless she had been intimately instructed by the Holy Spirit. She did not dare to spend one day without being refreshed by food unless she knew most certainly that she was rapt above herself and that her sensuality was absorbed within herself. Sometimes, however, when she was in this state, she would try to eat something to keep the peace of those who were near her, but she was utterly unable to do this and as a result nearly fainted for sorrow.

66. After she had obtained so much of the freedom she had previously requested, no one dared to ask 'Why are you doing this?' And when her manner of life passed beyond the boundaries of human reason and she had been left by herself with some kind of special privilege from God, she judged everything but was judged by no one. For the Holy Spirit frequently showed her the reason why some things should be done or not done, something that we were not able to achieve with our human senses. Sometimes, for instance, she would eat during

[92] Compare *VMO* 2, 47.

the week and on Friday, but on Sunday she would eat absolutely nothing at all. And when it seemed to us more reasonable not to eat at all on Friday which, after all is a day of penance and the day of the death of the Lord, but to dine on Sunday instead, she sometimes said to me, 'It is difficult for me to descend to sensible things when I have to interrupt the joy of contemplation by eating corporeal food. On Thursday, the day of the Holy Spirit, I am content with spiritual refreshment and on Sunday I am so overjoyed by the Resurrection that the eternal banquet is fully satisfying to me. I celebrate the whole day as a feast day and I do not need to descend to a lower level because I have no need for any sensible food.' When I heard this I was silent and did not open my mouth any longer against her and, reckoning my reason as naught, I was humbled in my own eyes for 'wisdom is justified by her children' (Matthew 11. 19).

67. She did not forsake sinners through indignation but was compassionate with them and often drew many back from the way of perdition by a prudent admonition. Nevertheless, her spirit greatly abominated the sins of men and she never presumptuously put faith in herself by living with or being on familiar terms with sinners. Sometimes depraved conversations corrupt good habits; and the Lord taught his disciples when they were entering a city that they ask who was in it and stay in a more respectable and secure inn (cf. Matthew 10. 11). It once happened when she was living in Oignies and went to Willambroux to visit some of her friends that she would pass through the middle of Nivelles on her return. Then she brought back to her memory the sins and abominations which worldly people had done in that town and she conceived in her heart such an indignation and abomination that she began to cry out for sorrow. After she had left the town, she asked for a little knife from her handmaid so that she could cut the skin from her feet because she had passed through places in which wretched men had provoked their Creator with so many injuries and irritated him with so many disgraces. Thus she suffered in mind and also, more marvellously, physical pain in her feet which had walked in the aforesaid places, and she could scarcely find rest after her feet had struck the ground so many times.

68. The prudent and discreet woman was adequately instructed in holy Scripture, for she frequently heard holy sermons. She guarded the words of the sacred writings in her heart and frequented the threshold of the church and wisely hid the holy mandates in her breast. And since good understanding is for all who perform it, when once she had devoutly heard these mandates, she undertook to fulfil them the more devoutly with actions.[93] Therefore, when she was in her last sickness and was failing and very near death, when anyone was preaching a sermon to the people in the church, her spirit would revive at the

---

[93] On Mary's vocation as a 'a living sermon' of the Gospel message, see above, note 1; see also the General Introduction for James's ideals of harmony between words and deeds.

word of God. Resisting death, she would prick up her ears, prepare her heart, and speak a few words about the sermon to those standing around her.

She loved preachers and faithful pastors of souls with such wondrous affection that, after their toil of preaching, it was bound to happen that she would provide them with hospitality or sometimes kiss and clutch their feet for a long time or to cry out from sorrow to prevent them from leaving.

69. With many tearful sighs, prayers, and fasts she insistently asked and obtained from the Lord that he recompense her with some other person for the service and office of preaching (which she could not herself exercise) and give her a preacher for herself as a great gift.[94] And so the boon was granted, and although a preacher is simply an instrument through which the Lord speaks, the preacher whom the Lord had given her brought the heart of the woman into spiritual readiness with prayers: he conferred virtue by bodily labour, ministered the word, directed her steps, and arranged his sermons for his audience in an agreeable and beneficial order through the merits of the handmaid of the Lord. While he was labouring in his duties of preaching, she supplicated the Lord and the blessed Virgin for him by saying the Hail Mary a hundred times just as Martin had prayed for Hilary while he was preaching.[95] She commended her preacher, whom she subsequently left at her death, most devoutly to the Lord. For just as he had loved his own to the end, so she loved them.

70. One day while she was in an orchard that belonged to a certain man in Willambroux, the devil appeared to her disguised as a shepherd. Then the impious one gathered together many knights who had to be at a tournament the next day near the town of Trasegnies[96] and who were staying at Nivelles that night. When the impious and disguised demon boasted that he was a shepherd, she said 'You are not a shepherd. Our masters who preach the word of God and faithfully feed our souls are the true shepherds.'[97] Then the worldly and proud enemy said, 'I have more flocks and more people who obey me than that master,

---

[94] The preacher whom God gave her was her biographer, James himself. Compare *VMO* 2, 79 and *VMO-S* 2, where Thomas exults at how James, thanks to her, 'reached in a short time such a pre-eminence in preaching that scarcely any mortal equalled him'. See also the General Introduction.

[95] I have been unable to locate the source for the story of Martin's recitation of one hundred Hail Marys for the preaching apostolate of Hilary. Although the recitation of the *Ave Maria* can be traced back to the seventh century, it was not until the eleventh and twelfth centuries that this devotion became widespread. See Herbert, '*Ave Maria*', in *DS* I: 1161–65 and above, note 52.

[96] Located near Binche in Hainaut.

[97] Caesarius of Heisterbach gives a fuller rendering of this anecdote with names of the pastors: *Die Wundergeschichten*, ed. by Hilka, pp. 128–29.

for I know them and they follow me[98] and hear my voice and follow my will.'
Then she could endure it no longer because he had usurped the name of the
Shepherd and had led his goats through the pastures of vanity to the pasture of
eternal damnation where death miserably devoured them. Thus groaning and
filled with compassion for the poor wretches, she left the demon and fled to the
church and for a long time afterwards she could not restrain from tears whenever
she remembered that most evil shepherd.

71. Although she was taught inwardly by the unction of the Holy Spirit[99] and
by divine revelations, yet externally she most gladly listened to the testimonies
of the Scriptures that were entirely in accord with the Holy Spirit. Although the
Lord could have illumined his disciples inwardly without verbally instructing
them, yet he taught them exteriorly through the office of the voice, and
expounded the Scriptures to them when he said, 'Now you are clean because of
the word which I have spoken to you' (John 15. 3). Therefore every day she was
more and more washed clean with the words of holy Scripture and was edified
by exhortations to virtue. She was illumined by faith, if indeed that could be
called faith for she perceived with the eyes of faith the invisible things which
God had revealed to her as if they were visible. Once, when she was present at
the door of the church in the village of Itère near Nivelles and a boy was being
prepared for baptism, she saw an unclean spirit coming out of the boy in great
confusion and when they lifted the boy out of the holy font, her eyes were
opened and she saw the Holy Spirit descending into the soul of the boy and a
multitude of the holy angels around the reborn child.

72. Frequently when the priest was raising the host she saw between the
hands of the priest the outward appearance of a beautiful boy and an army of the
heavenly spirits descending with a great light. When the priest received the host
after the Confiteor, she saw the Lord in the spirit who remained in the soul of
the priest and filled him with a wondrous brightness. If, on the other hand, he
received it unworthily, she saw the Lord withdrawing with indignation and the
soul of the wretched man remaining empty and shadowy. Even when she was
not present in the church but, as was her habit, was praying in her cell with her
eyes covered with a white veil, when Christ descended to the altar and when the
holy words were being said, then she was marvellously transformed and was
sensible of his coming. When the sick received the sacrament of Extreme
Unction and she was with them, she sensed the presence of Christ with a
multitude of the saints mercifully strengthening the sick, expelling demons, and
purging the soul. It was as if he were transfusing himself in light through the

[98] A blasphemous reference to John 10. 1.
[99] On the unction of the Holy Spirit, see Mulder-Bakker, *Lives of the Anchoresses*, pp. 142–43.

entire body of the sick person as the various parts of the body were being anointed.

Chapter VIII

Mary is fortified by the spirit of fortitude against adversity, and acts and gives council with the spirit of wisdom

V. The spirit of fortitude

73. It profits little to avoid evil through a spirit of fear,[100] to do good through a spirit of piety, or to have discretion in all things through a spirit of wisdom unless we resist threatening evil through fortitude, unless we persevere in good deeds through patience, endure until the end through constancy, and await the reward of eternal life through long suffering. Thus did her Father open his treasure chest and adorn his daughter with a most precious gem, that is he adorned her with the spirit of fortitude, and thus was she forearmed against all adversity so she might not be broken by any sudden attack of adversity and might sustain calumny with tranquillity, repay no evil for evil but, rather, might give a blessing to those who spoke ill against her and do good deeds to impious persons. She rendered good for evil and did not reply to calumniators but prayed for those who persecuted her, persevered in her plans through constancy of mind, bore everything through firmness of soul, willingly approached difficult things through magnanimity and did not fear threatening problems because of her serenity. Through a certain trustful hope, she was secure in a good plan that would lead to a good end and she gave a magnificent consummation to her holy and elevated plan.

74. Not only was she patient in the endurance of persecution and injuries, but she also rejoiced in tribulations and accepted the discipline of the Lord with great delight. When she was in her last illness and had already suffered grievously for almost forty days, we asked her if she found the pain irksome in any way, she said, 'If it please God, I would rather begin these forty days all over again.' Even more wondrous to relate, she added that whenever she had seen a sick person, she always desired whatever illness the person was suffering. Woe to you who are forced to carry the Lord's cross, who cast aside the discipline of the Lord, who carry the staff of the Lord, and all the while grumble against injury and bite it like mad dogs and make the pain of the body twice as great by impatiently enduring the pain of the heart. The precious gem of Christ was, as it were, inexplicably afflicted and sweetly tormented by a disciplined exultation of heart at the same time as an interior sweetness was anointing her exterior pain and

---

[100] *Timoris*: thus in the manuscripts. AASS reads *mortis*.

easing and alleviating the heavy weight of illness. Once, when she cried out from the pain of her paralysis and driven to beat her breast, one of her close friends had compassion on her and hid himself somewhere and prayed to the Lord for her. When she felt the illness diminish somewhat because of the prayers of the devout man, she said to her handmaid, 'Go and tell that man to stop praying for me. Although the medicine of his prayers has made me feel better, it is causing damage to my discipline.' Once when she was troubled by some grief, her distress caused one of her friends to become secretly heartsick. Through a revelation of the Lord, however, she knew the secrets of his heart and she sent her handmaid to him saying, 'Tell him not to sorrow any more for me for his grief aggravates the sorrow of my heart and I cannot endure that he sorrow for me.' She was more troubled by the sorrows of others than over her own infirmities.

75. She not only had patience for resisting those who were opposed to her with the spirit of fortitude but she was also patient in her abstinence from all carnal allurements. Thus she chastised her body and placed it in servitude so that it obeyed the bidding of the spirit and did not contradict it nor did she ever excuse herself with any pretence. She did not grumble against the Lord but by imitating the fortitude of the Lord, she never became careless through sloth and never or rarely did her body fail through hard work. Thus did that youthful drummer,[101] as it were, dry out her body by stretching it between two crosses so that she did not feel even the first stirrings of lust rise against her for many years. And from the great trust that she had towards men, from the abundance of her innocence and pure simplicity she thought them all to be like her. For this reason when one of her close friends clasped her hand from an excess of spiritual affection because he was very close to her although in his chaste mind he thought no evil — he felt the first masculine stirrings rising in him. She knew nothing about this and when she heard a voice from above saying 'Do not touch me' (John 20. 7) she did not understand what it meant. Truly the God of mercy has compassion on our weaknesses and he did not want to discompose the man in front of the holy woman but, as though he were jealous, he wished to guard the chastity of his friend. He therefore warned the man of the danger that was looming and when she said to him 'I just now heard a voice saying "Do not touch me" but I do not know what it means', he understood what was meant by it. And giving thanks that his weakness had not been discovered, he withdrew from her presence and thereafter he carefully guarded himself against such temptations whenever such occasions might occur.[102]

[101] *Tympanistria*: like Mary, Lutgard was surrounded by young girls with timbrels on her ascent to heaven (*VLA* 3, 16).

[102] In his *Life of Lutgard*, in *VLA* 2, 3, Thomas of Cantimpré has Lutgard pray for James because he was affected 'by an excessive human love' for, presumably, Mary. Is James hinting

VI. The spirit of counsel

76. Through the spirit of counsel she awaited him who would make her safe from both faintheartedness and turbulence of spirit. She was not precipitous nor did she show a lack of order in her behaviour, but she did everything diligently with foresight and showed deliberation in everything she did or did not do. She never omitted to do something through faintheartedness and never did anything with a turbulent, unconsidered or impetuous mind. In all her ways her eyes preceded her steps and she did everything with foresight lest she might repent even a little after the deed. Without seriousness, without the maturity of foresight, what could she do? He who said of himself 'I, wisdom, live in counsel and am among wise thoughts' (Proverbs 8. 12) filled her mind and lived in her soul. Although she inwardly experienced the intimate counsel of the Holy Spirit and although she was sufficiently instructed in holy Scriptures, yet from the extreme abundance of her humility, she did not disdain to subject herself willingly and devoutly to the counsels of others by renouncing her own will, lest she appear to be wise in their eyes.

77. Many of her intimate friends who had frequently had experience of her divine prudence did not dare to do anything important without her counsel, for what she could not know through human reason, divinely inspired, she knew by the prayers she had sent forth. Thus, when one of her friends who was content in his insignificance and humbly served the Lord the more securely because he was the more withdrawn from men's eyes and the more remote from worldly glamour, was asked by a certain nobleman to be his master and provide him abundantly with horses and clothing and many good things, he consulted the holy woman to ask what he should do. She who never presumed to do anything by herself, sent forth prayers and after she had returned from the bridal bed of divine counsels, replied, 'I saw in this deed a black horse prepared for you which neighed on its way to hell to the accompaniment of applause from an army of demons. My counsel therefore is that you remain in the vocation to which you were called by God lest you give an occasion to the devil through ambition and the glamour of the world.'

78. Among her other friends was one who was the dearer to her because he was the more humble. Once when he had a prebend that was barely sufficient for his needs, he received through prayers another that was greater in dignity as well as more highly paid. He was devout and of good morals and consulted the handmaid of Christ whether he had offended God in this deed. As was her wont, she answered hesitantly but, divinely inspired and assured of the certainty of her belief by divine revelation, she said with absolutely no scruple of doubt 'I saw a man attired in white vestments and ready enough for the race. He had a black

at the same incident?

mantle covering him and he was burdened with a useless encumbrance.' As she was saying this and other things of the same kind, he had a presentiment from God that those things that she had uttered were divinely inspired. He only remembered the first thing she said but it was enough for him and the prudent and God-fearing man agreed to the salutary counsel, He immediately resigned the other post lest he occupy the place of another man through ambition.

Forgive me brothers, you who join dignity to dignity and couple prebend to prebend (cf. Isaiah 5. 8)! What I have said is not mine but was revealed by Christ. Spare the handmaid of Christ. Do not slander the innocent. For how has she harmed you if she counselled her friend in a salutary fashion, if she told the truth as she had heard it from God? But if you who often pour over the pages of Gratian[103] ever look into this little book, you may scorn the visions of this handmaid of Christ as fantasies or dreams, laughing as is your wont. The Pharisees not only mocked the Lord when he spoke of avarice and said that a rich man could never enter the kingdom of heaven (Luke 18. 25; Matthew 19. 24; Mark 10. 25), but they judged him to be insane.

79. And lest I tell about the great deeds of the holy woman and omit to mention certain persons, I will not spare myself. Indeed I will tell a story of my own unhappiness. When, although unworthy, I began to preach the word of God to the simple laity, I had neither the experience nor the practice in composing sermons for the people and I was always fearful lest I perhaps fail by giving an imperfect homily. I gathered together many authorities from every source and, when I had collected very many of them, I could talk about almost everything from the top of my head, for a stupid man tells everything that is in his spirit while a wise man keeps back some for future use. After I had totally confused myself with such prodigality, it once happened after I had given a sermon, that I returned to myself and experienced a certain sluggishness of mind. It seemed to me that I had said much that was disordered and badly organized. The handmaid of Christ saw that I was depressed by this kind of sadness but that I was too embarrassed to tell her the cause of it. I became even more miserable when, as is the custom, anyone freely congratulated me after one of my sermons and told me how well and subtly I had spoken, I did receive some consolation and although I am ashamed to make my foulness public, I do not dare hide the praises of the holy woman. Once when she saw me confused and

---

[103] In the *Concordantia discordantium canonum* (*c.* 1140) of Gratian, women — especially laywomen — were forbidden to perform any function which pertained to the clergy, preaching, teaching, administering baptism. Women such as Mary would clearly unsettle those churchmen who were attempting to batten down the hatches of the ecclesiastical ship against all whom they thought would deprive them of influence. This probably is the reason why James, as Mary's advocate, is so scornful of those who 'read and reread the pages of Gratian'. See R. Metz, 'Recherches sur la condition de la femme selon Gratien', *Studia Gratiana*, 12 (1967), 377–96, and Lauwers, 'Entre Béguinisme et Mysticisme', p. 53, and notes 50–52.

overwhelmed by the sadness of which I have just spoken and while I was behaving erratically, she called me to her and wondrously opened the double wound of the temptation with which I was wounded. 'I saw', she said, 'the likeness of a man surrounded by clouds. He was entirely covered with an overabundance of hair, and I saw a harlot who was adorned with what looked like rays shining from beneath her clothing. She walked around him and looked at him fawningly and after she had circled him many times, she threw one of her rays at him and drove away a part of the darkness.' By means of this parable I understood most certainly and very quickly that I was sick with a triple disease: the superabundant hair produced my sadness; the adorned harlot betokened pride, and her rays signified that adulation which gave me wretched consolation. I do not know how to speak of you, O holy mother, with sufficient praises, you who knew the secrets of God. The Lord does not open the thoughts of men in vain, but confers strength for healing to the sick by your prayers.[104]

80. She was a friend of a certain holy and good young woman who was a recluse in Willambroux whose name was Heldewidis. She greatly loved her and for twelve years nourished her daughter in the Lord like a mother.[105] When the young woman was tempted by any difficult situation, she revealed the temptations and thoughts that young woman had in her heart. She knew what was in the mind of the astonished person and long before the event, she forearmed her against temptations that were threatening her. When the recluse received great comfort from the presence of Master Guido[106] (at that time chaplain in the church of Willambroux), she foretold that the master was going to leave Willambroux with his brother John,[107] six months before it happened: things like this happen very suddenly and greatly upset many people. She thus forewarned her with many exhortations[108] so that she might peacefully endure the absence of those whom she greatly loved. She foretold long before the event that a certain religious woman named Beslina who had served the handmaid of Christ for a long time religiously and faithfully, would leave her service. This

---

[104] James gives insight here in a much more active collaboration of Mary and James than in *VMO* 2, 69.

[105] This recluse must have lived at Willambroux in the twelve years before 1207, when Mary moved to Oignies. The anchorhold stayed inhabited until at least 1272. See Simons, *Cities of Ladies*, App. I. 81, p. 293.

[106] The man whom James calls Master Guido is not to be confused with Prior Giles (Aegidius) of the Supplement (as I mistakenly believed when I first read the *VMO*). This Guido (d. 8 September 1227) was the brother of Mary's husband, John, and was a 'priest of the beguines at Nivelles' (*BUA* 2, 30, 31: 338), ministering to the hospital chapel of St Sépulchre and its adjacent beguine community. See Simons, *Cities of Ladies*, p. 46, and notes 32 and 127.

[107] John was Mary's husband.

[108] Reading *exhortationibus* for the AASS *exportationibus*.

woman had been a great consolation to the recluse but she said that she would endure whatever the Lord would provide without anxiety.

Once a certain master who had been living in France planned to come to Oignies. When one of the brothers of the house at Oignies planned to go as far as Paris to guide him, she said, 'Wait and do not rush off, for the messenger whom the master is sending to us is already on the way.' Thus by her counsel the brother remained there and waited for the messenger whom she, with prophetic spirit, predicted would come to Oignies. And when the master had gone to Rome to visit the shrines of the apostles, false rumours were announced that he was dead. His friends believed the rumours and sorrowed but when they wanted to celebrate mass, she said 'He is not dead but lives and on such and such a day he will return alive and well from Rome'. Everyone marvelled and delayed the prayers of the mass and the outcome proved that her prediction had been correct.

Chapter IX

She contemplates the Divine through the spirit of understanding; she knows what is absent and to come

VII. The spirit of understanding

81. The daughter of Jerusalem, adorned with ornaments, shining with the lights of the aforesaid gifts of the Holy Spirit, turned to heavenly things with a purified heart by the spirit of understanding. Her soul chose suspension because it often flew higher for whole days at a time and she gazed on the sun of justice like an eagle,[109] not cast back down below by the rays of the sun. All the humours of her senses were dried out by these rays and, purged from the cloud of all corporeal images and from every fantasy and imagining, she received in her soul simple and divine forms as if in a mirror.[110] Having put away from herself sensible forms, the undivided and unchanging species of supra-heavenly things sprang back into her mind more purely as they approached more closely the highest, simple and unchanging majesty.[111] When her subtle and enfeebled spirit,

[109] The eagle representing contemplation and the soul's attentiveness on the heavenly secrets was a medieval commonplace. See John Steadman 'Chaucer's Eagle: A Contemplative Symbol', *Publications of the Modern Language Association of America*, 75 (1960), 153–59, note 159.

[110] On the mirror image in the medieval mystical tradition, see Ritamary Bradley, 'The Speculum Image in Medieval Mystical Writers', in *The Medieval Mystical Tradition in England* [...], ed. by Marion Glasscoe (Cambridge: Brewer, 1984), pp. 9–27 and her earlier 'Background of the Title Speculum in Mediaeval Literature', *Speculum*, 29 (1954), 100–15.

[111] James here grants Mary the highest form of vision, the *visio intellectualis*, as distinguished by Augustine in his *De Genesi ad litteram*, and quoted by Barbara Newman, 'What Did It Mean to Say "I Saw"?: The Clash between Theory and Practice in Medieval

consumed by the fire of holy love, penetrated above the heavens like the aroma of smoking green twigs,[112] she, as it were, walked through these sublime levels in the land of the living. 'She sought whom she loved through streets and lanes' (cf. Song of Songs 3. 2), now delighted with the lilies of holy virgins, now refreshed with the sweet-smelling roses of the martyrs. Sometimes she was received with veneration by a senate of the holy apostles and at other times she mingled with crowds of angels. When she ascended through all the levels, when she walked through all the places of paradise with such a gladdened mind, then she found him whom her soul ardently desired. There finally she found perfect rest; there she remained fixed without motion. When she ardently thirsted for him whom she loved, she forgot everything that had happened previously and she did not even pray any more for her dear friends. She did not think of the angels and it was as if she had even left all the saints behind her.

82. When she looked more closely into the book of life, she perceived many things in it through the spirit of understanding. When, for example, three years before men had taken the cross against the heretics in Provence, she said that she saw crosses descending profusely from heaven on a multitude of men. When this happened there had been no mention made about these heretics in our regions, but that was the time when God often spoke to her in the spirit and it was as if he were complaining that he had lost almost all his country and had been banished like an exile from his regions. When the holy martyrs of Christ who, for love of the crucifix, had come from distant places to a placed called Mongausy[113] to avenge the betrayal of Christ and were there killed by the enemies of the cross of Christ, she saw the holy angels rejoicing and carrying the souls of those who had been killed immediately to the supernal joys without purgatory. She saw all this although she lived far away. She therefore conceived such an ardour for this pilgrimage that she could barely be restrained, if she could have gone there in any way without scandal for her friends. When we smilingly asked her what she would do when she got there, she said, 'There I would honour my Lord by witnessing his name where so many impious men have blasphemously denied him'.

Visionary Culture', *Speculum*, 81 (2005), 1–43 (pp. 6–7). James clearly tries to evaluate Mary's sapiential knowledge in theological terms.

[112] Miriam Marsolais, 'Marie d'Oignies: Jacques de Vitry's Exemplum of an Ideal Victorine Mystic' (unpublished master's dissertation, Berkeley Graduate Theological Union, 1988), argues that James used Victorine spirituality as particularly developed by Richard of St Victor in his *Mystic Arc* to structure Mary's *Life*. She recognizes here, and elsewhere in the *Life*, metaphors invented by Richard in his *The Twelve Patriarchs, The Mystical Arc, Book of Three of the Trinity*, trans. by Grover A. Zinn (New York: Paulist Press, 1979), pp. 149–376 (here *Mystic Arc* 5. 5).

[113] *Mons-gaudii*: this event occurred in 1211.

83. When it happened that one of our close friends who lived at our house in Oignies and who had been signed with the cross was dying, she saw a multitude of demons roaring as if preparing for a feast. When she berated the demons and ordered them to withdraw from the servant of Christ who was protected by the banner of the cross,[114] they maliciously charged him with many sins, bringing up the fact that he had not yet walked in truth. But she prayed to the Lord for the sick man and saw a shining cross descending upon him, which protected him on all sides. Although this man had been overtaken by death before he had completed his pilgrimage, a great part of purgatory was taken from this man who had been signed by the cross because he had had the desire to go but could not fulfil it, just as the Lord had revealed it to the holy woman.

84. One of our friends who was noble by birth but nobler in faith, had served God devoutly and had left everything for Christ. His wife, however, was very worldly and vigorously opposed his plan. It is concerning this kind of thing that Solomon spoke when he said that there are three things which cast a man from his house: smoke, a leaking roof, and a wrangling wife (cf. Proverbs 19. 13; 27. 15). The man was very frightened lest his evil wife throw him out of his house, but the holy woman had compassion on his youth and said many prayers for the wife. Unperturbed, she consoled this noble man and predicted that his wife would soon be converted to God. As we now know, this in fact did happen and we thank God for it. Thereafter the wife despised the vanity of the world to the same degree that she had previously opposed the will and plan of her holy husband. Afterwards she encouraged him and induced him to follow the woman whom she had previously had thwarted and whose progress she had impeded.

It once happened that one of the canons of the church of St Gertrude in Nivelles was suffering from a terminal illness and the brothers at Oignies wanted to know the day of his death for a legitimate reason. A layman from Nivelles was at that time staying at Oignies and when they asked him to go back home and let them know when the canon died, the holy woman said to him, 'If you want to give them the news that they are asking for right away, you will have to leave tomorrow and begin your journey.' When he entered Nivelles the next day, the bells were already tolling for the dead man.

85. Once on the evening of Shrove Tuesday, when even worldly men are wont to refrain from eating, she saw some demons who were waging a grievous battle against a certain religious woman. They, however, turned back in sorrow and confusion because the Lord was helping her and, for this reason, they could not prevail against her. A little later she asked the woman how it was with her

[114] This is a reference to the metaphor of the cross as a military banner and irresistably recalls the famous hymn, *Vexilla regis*: I vespers, 3 May, 'The Finding of the Holy Cross', in *Liber usualis missae et officii* (Paris: Desclee, 1960), p. 575.

and she said, 'I was suffering grievously but at such-and-such an hour I was delivered by the grace of God.' She knew that it was at that very hour that she had seen the routed demons leave.

Once she was present when a certain priest was celebrating mass for whom she had frequently prayed. This priest planned to say mass for her because he did not have anything else to give her and did not want to appear ungrateful. After he had finished mass, she said to him 'This mass was for me. Today you have offered the Son to the Father for me.' When he marvelled and asked how she knew this — for only the Lord God 'knows the thoughts of men' (Psalm 93. 11) — she said, 'While you were at the altar, I saw a most beautiful dove descending upon your head and it extended its wings towards me as if it were flying. I therefore knew in the spirit that the Holy Spirit had passed the merits of this mass to me.'

86. When priests celebrated mass worthily and devoutly, she saw the holy angels rejoicing and very gladly helping them, and they gazed on them with an affectionate countenance and venerated them most devoutly.

Woe to those wretched priests, companions of the traitor Judas, who again crucify Christ as much as they are able! They defile the blood of the Testament with polluted hands, with immodest eyes, a venomous mouth, and an impure heart while they irreverently approach the Sacrament that must be venerated. They offend the holy angels who assist them and, wretchedly, obtain for themselves death instead of the medicine that gives salvation.

Once when one of her dearest friends was ordained a priest in Paris,[115] she was present in spirit although absent in body. She saw how it was with him when he was anointed a priest and what the place of his ordination and his priestly vestments were like, as well as the state of mind of the ordained man and other things of this sort. The priest was amazed when she told him what she had seen. When she sent him letters to Paris through her messenger, she wrote, among other matters, some things that the priest could not understand until they were fulfilled. For instance, she made this prophecy (as well as others like it): 'A new tree has just now flowered whose first fruits the Lord has destined for me'. When the priest planned to celebrate his first mass in France, it happened (just as it pleased God) that he celebrated it in Oignies in the presence of the holy woman.

[115] This priest was James himself.

Chapter X

Mary is attracted by the spirit of wisdom to taste the sweetness of God, in the feasts of Christ and the saints

VIII. The spirit of wisdom

87. In order that the prudent Craftsman may bring his work to a perfect end, the supreme Priest decorated his temple richly and the supreme King adorned his daughter with the sevenfold gifts of the Spirit and beautified her most excellently: that is to say, he adorned her with the spirit of wisdom which is first in dignity but last in fulfilment. With the savour of this wisdom she 'saw and tasted how sweet is the Lord' (Psalm 33. 9) and it was as if 'her soul were filled with marrow and fatness' (Psalm 62. 6). When, 'leaning upon her Beloved' (Song of Songs 8. 5), she grew merry with Joseph at noonday around the table of the Lord which was overflowing with delights. When she ate milk and honey from the lips of the Bridegroom (cf. Song of Songs 4. 11), her heart was affected in its innermost parts with a gift of honey-dripping wisdom: her words were made sweet and all her works made fat (cf. Proverbs 13. 4) with the unction of a spiritual sweetness. Amiable in works and inebriated with charity, her heart was meek and her mouth gentle. Indeed she was so inebriated and so withdrawn from sensible things that once when we were ringing the bell for none or vespers, it was as if she had just awakened and she asked if it were still prime. Once when she had lain continuously in bed for three days and had been sweetly resting with her Bridegroom, the days slipped by most stealthily because her joy was so great and so sweet, and it seemed to her that she had been lying like this for barely a minute. At other times she hungered for God with a wondrously changing affectivity, and at other times she thirsted for him. And since it is written 'They who eat me shall yet hunger and those who drink me shall yet thirst' (Sirach 24. 29; John 6. 35), the more she knew God with her senses, the more her desire increased. She was tormented, she cried out and begged that he remain and it seemed that she embraced him within her arms lest he leave and tearfully prayed that he show himself more clearly to her.

88. Sometimes it seemed to her that she held him tightly between her breasts like a clinging baby for three or more days and she would hide him there lest he be seen by others and at other times she would kiss him as if he were an infant. Sometimes the holy Son of the Virgin showed himself to her in the form of a gentle lamb beside her skirts. On other occasions, the holy Son of the Virgin appeared to her in the form of a dove for the consolation of his daughter, and sometimes he would walk around the church as if he were the zodiacal ram with a bright star in the middle of his forehead and, as it seemed to her, would visit his faithful ones. And just as the Lord showed himself to his doubting disciples in the form of a pilgrim (Luke 24. 15–31) and took the shape of a merchant when he sent St Thomas to the Indies,[116] just so he deigned to manifest himself to his friends in the form of a friend. St Jerome testified that when St Paula came to Bethlehem, she saw him in the form of a baby lying in a crib,[117] thus showing himself in a form suitable to the feast that was being celebrated. When, at the Nativity, he appeared as a baby sucking at the breasts of the Virgin Mary or crying in his cradle, she was drawn to him in love just as if he had been her own baby. In this way the various feasts took on a new interest according to how he manifested himself, and each produced a different state of affective love. At the feast of the Purification, she saw the blessed Virgin offering her Son in the temple and Simeon receiving him in his arms. In this vision she exulted no less from joy than if she had been present herself at this event in the temple. It sometimes happened during this same feast that after she had been walking in procession for a long time with her candle snuffed out, it suddenly burned with a most brilliant light that no one except God had kindled. Sometimes the Lord appeared to her on the cross during Passiontide, but this only happened rarely because she could scarcely endure it. Often when a great solemnity was approaching, she would feel joy for the entire octave before the feast. Thus, in different ways, was she transformed throughout the course of a whole year and wondrously filled with love.

89. When the feast day of a saint was approaching, the saint in question would announce his feast to her and on the day itself would visit her and come to her accompanied by a multitude of his heavenly companions.[118] As a result of the many intimate conversations she had had with the saints, she was able to distinguish one angel or saint from the other as well as she could distinguish one neighbour from another.[119] When any saint who was unknown in these parts brought her news that his feast was being celebrated in some distant place, she would rejoice in this solemn feast. Even when she did not know about the feast, she could distinguish in the secrecy of her heart those days which were festive

[116] See 'The Acts of Thomas', trans. by R. M. Wilson in *New Testament Apocrypha*, ed. by Wilhelm Schneemelcher, 2 vols (Philadephia: Westminster Press, 1963–65), II, 442–531.

[117] Jerome, *Life of Paula* 9: 'And in my hearing she swore that she had seen the Lord with the eyes of faith wrapped in swaddling clothes and lying in a manger', in AASS, 26 January, I, 327–37.

[118] On the thirteenth century as a crucial moment in the development of personal veneration of saints in the Low Countries, see Anneke B. Mulder-Bakker, 'Saints without a Past: Sacred Places and Intercessory Power in Saints' Lives from the Low Countries', in *The Invention of Saintliness*, ed. by Mulder-Bakker, pp. 38–57, and the contribution of Brenda Bolton to this volume.

[119] See in Lutgard's *Life*, in *VLA* 3, 13: 'When she was asked by some friends how she could distinguish among the saints, she said "From Christ himself, the holy of holies, there comes forth a splendour which shines in the soul and in which I perfectly and directly know each one of the saints who appears to me"'.

and those which were not, because solemn days were more sweet to her taste than ordinary days: she celebrated these festive days since they were written in her spiritual consciousness and impressed in her heart as if in a martyrology.

Once, when she was in a church dedicated to St Gertrude in the village of Lenlos, one of the feasts of this saint was to have been celebrated the next morning. The parish priest knew nothing about the feast, but she felt that a solemnity was approaching. When the priest did not show up — as he should have done — or another did not ring the bells at the vespers preceding the feast — she rose from her place and began to ring the bells as hard as she could. When the priest heard them ringing, he was filled with amazement and ran to the church and asked, 'Why are you ringing the bells as if it were a feast day? We are not accustomed to ring the bells at this hour except on feasts.' Then embarrassed and timid, she said, 'Forgive me, my lord, but tonight is a great feast and although I do not know whose feast it is, I feel that this church is full of joy.' Then the priest opened the calendar and discovered that the next day was the feast of St Gertrude.

90. She had so many and such great consolations from the Lord that even while she was at recreation, she would pay no attention to outward things and could always sit in one place without any companionship or boredom or sloth. Sometimes when she was in her cell, she heard the most sweet voice of the Lord saying 'Here is my beloved daughter in whom I take great delight' (cf. Matthew 3. 17, 12. 18, 17. 5; Mark 1. 11, 9. 7; Luke 3. 22, 9. 35). When she was rapt outside herself, it seemed to her that her head was lying upon the knees of the glorified Christ.[120] Sometimes at the moment when an angel brought a message, she was saluted by some of the saints of heaven. When she prayed before the altar of St Nicholas, it sometimes seemed to her that milk flowed from his relics.[121] Sometimes she saw rays coming out of the image of the crucifix that came towards her and penetrated as far as her heart. In all these things she was greatly delighted and wondrously comforted in her spirit.

[120] This recalls the iconography of the so-called 'Christus-Johannes-Gruppe', very popular in religious women's circles. See *Krone und Schleier: Kunst aus mittelalterlichen Frauenklöstern* (Munich: Hirmer, 2005), cat. no. 310, pp. 409–11.

[121] The church at Oignies was dedicated to St Nicholas. Although James says that Mary saw milk flowing from his relics, this might be an error for 'oil' or might perhaps refer to an oleaginous water resembling milk. The oil that seeped from Nicholas's bones at Bari was counted as a great treasure and many churches dedicated to him possessed a phial of it. Even his bones were said to drip oil. See Charles W. Jones, *Saint Nicholas of Myra, Bari, and Manhattan: Biography of a Legend* (Chicago: University of Chicago Press, 1978), pp. 69, 75. Further investigation into the unctuous miracles of Nicholas — and, by extension, of Catherine — might well clear up my interpretation of the oil which dripped from the fingers of Lutgard (VLA 1, 16), and the breasts of Christina Mirabilis (*VCM* 19), whose life was intimately connected to the monastery of St Catherine in Sint-Truiden.

Once St Bernard, the father and luminary of the Cistercian order, appeared to her as if with wings and he stretched his wings around her. When she had been sitting with him for a long time in the choir of the church and asked him what kind of wings they were, he replied that, like an eagle, he attained the high and subtle things of divine Scripture through high flying and that the Lord had opened to him many of the heavenly secrets.

She had a great veneration for St John the Evangelist and loved him with a special love. Once when she had confessed a very little venial sin to a certain priest with many tears and groans and he asked her why she was weeping, she said, 'I cannot restrain my tears', for she saw an eagle on her breast which plunged its beak into it as if into a well and filled the air with great cries.[122] Thus in the spirit did she understand that St John had borne to the Lord her tears and groans.

91. Once she saw a certain priest devoutly and tearfully celebrating mass and it seemed to her that a dove descended on the shoulders of the priest and that a fountain sprang up from his shoulder. Once she saw the Son of the Virgin in the form of a boy and the pyx on which reposed the Body of Christ surrounded with a great brightness. When we asked her to describe this brightness, she replied that as the light of the sun so far exceeds the light of a candle, so much the more did this brightness exceed the brightness of the sun. And when some relics were brought to our church, she felt the arrival of these relics in the spirit even before they arrived. She exulted with the holy relics for the whole night and she saw that Christ was also rejoicing and that the other relics received the new relics with exultation and joy. It was in this way that her spirit marvellously perceived whether they were true relics or not. When she looked at the little cross in the church of Oignies which contains a piece of the holy cross, it seemed that it shone very brightly and that a ray of heavenly brightness came out of it.

A close friend of ours and of our house discovered, among other relics, a bone of a certain saint that had no written verification. When he brought these relics to her to guarantee them as true relics, she perceived their power and truth in the spirit and when she prayed that God show her whose bones they were, a certain saint appeared to her, shining with very many merits. When the holy woman

[122] See *VLA* 1, 15: 'An eagle appeared to her in the spirit, his wings brightly shining with such lustre that all the universe could have been enlightened by the dazzling clarity of its rays. She was so astonished at this vision with a wonderment which exceeded any words to describe it that she had to wait until the Lord moderated the glory of such a vision to the capacity of her weak sight. And so it happened. When the intensity of the vision was thus weakened, she saw in contemplation that the eagle was placing its beak on her mouth and filling her soul with such a flashing from such an ineffable light that no secrets of the divinity lay hidden from her insofar as is possible for mortal people, and she drank so deeply and abundantly from the torrent of voluptuousness that the eagle found the vessel of her heart made that much more enlarged and widely open because of this desire.'

asked the saint who he was, he did not give his name but wrote four letters before the eyes of her mind. Later, when she recalled them to her consciousness, she did not know what they meant and, calling a cleric, she told him that the letters were a, i, o, l and asked him what they meant. He spelled them out together and told her their meaning and then she knew clearly that these relics were those of St Aiol[123] who had great honour in Bourges in Champagne.

92. When she languished in this exile from her desire for the satisfactions of eternity and grew faint from her love of the vision of God and from her yearning for eternal beatitude, then the only and best remedy for her was the manna of the heavenly bread that was her only solace until she could arrive at the promised land.[124] The anxiety of her heart and her desire was moderated by this; by this, all her sorrows were soothed and her spirit strengthened; by this highest and most excellent sacrament, she patiently endured all the perils of this pilgrimage. She overcame all the labours of this desert and having been invigorated by this food, set as naught all the failings of this wretchedness. The holy bread strengthened her heart; the holy wine inebriated her mind, filling it with rejoicing; the holy Body made her fat and the life-giving blood washed and purified her. She could not long endure without this consolation. Life itself was for her the same as receiving Christ's Body, and to be separated from this sacrament for a long time or to abstain from it was like death to her. She had learned from experience in this world what God had said in the Bible: 'Unless you eat of the flesh of the Son of Man and drink his blood, you will have no life in you; who eats my body and drinks my blood will have eternal life' (John 6. 54). These words were not as hard for her as they were for the Jews: on the contrary, they were sweet, for she felt all delight and all sweetness of taste in the reception of the holy Sacrament. She felt this both inwardly in her spiritual consciousness and [externally in her body], for it was tasted like honey dripping in her mouth. When the Lord appeared to her in the likeness of a boy tasting of honey and smelling of spices, she would often gladly admit him into the pure

---

[123] Aigulph [Ayoul] was either Aigulf, abbot of Lérins, who verified and translated the bodies of St Benedict of Nursia and his sister from Monte Cassino to Fleury *c.* 690–707, or a ninth-century solitary who lived in the forests near Bourges (Pruvium) whom the clergy and the people of the diocese unanimously chose as their bishop. Although he accepted the position reluctantly, he reigned wisely and well for twenty-four years and was one of the signatories of the Council of Toulouse in 829. He died in 836. Lutgard had a similar experience when she discovered the name of the hitherto forgotten Osanna (*VLA* 2, 34).

[124] Mary experiences communion in a similar way as Juliana of Cornillon was going to proclaim in her liturgy of the Feast of Corpus Christi, *Animarum cibus*: as a foretaste of heavenly bliss, more than as a reminder of the Passion. As is alluded to in *VMO* 2, 106, Mary, or James, had already learnt about the Eucharistic theology and the new feast that Juliana had just begun to think about in these years. See Mulder-Bakker, *Lives of the Anchoresses*, pp. 86–117.

and richly decorated chamber of her heart. Sometimes after the solemnity of mass when she was thirsting for the life-giving Blood and could not endure its absence any longer, she would beg that she might at least look for a long time into the empty chalice on the altar.

Chapter XI

Her arrival at Oignies, her pious preparation for death

IX. Her arrival at Oignies

93. Now that we have depicted, as well as we could — although not adequately — the precious ornaments of the daughter of the King and the fragrant clothes of the bride of Christ, we will hasten to a description of the hems of her garments, that is to say, to a description of her blessed passing; may we thereby offer to the Lord this final part of our sacrificial offering.[125]

After she had immolated herself to God for a very long time in Willambroux, she wanted to occupy herself with God alone because she could not endure the company of the men whose devotion frequently impelled them to visit her since she lived so close to Nivelles.[126] It was for this reason that she begged the Lord with many prayers and for a long time that he provide his handmaid with a place suitable to her purpose, and with people who would humbly give in to her desire according to God's will. A place in Oignies[127] was shown to her that she had never seen before and which, before her arrival, had barely been known among men because it was so new and so poor. She deliberated within herself for a long time what she should do since she did not know what kind of place it was, but she had trusted in the promise of the Lord long before she came to that place and, like an obedient daughter,[128] she asked for and received permission from her

---

[125] The ME translation reads 'we offer the head as well as the tail', reading *cauda* ('the tail' [of an animal] for *caudem* ('a note book, often containing public records'), as I did in the earlier editions of this translation.

[126] Mary was now about thirty years old, an appropriate age for choosing the life of a recluse, as was the case for Yvette of Huy and Bertke of Utrecht. See Mulder-Bakker, *Lives of the Anchoresses*. See also the General Introduction.

[127] The priory at Oignies was founded around 1187 by Aegidius (variously called Giles, or Gilles), whose career is outlined in *History of the Foundation*, 37–41, published hereafter. James mentions Oignies in his *Hist. Occ.* 21: 144. Oignies was located on the Sambre some 15 miles south-east of Nivelles. After her move to Oignies Mary seems to have shuttled between this place and Willambroux.

[128] Mary was 'like an obedient daughter' in things having to do with Church law but 'like a master' in matters of the spirit. See above, notes 12 and 76.

husband John and his brother, her spiritual father Master Guido,[129] to visit that place and, if it were pleasing to her, to remain there. They easily gave in to her because they feared to sadden the woman whom they loved deeply and because God had inspired them to yield. They did not, in fact, really think that she would remain in such a place because it was unknown to her and she did not have any close friends living there.[130]

94. Then, through the guidance of God, she made her way to that predestined place and when she was still a little distance away, St Nicholas who was the patron saint of that village came to meet her with great exaltation and he led her to his church. All that day, while she was on the road, she felt that the great solemnity of St Nicholas was present in her heart. She wondered greatly at this because she did not know that the feast of St Nicholas was usually celebrated there before the Nativity of the Lord and not in May. On the day that she arrived, the brothers of Oignies were making a great feast on the occasion of the translation of the saint.[131] As soon as she arrived there, she knew in a wondrous manner how it was laid out and knew who each of the brothers were who lived there, just as God had already shown it to her, and she also knew that it was the feast of St Nicholas. As well, she predicted that she would die there and she later secretly showed me the very place in the church where her dead body would lie in its tomb. Later events proved the truth of this prediction, for it was in Oignies that she paid the debt of nature by dying, although many people had tried to bring her back. After her death she was buried in that very part of the church that she had indicated, although some people wanted her to be buried elsewhere.

x. Her house in Oignies and her visitors
95. After she left her home region and her relatives[132] through the bidding of our Lord, she sat the more safely and the more sweetly 'under the shadow of him whom she desired' (Song of Songs 2. 3). I can neither conceive in my mind nor tell in words how much good the Lord wrought in her in that place — how

---

[129] Mary was therefore the sister-in-law of Guido, concerning whom see above, notes 32, 106, and 107.

[130] This story would seem to be a little exaggerated to say the least. When Mary moved to Oignies in 1207, the priory had already been in existence for twenty years, having been founded in 1187.

[131] The Feast of the Translation of St Nicholas to Bari is celebrated on 9 May and his regular feast on 6 December.

[132] Thus, does Mary finally make the pilgrimage for which she had so longed. For the previous twenty-two years she had been a pilgrim in spirit only who, according to James, had been prevented from taking to the road by the worried concern of her spiritual friends. For pilgrimage, see Jean Leclercq, 'Monachisme et pérégrination du IXe au XIIe siècle', *Studia monastica*, 3 (1961), 33–52; G. B. Ladner, 'Homo Viator: Medieval Ideas on Alienation and Order', *Speculum*, 42 (1967), 233–59.

many times — even more frequently than before — he visited her with the consolations of the holy angels, how many times she had intimate conversations with the mother of God in the church,[133] how many times the Lord himself appeared in person to her. The closer her desired end approached and the nearer the final year of her temporal life came, by so much the more abundantly did her Lord show her his treasure with overwhelming generosity.

When her last year was approaching which the Lord had promised her, she could not conceal her joy because six years previously she had predicted to Master Guido of Nivelles — and frequently to us — the year and the time of her death, although she did not tell us the day. Even more than before, she now could not contain herself (it was as if she were impatient that there be any delay before she was able to embrace the Lord), but from her desire she gasped and sighed and cried aloud, 'Lord, I do not want you to depart without me! I do not want to remain here any longer! I want to go home!' While she was being tortured with such violent desire and rapt outside herself, her entire body almost seemed to burst from the fullness of her heart in a wondrous manner and for a long time after she had returned to herself, she could not stand on her feet. While she was being drawn out of herself, she would cry aloud and her face would burn from the fervour of her spirit and, what is more marvellous, while she was in ecstasy of mind, she could see the wheel of the material sun with unblinded eyes. Then she was inebriated and could not be silent and she cried out, 'It has been said to me by the Lord that I will go into the holy of holies. O what sweet words! Tell me, Clementia, what is the holy of holies?'[134] Clementia was the name of her handmaid and often, when she was inebriated, she would ask her what some words she had heard meant, but neither of them knew. Nevertheless she frequently repeated that word, for it savoured sweetly in her heart. When she returned to herself, she marvelled that she had been even more vehemently ravished than usual and it was said to her, 'Do not marvel. This is your last year. There is not much time left to you', and she heard the voice of the Lord calling to her, 'Come my friend, my turtle dove! You shall be crowned.' Once when she was stirred up with a vehement spirit and more forgetful of herself than usual, from the fullness of her heart, among other things, she said, 'The garments of the daughter of the king smell like aromatic herbs and the limbs of her body are sanctified by the Lord like precious relics'.

[133] On Mary as the beloved teacher and guide of recluses, see now Mulder-Bakker, '*Maria Doctrix*: Anchoritic Women, the Mother of God, and the Transmission of Knowledge', in *Seeing and Knowing*, ed. by eadem, pp. 181–99.

[134] In the same way Lutgard 'did not find perfect rest for her spirit until she found the holy of holies' (*VLA* 2, 42).

96. In the year that she passed to the Lord, I was getting ready to preach and to sign those whom God had inspired to fight against the heretics.[135] This office had been placed on me by the Lord's legate — that is to say, the pope — and she asked me when I planned to return. When I replied that I would have to remain there a long time, she (who had not been ill at all and did not become sick until just before Quadragesima Sunday) said, 'I am leaving my testament to you because I want you to have it after my death'. She told me that the dissolution of her body was imminent for, as I mentioned above, she had foreseen her death a long time before the event. Since she did not know when I would return, she hastened to make her will and left to me the piece of lace with which she was girt and a linen kerchief with which she wiped away her tears and a few other little things dearer to me than gold or silver. When the time of her greatly desired illness was imminent and her final sickness was near, she said to her servant, a certain devout virgin who ministered to her, 'I fear that perhaps I am a burden to you and to others, for I must pass from this world after a long and grave illness. Who can assist me for such a long period of time?' She always feared lest anyone be grieved by her illness, but almost anyone would have grieved more had they not been able to assist and minister to her more frequently. She predicted that she would lie dead upon the earth on a Monday and for that reason she almost always fasted on Mondays and, for a whole year, she ate no meat at all.

97. When the time of her death was coming closer and closer, she busied herself even more to serve and please God day and night without ceasing. Thus from the feast of the Annunciation of the blessed Virgin until the feast of John the Baptist, she only ate corporeal food eleven times and then only in small quantities, always rejoicing and exultantly awaiting her wedding day. She loved the apostle St Andrew most among all the saints and he was her intimate friend, he who clung to the cross of the Lord with so much love that he would not come down from it.[136] This blessed apostle of Christ made this prediction to the handmaid of Christ before her last sickness: 'Be confident, daughter. I will not desert you, for just as I was a witness of Christ and did not deny him, so on the day of your passing, I will be by your side when you are in the presence of God and will attest to your character and be your witness.'

[135] In 1213, the year of Mary's death, James was commissioned by the papal legate to preach the crusade against the Albigensians.

[136] This is a reference to the apocryphal account of the martyrdom of St Andrew. See the reconstructed text in *The Acts of Andrew*, trans. by E. Best, in *New Testament Apocrypha*, ed. by Schneemelcher, II, 421.

XI. Her song before her illness

98. When the promised time was near which she had so tearfully anticipated and, groaning and sighing, had begged for, behold, a sound was suddenly made and 'the voice of the turtle was heard in our land' (Song of Songs 2. 12), the voice of exultation and testimony, a sound of feasting and jubilation which was like the sound coming from the high God, for he shook every tear from the eyes of his handmaid and filled her heart with exultation and her lips with harmony.[137] She thus began to sing in a high and clear voice and for three days and three nights did not stop praising God and giving thanks: she rhythmically wove in sweet harmony the most sweet song about God, the holy angels, the blessed Virgin, other saints, her friends and the holy Scriptures. She did not think about composing sentences, nor did she spend time arranging what she had composed rhythmically, but the Lord gave it to her just as if it had been written out before her at exactly the same time as it was spoken.[138] She rejoiced with a continuous cry and did not have to deliberate over it, nor did she have to interrupt her song in order to arrange its parts. It seemed to her that one of the seraphim was stretching his wings over her breast, and with this help and sweet assistance, she was inspired to sing without any difficulty.

When she had declaimed aloud for the whole day, from dawn to dark, her throat became so hoarse that by the early evening she could barely speak. The next day was Sunday and our prior was very relieved when she lost her voice because he was afraid that the worldly men who used to come to our church from different places might be scandalized by the incessant singing with such a piercing and subtle voice, and might think her a fool. The sons of the world, the sons of sorrow, are not surprised when someone cries out in agony or sorrow during the pangs of childbirth, but they are amazed and marvel if someone cannot be silent from a fullness of heart and cries out for joy. When, on the other hand, the sons of joy hear such things, they do not murmur and are not scandalized, but they humbly venerate the great things of God in his saints.

99. The next morning our percussionist began to play her lyre even louder and more piercingly than usual, for that night an angel of the Lord had taken

---

[137] On teaching in song see the illuminating study of Muessig, 'Prophecy and Song', and elaborating on that Ulrieke Wiethaus, 'The Death Song of Marie d'Oignies: Mystical Sound and Hagiographical Politics in Medieval Lorraine', in *The Texture of Society: Medieval Women in the Southern Low Countries*, ed. by Ellen E. Kittel and Mary A. Suydam (New York: Palgrave, 2004), pp. 153–79.

[138] Searching for comparable cases, Muessig, 'Prophecy and Song', p. 148, quotes Hildegard of Bingen: 'untaught by anyone, I composed and chanted plainsong in praise of God and the saints although I had never studied either musical notation or any kind of singing'. See *Saint Hildegard of Bingen: Symphonia: A Critical Edition of the "Symphonia armonie celestium revelationum"*, ed. by Barbara Newman (Ithaca: Cornell University Press, 1988), p. 17. For more information see the General Introduction.

away all her hoarseness and put into her breast an unction of wondrous sweetness. Her windpipe was opened and her voice renewed and for almost the entire day she did not cease from praising God, and men heard a voice of great exaltation and harmonious modulation, although the doors were shut and everything blocked up. Our prior remained in the church with the woman's servant but they could not understand many of the things that she was saying about heavenly secrets nor, alas, could they even remember those things, few as they were, which they had understood. At first she began her antiphon, in a very high and supreme tone, about the holy Trinity, about the Trinity in unity and the unity in Trinity.[139] She sang these praises for a very long time and inserted marvellous and, as it were, ineffable things into her song. She expounded the holy Scriptures in a new and marvellous way and subtly explained many things from the Gospels, the Psalms and the Old and New Testaments which she had never heard interpreted. From the Trinity she descended to the humanity of Christ and from there to the blessed Virgin, the holy angels, the apostles, and the other saints who followed them. Then, as it were, having come to the last and lowest point, she said much about her friends who were still in the world and commended them in order, one by one, to the Lord, and poured out many prayers for them to the Lord, and she spoke all this rhythmically and in the Romance tongue.[140]

XII. Her illness before her death

100. Among many other things, she said that the holy angels received their understanding from the light of the holy Trinity and that they have their fruit and exultation from the light of the Body of Christ that is glorified in holy souls. She constantly asserted that the blessed Virgin is already glorified in the body and that the bodies of the saints who rose from the death in their passion, will never turn to dust. She said (and was greatly gladdened by the fact) that the Holy Spirit would be visiting the Church soon and would send holy labourers throughout the whole Church for the profit of souls and illumine most of the

---

[139] 'Her antiphon': Mary composed her theological thoughts in liturgical forms just as Juliana would do in her *Animarum cibus*, which she composed for the liturgy of Corpus Christi in the 1240s. See *L'Office de la Fête-Dieu primitive: Texts et mélodies retrouvés*, ed. by Cyrille Lambot and I. Fransen (Maredsous: Éditions de Maredsous, 1946). Juliana also focused on the Trinity and the Incarnation, the humanity of Christ: see Mulder-Bakker, *Lives of the Anchoresses*, pp. 140–42. As we learn from the Prologue and *VMO* 2, 101, Mary kept in close contact with the religious women in Liège, and she knew about the young Juliana and her ideas, see *VMO* 2, 106, and note 144: therefore her own thoughts can be seen as pointing ahead to what was coming. On the Trinity see F. Boespflug, 'Le dogme trinitaire et l'essor de son iconographie en Occident de l'époque carolingienne au IVᵉ Concile du Latran (1215)', *Cahiers de Civilisation Médiévale*, 37 (1994), 181–240.

[140] *Lingua romana*: as Judith Oliver has rightly pointed out, refers to the French language.

world.[141] When she sang of St Stephen, the first martyr who is called 'the rose of heaven',[142] she also said that when he prayed at his death, the Lord gave him St Paul as a gift.[143] When St Paul was crowned with martyrdom in his turn and breathed out his spirit in death, St Stephen was present and offered St Paul's spirit to the Lord, saying to him 'You gave me this great and singular gift and I, with the fruit multiplied, give it back to you'.

101. She then asked the Lord, beseeching him profusely, on behalf of a certain preacher, that the Lord should first preserve him so that she could offer his spirit to the Lord at her death, in order that she could give back to the Lord as usury the one whom the Lord had given to her.[144] In a wondrous manner, she described all the temptations her preacher had suffered and almost all the sins he had committed at some time or other, and she begged the Lord that he vouchsafe to keep him from such things. Our prior (who knew the conscience of this man) heard her and since he had heard this preacher's confession, he went to him and said, 'Have you ever told lady Mary your sins? While she was singing she told your sins as if she had seen them written plainly in a book'.

She frequently repeated the song of the blessed Virgin (that is to say, the *Magnificat*) by setting it forth in the Romance tongue and in rhythmic prose and she found therein much joy and sweetness. When it seemed as if she finished her song, she continued on to the Canticle of Simeon, and afterwards most devoutly commended to the Lord her friends (that is to say, the religious women who dwelt in the city of Liège) and prayed for their peace. Throughout the first verse and at the end of each of the Canticle verses, she would repeat the *Nunc dimittis*.

---

[141] Joachim of Fiore's ideas about the Holy Spirit may have influenced Mary here, see Marjorie Reeves, *The Influence of Prophecy in the Later Middle Ages: A Study in Joachimism* (Notre Dame: Notre Dame University Press, 1993).

[142] The epithet *rosarium paradisi* which James applies to St Stephen, the proto-martyr, is not, as I previously translated it, 'the rose of heaven' but, rather 'the crown of heaven'. Although *rosarium* originally meant a rose garden, by the thirteenth century in the Lowlands, it had also come to refer to a type of head-covering, often adorned with flowers: *hodekin* in Flemish, *chapelet* in French, *Rosenkranz* in German, and *rosarium* (or *sertum* or *corona*) in Latin. See André Duval, '*rosaire*' in *DS* XIII: 942. The application of this epithet to Stephen is probably due to the etymology given to his name: *corona*: 'crown'. See for example, Augustine, *Sermo* 211a, in PL 39, col. 2140.

[143] See Augustine: 'If St Stephen had not prayed in this fashion, the Church today would not have had Paul'. See Augustine, *Sermo* 225: 5, in PL 39, col. 2144.

[144] This is the logical extension of Mary's description of Stephen's speech to the Lord in the previous chapter, when Stephen had referred to the interest (*fructu multiplici*) earned from the Lord's gift. It is surely an allusion to the words of the master to the wicked servant of Matthew 25. 27: 'You knew that I reap where I have not sown, and gather where I have not scattered? Then you ought to have put my money on deposit, and on my return I should have got it back with interest.'

She always repeated the *Nunc dimittis* in this way when she prayed for the religious of Nivelles and for many who lived in the diocese of Liège.

Chapter XII

Her last illness, her devout death

102. After three days of jubilation, she had her bed set up in the church in front of the altar and, returning to herself, she called the brothers and said, 'The Book of Lamentations went on while I was weeping for my sins, and a song while I was exulting and rejoicing in the thought of eternity. Then followed: "Woe to sickness and death", I shall not eat again.[145] I shall never again read from this book.' She then gave to the brothers the little book from which she was wont to sing her prayers and the songs of Our Lady and she patiently submitted to the discipline of the Lord and joyfully awaited her blessed end in silence and hope.

103. Although externally she suffered grievously in this illness, inwardly she sweetly rested because the saints who had been with her so often while she was healthy, now visited her more frequently in her illness. Christ often appeared to her and looked at her with a face full of compassion. The mother of Christ almost always helped her and, among others, St Andrew the apostle came to her many times and gave her great consolation and it seemed as if he made her unaware of her illness. Holy angels assisted her and devotedly ministered to her. One night when she was thirsty and was so weak that she could not get up or even walk by herself, two holy angels held her up and led her to the place where the water had been placed and after she had drunk, they led her back and she regained her bed without any effort. After she had been forewarned, she received Extreme Unction with all the apostles present, and St Peter showed her the keys and promised that he would open the gates of heaven for her, and Christ affixed the sign of the cross (the mark of his victory) to her feet.[146] When she received the sacrament and the different parts of her body were being anointed, she felt

---

[145] Thus Jerome: 'Eating the book is the starting-point of reading and of basic history. When, by diligent meditation, we store away the book of the Lord in our memorial treasury, our belly is filled spiritually and our guts are satisfied': Jerome, *Commentary on Ezekiel* 3, 5, quoted by Carruthers, *Book of Memory*, p. 44. There is a large body of monastic literature on the *lectio divina* and on rumination and the spiritual digestion of Scripture. See, for instance, Jean Leclercq, *The Love of Learning and the Desire for God*, trans. by Catherine Misrahi (New York: Fordham University Press, 1960).

[146] Were these the stigmata? See above, *VMO* 1, 22 for the wounds on her feet that were self-inflicted.

that each part was filled with a great light through the operation of the Holy Spirit.

104. Some of her friends who had already died were sent to console her: John of Dinant who was then reigning with Christ, and Brother Richard of Menehen-Capella, a good man and holy in life but still in purgatory. A certain man also appeared to her who had begged help from the handmaid of Christ while he had been ill and who was greatly tormented by purgatorial pains. Once he had the name and the habit of a religious and seemed to be in a state of perfection, but later he returned to the world to the scandal of many. Although the religious authorities reproached him, he entered into a relationship with a woman who, like him, had appeared to lead a perfect life but had broken her first vows. He said that he tormented himself above all because he had harmed the Church of God through scandal.

When the holy bishop of Toulouse came to visit her,[147] she received very great consolation from his presence and, for a time, strength of body as well and it seemed to her that the holy Virgin lifted her up in the air in front of the holy bishop. When this bishop solemnly celebrated mass in the church at the blessed Virgin's altar, it seemed to her that a white dove put the sacred host in the mouth of the bishop when he received the sacrament and a great brightness shone inwardly through him and she knew, by a revelation from the Lord, that his soul was illumined.

105. When she was so sick that she could eat nothing at all and could not even endure the faintest odour of bread, she easily and frequently partook of the Body of Christ. It was as if the host immediately melted and, passing into her soul, it comforted not only her soul but immediately alleviated her bodily illness as well. Twice it happened to her while she was ill that as she was receiving the Body of Christ, her face shone as if with rays of light. Once when we tested her to see whether she could consume an unconsecrated host, she was immediately revolted by the smell of the bread. As soon as her teeth touched the tiniest part of it, she began to cry out and to spit, and it was as though her breast would break from her retching, and she began to gasp with a monstrous anxiety. After she had cried out for a long time from her sorrow, and had rinsed her mouth repeatedly, she could barely rest for most of the night.[148] No matter how weak her body was, no matter how empty and lifeless her head (for she ate absolutely nothing for fifty-three days before her death), she could always endure the light

[147] Fulk, the patron of Mary's *Life*, apparently came to visit Mary on her deathbed and consecrated an altar in the church: *VMO* 2, 105.

[148] James also refers to this incident in his *Historia occidentalis*, in his long chapter on the sacrament of the altar. There he records two exempla, or miracles, of saints who recognized unconsecrated hosts, Maurice of Sully, bishop of Paris, and Mary. See *Hist. Occ.* 39: 276–77.

of the sun and never closed her eyes against the brightness of this light. Even more wondrous was the fact that she was untroubled by any sound which she knew pertained to God or to his Church. For instance it did not bother her when we were sitting beside her in the church and were singing in a loud voice almost directly into her ears. She was equally undisturbed when a large group of masons were hammering right next to her during the erection of an altar that we had arranged to be built and which was to be consecrated by the bishop of Toulouse. When we sympathized with her, she assured us that the sound did not hurt her head nor did it strike her brain, but she accepted it in her soul with great joy.

106. Family and friends from various regions came to visit her. When we mentioned some of them who were absent and had not come to her, she said 'I will still see them.' Of others, she said 'I will never see them in this world again', and we know that this happened. A long time before she died, a certain noble woman who had once been the wife of the duke of Louvain and had left the world to enter the Cistercian order as a nun had come to visit her when she was still living in Willambroux. When she left, she said, 'Lady, I do not know if I will see you again.' The holy woman said, 'Yes, you will see me again.' When this noble woman, who was then living in Cologne and far from our region, heard that the holy woman was labouring in her last pangs, she said 'I trust in the Lord that as she promised, I will yet see her.' And so it happened. When she arrived at our place, the bells were still ringing for the dead woman and she was present while they were washing and burying her.

She privately told certain things to one of our men through the revelation and promise of the Holy Spirit which, after her death, happened as we ourselves know. We will add these things as an appendix so that when they occur they can easily be examined in writing, [but we will not mention them here] lest they become a stumbling block to people of irresolute spirit. In the meantime we have written it all down but with no regrets have sealed up the book, so that knowledge of these events can be spread abroad after most of these people have died. This has been done since some men, unless they immediately see what God has in mind for the use of those coming afterwards, begin to murmur and say like the Jews, 'Command, command again; expect, expect again' (Isaiah 28. 10, 13).

We have already seen things happen which she foretold, such as those concerning the place where she lies buried and how her clothes have been sanctified and honoured against the cold, and how she lay dead upon the ground on a Monday. These things happened just as she predicted and, for the rest, we are expecting with the greatest certainty that they also will happen. For instance, we are awaiting the solemnity of a new hymn[149] that was promised to her by the Lord through angelic voices as well as the miracles that she saw with great clarity because, as I mentioned above, God frequently appeared to her in great brightness. Since she frequently ate meat on the day after a two-day fast, we are looking forward to a fast of two days before a double solemnity, and we are also waiting for a special veneration of the image of the blessed Virgin, because she frequently venerated and prayed.

XIII. Her death

107. When her last hour was approaching, the Lord showed to his daughter among the brothers the portion of her inheritance (cf. Luke 15. 12) and she saw the place in heaven that the Lord had prepared for her. She saw and rejoiced.[150] We could in some way estimate the height of the place and the magnitude of its glory if we could remember the precious stones and the virtues of gems which she herself wondrously described: if, that is, we could remember the names of the stones which the Lord had named when he showed them to her. We cannot understand but, because it is written 'Eye has not seen, O God, those things which you have prepared for those who love you' (Isaiah 64. 1): we can understand only with what glory she was worthy to be adorned. She who served the Lord so devoutly, who loved Christ so ardently, is the one whom the Lord singularly honoured with so many privileges on earth. When we were with her on the Thursday before her death and were helping her at vespers, she could neither speak to us nor turn her eyes towards us. She was lying outside her cell in the open air and her eyes were fixed immovably towards heaven and her countenance began to brighten with a certain peacefulness. Then it was as though she were smiling and from her joy she began to sing I know not what in a low voice for a very long time, for at that time she could not raise her voice. When I approached closer, I could understand only this little bit of her song: 'How beautiful you are Lord, our King'. After she had sung and smiled and occasionally clapped her hands and had remained for a long time in such joy, she returned to herself and it was as if she once again felt how sick she was, and she began to groan a little. When we asked her what she had seen and if she was able or wished to tell us a little, she said 'I could tell marvels if I dared'. On the Saturday at vespers, when her wedding day was close at hand, the handmaid of Christ (who had eaten nothing now for fifty-two days) began to sing the Alleluia

---

[149] 'De cantu novae solemnitatis': this is a reference to the new feast of Corpus Christi which was first celebrated at Liège in 1246 and which Juliana of Cornillon was already attempting to promote in 1208. James uses the same allusion to Psalm 39. 3 (40. 3), as the author of the *Vita Julianae* would do a few decades later, see *VJC* 2, 7: 124: 'Immisit in os meum canticum novum.' On this feast, see Rubin, *Corpus Christi*.

[150] This echoes James's words to Fulk in the Prologue, wherein he draws a parallel between the *mulieres sanctae* of the diocese of Liège with the inhabitants of heaven.

in a sweet voice, that is to say on that day of rejoicing and exultation, that day which the Lord had made, that day which the Lord had foreordained and promised for his handmaid, that day of the Lord, that day of the Resurrection, that day of the vigil of St John the Baptist when, it is said, the apostle John left this world although the Church is accustomed to celebrate his feast at another time.[151] For almost the whole night she was as joyful and exultant as if she had been invited to a banquet.

108. Satan appeared to her on Sunday, 'lying in wait at her heel' (Genesis 3. 17).[152] He disturbed her greatly and she began to fear for a little time and asked for help from those who were standing around her. She, however, took confidence again from the Lord and with strength 'broke the head of the worm' (Psalm 73. 14) and, making the sign of the cross, she said 'Get behind me filth and foulness': she did not call him 'foul' but 'foulness'. When he had departed, she began again to sing the Alleluia and to give thanks to God. When, on the day of the feast of St John the Baptist, the time of holy vespers was drawing near and at about the hour when the Lord sent out his spirit on the cross (that is to say, about the ninth hour), she also migrated to the Lord. Neither the gladness of her countenance nor the exultation of her face was changed by any of the pain of death. I do not ever remember that her face had more serenity even when she was healthy, nor had it ever shone with a greater expression of joy. Her face did not appear pallid or blue after death, as is usual. She brought many to devotion in and after her death by her angelic dove-like face, bright and clear in its simplicity and expression. Many were sweetly moistened with an abundant flood of tears at her death and they understood that they had been visited by the Lord through her merits in exactly the way that a certain holy woman had foreseen through the Holy Spirit when she had predicted that those who were present at her passing would receive much consolation from the Lord. When her tiny holy body was washed after death, it was found to be so small and shrivelled by her illness and fasting that her spine touched her belly and the bones of her back seemed to lie under the skin of her stomach as if under a thin linen cloth.

---

[151] Although the normal practice of the Catholic Church is to celebrate a saint's feast on the death day (*dies natalis*), the feast of John the Baptist is celebrated on 24 June in commemoration of his birth. John the Baptist's death by beheading is observed on 29 August.

[152] Compare Luke 10. 19: 'Behold I have given you power to tread upon serpents and scorpions and upon all the power of the enemy: and nothing shall hurt you.' See Gregory the Great, *Moralia on Iob*, ed. by M. Adriaen, CCSL 143 (Turnhout: Brepols, 1979), I, 36: 'because the end of the body is in the heel, what is signified thereby but the end of an action? Whether then it be evil spirits, or all wicked men that follow in the steps of their pride, they "mark the heel" (Psalm 56. 6) when they aim at spoiling the end of a good action.' Similarly, Bede, *Commentary on Genesis* I. 3, in *Opera exegetica*, ed. by C. W. Jones, CCSL 118A (Turnhout: Brepols, 1967), line 2120: 'the heel is the end of the body, so not without reason is the end of our life called the heel.'

109. After her death, she did not desert those whom she had loved in life and returned to many and she frequently spoke to holy women of proven conduct[153]. She taught her friends what they should do and warned them of dangers and removed from their hearts all doubt by certain and secret signs. We believe that by her prayers she obtained from the Lord the splendour of wisdom and fervour of charity for some of her friends. After the death of the servant of Christ, a certain holy Cistercian monk saw in a dream that a golden chalice was coming out of her mouth which she gave to certain of her friends to drink therefrom. Another person told me that in a dream he had seen her body as if transformed into a very brilliant precious stone.

In the year 1213 of the Incarnation of the Word, on the ninth kalends of July, on the vigil of St John the Baptist, on Sunday around the ninth hour, the precious pearl of Christ, Mary of Oignies was borne away to the palace of the eternal kingdom at the age of about thirty-six to where there is life without death, day without night, truth without falsehood, joy without sadness, security without fear, rest without labour, eternity without end, where one is not troubled with cares, where the body is not afflicted by sorrow, where a torrent of the divine will fills and satiates everything with the spirit of full liberty, where we both know and are known. Then 'God will be all in all' (I Corinthians 15. 28) and our Lord Jesus Christ 'will deliver up the kingdom to God the Father' (cf. I Corinthians 15. 24), he who lives and reigns with the same Father and the Holy Spirit, world without end. Amen.

---

[153] For example, Mary appeared to Lutgard and asked for her prayers on behalf of Baldwin de Barbençon who had succeeded Giles as prior of Oignies (*VLA* 3, 8).

THE SUPPLEMENT TO JAMES OF VITRY'S *LIFE OF MARY OF OIGNIES* BY THOMAS OF CANTIMPRÉ

Translated by Hugh Feiss OSB

INTRODUCTION

The Supplement to *The Life of Mary of Oignies*[1] was written by Thomas of Cantimpré and dedicated to Giles, the founder and prior of the community of canons regular of St Nicholas at Oignies. Thomas's work is a supplement to James of Vitry's *Life of Mary* [*VMO*] and deals especially with events concerning James. It ends with a two-fold complaint (*querela*) addressed to James urging him to return to Lotharingia. Apart from what is said in the General Introduction and the notes, here it will be helpful to introduce the author.[2]

---

[1] This translation was made during a National Endowment for the Humanities Summer Seminar held under the direction of the late Professor Robert E. Kaske at Cornell University in 1986. I wish to thank Professor Kaske, The Olin Library of Cornell University, and my colleagues in the seminar whose knowledge and good humour greatly facilitated my work. Special thanks are due Professor Ronald Pepin who read through a draft version. The Supplement, referred to as *VMO-S*, is translated here from AASS, 23 June, XXV, 572–81. Words that were in brackets or parentheses in the Latin edition appear in brackets in the translation. At two places (*qui/quid, sibis/cibis*), misprints in the Latin edition have been corrected. For this fourth edition, I have checked the translation and adapted the notes.

[2] Some of the more useful studies of Thomas of Cantimpré which I have been able to consult include: Paul Kirsch, *Des Thomas von Cantimpré Buch der Wunder und denkwürdiger Vorbilder* (Gleimitz: David, 1875); Alexander Kaufmann, *Thomas von Chantimpré* (Cologne: Bachem, 1899); Henry Platelle, 'Vengeance privée et réconciliation dans l'oeuvre de Thomas de Cantimpré', *Tijdschrift voor Rechtsgeschiedenis*, 42 (1974), 269–81; Henry Platelle 'Le Receuil de miracles de Thomas de Cantimpré et la vie religieuse dans les Pays-Bas et le Nord de la France au XIIIe siècle', *Actes du 97e Congrès National des Sociétés Savantes, Section de philologie et histoire jusqu'à 1610, Nantes, 1972* (Paris: Bibliothèque nationale, 1979), pp. 469–98. On his education: Alfred Deboutte, 'Thomas van Cantimpré: zijn opleiding te Kamerijk', *Ons Geestelijk Erf,* 56 (1982), 283–99. Additional bibliography may be found in G. J. J. Walstra,

Thomas of Cantimpré was born about 1200 AD at Leeuw-Sint-Pieter, a town of Brabant, a short way to the southeast of Brussels. His family were nobility of Brabant; his father served under Richard the Lionheart in England. During a pilgrimage to the Holy Land, he made his confession to a hermit who told him that he would surely obtain God's mercy should he encourage his son to become a priest.[3] Thomas, therefore, was sent to school at Cambrai (or perhaps Liège) from about 1206 to 1217.[4] While he was a young student, Thomas heard James of Vitry preach and was struck with such admiration for him that he remained attached to him all his life.[5]

About 1217, Thomas entered the monastery of Cantimpré outside Cambrai, a choice perhaps suggested by familiarity with its dependent priory at Bellingen near Leeuw-Saint-Pieter. The monastery of Cantimpré had been founded about 1180 by St John of Cantimpré (d. 1205/1210) whose *Life* Thomas later wrote.[6] The community was composed of canons regular who followed the observances of the abbey of St Victor at Paris. Thomas spent fifteen years as a canon regular of Cantimpré, where he was a zealous pastor of souls, dedicated to preaching and hearing confessions. As James of Vitry had found a spiritual mother in Mary of Oignies, so Thomas found a spiritual guide in Lutgard of Tongeren (or

'Thomas de Cantimpré, *De naturis rerum*: état de la question', *Vivarium*, 5 (1968), 146–71 (pp. 164–71); 6 (1968), 48–61.

[3] In his *Bonum universale de apibus*, Thomas writes: 'Hoc idem audivi a patre meo ante annos quadraginta, qui illis in partibus sub rege Richardo Angliae militavit': *BUA* 2, 27, 28: 560; and *BUA* 2, 53, 32: 513: 'Sed et patrem meum, ut me adhuc puerum ad litterarum studium, et vitam caelibem provocaret, saepius mihi cum lacrymis et devotione referentem audivi. Cum mare, inquit, transissem, terram sanctam, ac Hierosolymam visitare, veni in montem, quem Nigrum vocant: ubi sparsim multi viri sancti vitam eremiticam ducentes, Domino serviebant. Uni ergo eorum peccata mea confessus, responsum accepi, me de facili culpas meas per poenitentiam non posse diluere, sed si filium haberem, et hunc ad litteras ponerem, fieretque sacerdos idoneus Christo, potissime per hunc me posse iuvari.'

[4] *BUA* 1, 19 10: 74–75: 'Ego in quadam civitate episcopali annis undecim adolevi, ubi sexaginta duo canonici [...] in matrici ecclesia serviebant [...]'. See Deboutte, 'Thomas van Cantimpré, pp. 283–99.

[5] *VMO-S* 27.

[6] 'Une oeuvre inédite de Thomas de Cantimpré: La "Vita Ioannis Cantimpratensis"', ed. by Robert Godding, *Revue d'histoire ecclésiastique*, 76 (1981), 241–316. An English translation by Barbara Newman is forthcoming.

Aywières, (d. 1246) who helped him with the scruples he experienced as a young priest. He later wrote her *Life*.[7]

In 1232 or slightly before, Thomas left Cantimpré to join the Dominican order, that was then in its pristine fervour. Thomas entered the community of Louvain, which had been founded in 1228. He was sent for further studies to Paris and also studied under Albert the Great, probably at Cologne.[8] He returned from Paris in 1240 and devoted himself zealously to pastoral work. In 1246 he was sub-prior of the Dominican community at Louvain. For much of the rest of his life, Thomas preached in Lotharingia and adjoining areas. He was probably bilingual from childhood, which would have been an asset in his preaching work. He died around 1270.

Thomas managed to do considerable writing in the course of his long and busy life. Besides the Lives of John of Cantimpré, Mary of Oignies, and Lutgard of Tongeren (or Aywières), he wrote the Lives of Christine of Sint-Truiden [*VCM*], called the Astonishing (d. 1224) and of Margaret of Ypres [*VMY*] (d. 1237). The *Life of John of Cantimpré* was the first work that Thomas started and the last he completed. The Supplement to the *Life of Mary* was written about 1230, the *Life of Christine* in 1232, Margaret's in 1240, and that of Lutgard about 1248. Thereafter Thomas worked for fifteen years on an encyclopaedic work, the *Liber de natura rerum* [*De nat. rerum*] and later drew moral examples from the section on bees for his *Bonum universale de apibus* [*BUA*] that is dedicated to Humbert of Romans, the master general of the Dominicans from 1254 to 1263.

Thomas was a well-educated man who declared that he wished to relate only events vouched for by trustworthy witnesses. In the Supplement he first addresses Prior Giles, then James of Vitry. Most of the marvels he discusses involve these two men who were, in fact, in a position to confirm his veracity. Nevertheless, modern readers are likely to read the Supplement and Thomas's other works with mixed feelings. On the one hand, much of what he says seems fantastic: the devil looms very large; miracles occur with unsettling frequency; Eucharistic devotion is extremely intense; purgatory is a preoccupation. On the other hand, Thomas is a spokesman for the high ideals of clerical and lay life

---

[7] *VLA* 3, 38.

[8] *BUA* 2, 57, 50: 576: 'Vidi, et certissime expertus sum, sicut auditor eius per multum tempus, quod venerabilis ille frater ordinis Praedicatorum, magister Albertus'; 1, 19, 5: 70: 'Volo ut quicunque haec legerit, sciat me anno ab incarnatione Domini MCCXXXVIII fuisse Parisiis, ubi venerabilis Guillielmus Parisiensis Episcopus [...].' See Alfred Deboutte, 'Thomas van Cantimpré als auditor van Albertus Magnus', *Ons Geestelijk Erf*, 58 (1984), 192–209.

which motivated reformers from the middle of the eleventh century to the middle of the thirteenth; he portrays a close interaction between professed religious, holy women and laity; like James of Vitry and Mary of Oignies herself, he is very alert to the injustices of the growing market economy; he manifests a lofty regard for the religious gifts of women.[9]

Thomas wrote as a pastor of souls. He found in nature moral lessons for Christian life. The stories of those holy women and men of different social and religious milieux about whom he wrote manifest the work of the Holy Spirit stirring up the faith of the people of lower Lotharingia.[10] From the Holy Spirit come prophecies and visions, miracles and sudden conversions, wordless praise and dancing for joy — the manifestations of devout enthusiasm not without parallel in charismatic Christian communities of the present day. These devout Christians Thomas presents as models of consecrated chastity, simplicity of life, humility and service to the needy. Their compassion is nourished by prayer, vigils, and fasting. As Thomas shows, these holy women and men lived in a world where the clergy were sometimes avaricious or inert. Greed was rampant and heretics were winning converts.[11] Mary, like the other religious women who figure in Thomas's writings, was a devout daughter of the Church and the handmaid (*ancilla, famula*)[12] of Christ or of God, but she was also lady (*domina*), mother and nurse, very much filled with the Holy Spirit. One disregarded her word at considerable risk. The flourishing of piety, especially among women, was one key manifestation of the spiritual enthusiasm abroad among Thomas's contemporaries. The other was crusading. In the *Bonum universale de apibus*, Thomas mentions seven crusades that had been preached during his lifetime.[13]

[9] Platelle, 'Le Recueil des miracles', pp. 478–93; Kaufmann, *Thomas von Cantimpré*, p. 65; Kirsch, *Des Thomas*, pp. 24–40.

[10] In the translation 'spirit' is usually left uncapitalized and therefore as ambiguous as it is in the Latin text, but it almost always refers to the Holy Spirit.

[11] In addition to the works cited in the above notes, one might consult the fine summary of the state of Christendom as seen through Thomas's eyes in Robert Godding, 'Vie apostolique et société urbaine à l'aube du XIIe siècle', *Nouvelle revue théologique*, 104 (1982), 692–721.

[12] For a more specific use of this term, see Goodich, '*Ancilla Dei*', pp. 119–36. Unlike the servant girls whom Goodich discusses, Mary was originally a lady and wife. She voluntarily became God's *ancilla* and, precisely in that capacity, was filled with the Holy Spirit and empowered to deliver God's word.

[13] *BUA* 2, 3 9: 137–39: 'Prima crux nostri temporis contra terram Albigensium praedicata est. Secunda in terram sanctam, contra Saracenos. Tertia iterum contra Albigenses. Quarta

Mary, Thomas implies, should be a model for James of Vitry. James had felt the spiritual power of this handmaid of Christ who had left all to lead the *vita apostolica*. James had emulated Mary by leaving Paris and joining the community at Oignies. But now that he had become a cardinal at Rome, he was risking betrayal of the ideals he had espoused with Mary. He might not be susceptible to the 'gifts of Rome' which cardinals could receive from those who wanted judicial or administrative favours, but his comfortable life and his power were suspect to Thomas who was something of a stern moralist and chastening prophet.

Mary's mortal remains, her friends, and the people of Lotharingia were waiting for James's return. He might send presents, but material gifts were problematic to a community committed to following Christ who was stripped of everything on the cross. The present that the community wanted most was the return of James to them.

contra Stadingos, quos in Theutonia Henricus Dux Brabantiae cum suis stravit. Quinta iterum in terram sanctam. Sexta contra Aquenses, qui se pro scismatico Frederico quondam imperatore, contra Guillelmum regum Romanorum electum, stultissime opposuerunt. Septima contra Hezelinum nobilem Italiae.' Compare Platelle, 'Le Recueil des miracles', p. 471.

PROLOGUE

To his father in the Lord, most reverend in everything, Giles,[1] Prior of Oignies, N. [Thomas], a humble canon of the monastery of Cantimpré, wishes salvation in Christ Jesus, the author of our salvation

1. I have been asked by some friends and brothers of your charity to write about the many things which James,[2] formerly bishop of Acre and now bishop of Tusculum and cardinal in the Roman curia, omitted from his *Life of the Venerable Mary of Oignies*.[3] For a long time I postponed doing it, since I was very fearful of incurring the reproach of presumptuous audacity. This was especially so since that man had such knowledge and foresight, discretion and holiness, that to add anything to his words seemed to be the height of foolishness. However, in the face of my reluctance, some of them repeatedly drove home to me that often they had heard from his truthful mouth that he had not set down in writing a fifth of the deeds of the handmaid of Christ, lest he bore his readers by including too much of the incomparable magnitude of revelations and miracles which is the fragrance of life in the hearts of believers but the odour of death [in the hearts of the unbelieving]. Convinced by this argument, I then

---

[1] Giles (Aegidius) was one of the founders of the monastery of Oignies, but is not to be confused with Guido, Mary's brother-in-law who is mentioned several times in *VMO*. Giles's career is outlined in the history of the priory, translated below. According to that history, he was prior of the community from its inception in 1187 until his death in old age in 1233. The founding of a community could be a rather prolonged process. There is some disagreement about the precise moment when St Nicholas of Oignies was founded. Giles was Thomas's main informant: 'the man who reported to us so many miracles about the handmaid of Christ', *VMO-S*, see 3, 12, 13, 14, 19.

[2] For James of Vitry see the General Introduction and Margot King's Introduction to *VMO*.

[3] See translation of *VMO*.

prudently yielded to the prayer of these suppliants. There is nothing to be afraid of at this time when the ardour of holy religion has increased in intensity especially in the territory of Lotharingia, and in almost all Christian lands there shines forth the joyous veneration of Christ's handmaid. So, like speedy Ruth, I advance quickly to collect whatever things in the wide field of the life of Christ's handmaid escaped the diligent hands of that great harvester (Ruth 2. 2–18; Revelations 14. 14–16). So, holy father, Prior Giles, accept this work, exceptional at least in the deeds it recounts, which for the praise of Christ and the glory of his handmaid I have written with fear and reverence about the friend of your love. If I have made a human error anywhere, you will correct it. It is a perfect man who never errs in speech. I am not such a man but a sinner. May your kindness and genuine paternity prosper, and may Christ the Lord keep you safe and mindful of me in this endeavour.

Chapters[4]

[4] The AASS does not insert these chapter headings into the text. Instead the Bollandists divided the contents into four large chapters, whose contents can be characterized as follows: (i) Mary's revelations (2–7); (ii) Further miracles and revelations (8–13); (iii) Mary's death, posthumous miracles, and revelations (14–18); (iv) James of Vitry (19–27). I have included both sets of headings in the text, referring to the four large divisions as chapters. The text is further divided into twenty-seven numbered paragraphs.

XIV.   How she predicted that after her death, she would not allow her teeth to be removed from her mouth unless prayers had been offered beforehand (ibidem)

XV.   How Lord Hugolino, cardinal bishop of Ostia, was freed from a spirit of blasphemy by the relic of Christ's handmaid (15)

XVI.   About another holy woman, tempted by the spirit of blasphemy and freed by the Lord (18)

XVII.   How the handmaid of Christ was seen to pray for a bishop who was visiting her tomb (19)

XVIII.   How, in freeing her fifth confessor, venerable Master James of Vitry, from the danger of death, she revealed some future events (20)

XIX.   How the same venerable James consecrated the church at Oignies in accordance with a vision shown earlier by the handmaid of Christ (21)

XX.   How the handmaid of Christ appeared to the venerable James in a dream and tried to dissuade him from a plan he had formed (22)

XXI.   How the same James made a journey to the curia despite warnings to the contrary from the handmaid of Christ (23)

XXII.   A complaint for the return of James of Vitry, and how dangerous it is to follow one's own will (24)

XXIII.   Another admonishing complaint by the author of this little work about the situation of Master James (26)

Chapter I

Activities with James of Vitry; conversion of a merchant, and miracles done for him and his son

1. How Master James of Vitry, when he heard of her renown, came from Paris to see the handmaid of Christ, Mary of Oignies, underwent a conversion through her prayers and became a preacher

2. When Master James of Vitry, who later became bishop of Acre and now is bishop of Tusculum and a cardinal of the Roman see, heard among the French, in Paris, the name of the blessed handmaid of Christ, Mary of Oignies, he abandoned his theological studies in which he was immoderately interested and came to Oignies where she had recently gone. The handmaid of God welcomed his pilgrimage with great devotion and urged with insistent entreaties that he abandon France and remain with the brothers at Oignies. It is he himself to whom the venerable James refers in his *Life of Mary*, without mentioning his own name, because he reports that the Lord gave his handmaid a certain preacher whom, at her death, she commended to the Lord with many prayers.[5] The handmaid of Christ compelled this venerable man to preach to the people, to call back souls that the devil was trying to take away. There shone forth in him a special miracle: by the prayers and merits of the most blessed woman he reached in a short time such a pre-eminence in preaching that scarcely any mortal could equal him in expounding the Scriptures and destroying sins. It was only right. For the love of Christ's handmaid he had left his country, relatives and the mother of all arts at Paris. Divine grace bestowed on him even in the present life the summit of knowledge and teaching. At the urging of the brothers and especially of the holy woman of God, he ascended to the rank of priest: actually he was worthy of an even greater rank. When he had come to Oignies from Paris where he had been ordained, the handmaid of Christ went out with the brothers to meet him while he was still on the road a distance away. He was sitting on a horse and dismounted to meet those coming and, as is customary in such circumstances, they kissed his hands that had been anointed with sacred chrism. While he went ahead with the brothers, mistress Mary with a certain Rainer, a noble and devout man, followed in his footsteps, suppliantly kissing on bended knee the places where he stepped. When Rainer saw her doing this, he chided her and said, 'Mistress, what are you doing? If those ahead of us see this, what will they say? I beg you, stop, don't do it.' She replied, 'No, no, I can't. I am forcefully impelled by the spirit who now reveals to me inwardly that God has chosen him from among mortals to exalt him gloriously so that through him the salvation of souls will be miraculously achieved.'

II. How she predicted that Master James was going to be a prelate in lands across the sea

3. When she and the venerable Prior Giles of Oignies were discussing this, she said, 'Truly the Lord has sworn and will not regret it (Psalm 110. 4), for he will raise this man up to an episcopal see in the holy land across the sea.' The prior replied, 'Please be quiet, my lady, for if you say such things, someone who may hear you will not credit them to your honour. When could these things happen?' She said to him, 'They will happen, but I will not see them, though you will. You will be saddened, but your sorrow will be turned to joy (John 16. 20) when you see him return from those lands to this place to live with you away from the public eye.' When she had said this, the prior trembled with fear and, pondering

---

[5] Compare *VMO* 2, 69 and 2, 101.

her words, he quietly awaited the outcome. When she was led to forewarn James himself about her prediction, she added, 'Do not oppose the divine judgement if any honour is offered you in the lands across the sea. The Lord has arranged to work there through you for the salvation of souls.' Scarcely four years had passed after this when the prediction of the blessed woman was fulfilled and venerable James was elected and consecrated bishop of Acre. As she had predicted, she had already departed this life before these things happened. But before we come to what occurred at her death, let us, for the praise of Christ's name, mention some of the things that Bishop James did not describe in his book about her life.

III. How she predicted that a certain man, signed with the cross, would have to return to his own place, safe and sound; and on the pains of purgatory

4. It happened during the time when the same handmaid of Christ shone forth by her angelic life on earth that a rich merchant, still given to secular pursuits, went forth from Nivelles with some other inhabitants of the town to visit her at Willambroux.[6] As soon as she saw him, she knew this man was going to be a vessel of election (Acts 9. 15). For his part, he instantly drank in so much perfection from her face alone that he experienced completely unclouded self-knowledge and felt the spirit of God miraculously at work in him. After this he made his confession and then often returned to the mother of his salvation. He grew in virtue and the grace of God overflowed in him. Not long afterwards, he took the cross[7] and was about to set off to fight against the adversaries of Christ, the Albigensian heretics. Since he was travelling with some of his neighbours who were stupid and irreverent people, he reprimanded them about their dirty and immodest conversations. He said that pilgrims on the sacred path ought not to engage in such things, but should try to know God and gain divine favour by prayers and exhortations. They were very angry at his admonition and assailed him greatly with taunts and insults. But, filled with the grace of God, he confounded their follies with wondrous and limitless arguments. For this reason,

---

[6] Nivelles is twenty kilometres south of Brussels. Willambroux was a leper colony outside Nivelles where Mary and her husband went to serve. In visiting Mary, the rich merchant was visiting someone who had sprung from the same town and class.

[7] 'Cruce suscepta' and phrases like 'cruce signatus' were used in reference to the Crusades. 'Pilgrim' had a similar use at this time. The term 'crucesignatus' seems to have been gradually extended from the effort to conquer the Holy Land to other papally endorsed campaigns. See Markowski, '*Crucesignatus*'.

they were so upset that they arranged to kill him in revenge for having been embarrassed. When a certain intimate who was travelling with him became aware of this; this person informed him that unless he stopped rebuking those evil deeds, he knew they would kill him. Aroused with wondrous fervour for martyrdom, he told his companion, 'Now I will correct them [all the more] in hopes that for the truth of my Lord Jesus Christ, I may be killed by his enemies.' However, although [they were evil], the Lord did not want them to be stained with the blood of a just man, but to lead them to knowledge of truth through his exhortation and to keep safe the man whom the handmaid of Christ had predicted would return in peace.

After he had returned home, he went one day to this same woman to be edified. A conversation arose between them about the fire of purgatory.[8] She undertook to explain what one should think on the subject: 'It is certainly fitting and right[9] that the Lord has prepared a fire for the cleansing of souls which have not been purified in this world by penance, so that, because no evil deed passes without being punished, the souls of penitents may be temporally cleansed according to their deeds by this admittedly most severe punishment so that, without spot or wrinkle (Ephesians 5. 27), they may pass to those eternal abodes with the saints.' Then the man said to her, 'Is that fire as severe as it is said to be?' She replied, 'It is incomparably more severe. I tell you that purgatorial fire is as much more severe than our material fire as our material fire is more severe than imaginary fire painted on a wall.' Hearing this, he trembled with fear. Disturbed in spirit, he cried out to her with a grave voice, 'What shall I do, mistress? The horror of purgatory blots out the memory of Gehenna's everlasting fire.' She replied, 'Be strengthened, be comforted in the Lord your God'.

5. Saying this, she ordered him to enter the church that was nearby. Getting up immediately from that place in obedience to her command, he prostrated himself before the holy altar. With an intent gaze, he contemplated the pyx that contained the body of Christ and hung down from the altar. Instantly his eyes clung where his spirit was fixed and, before his gaze, the pyx moved from its place and came towards him as he prayed. It stopped, but did not go back. After a while it moved a second time from the place where it had stopped and approached him. Again it stopped and did not go back. When again a third time

---

[8] Compare for the relatively new belief in purgatory *VMO* 2, 50–52 and note 78 there.

[9] This phrase echoes the opening words of the prefaces of the Roman canon: 'Vere dignum et iustum est [...]'.

the pyx moved and came closer, his gazing eyes were suddenly covered by his eyelids and he was rapt inwardly to contemplation. He saw hidden and secret things which it is not permitted a person to reveal. Returning to himself, although not completely, he quickly ran to his mother emitting flames of divine fire and said, 'Mother, I will love God without discretion.' She replied, 'No friend, certainly not.' The handmaid of Christ continued, 'At the hour I saw you leave I felt Christ show you good things. Afterwards, when the pyx approached you the third time, like a white dove he went out of the pyx, encircled your face with his wings with a gentle flame and thus, through your soul, made his way towards me. So pay no less attention to what I saw: for our Lord Jesus, holding a white cross in his hand, gave testimony on your behalf. Because you had wished with a perfect will to suffer for his truth, you were made his martyr. He promised therefore you that after your death you will pass to the heavenly realm with little or no additional suffering in purgatory.' As she said these things, the man remembered that when he corrected his fellow pilgrims about their stupid talk while they were on the road, he accepted abuse from others and formed the intention to die. Then, having poured out praises to Christ, he also blessed God's handmaid magnificently.

IV. How this same man by touching the hair of Christ's handmaid was healed of an illness that afflicted him

6. Another time, when this man travelled to more distant places in order to buy things which he needed to take advantage of his opportunities at that time, it happened that he was weakened by a grave illness in some part of his body so that he was not well enough either to proceed or to return. Although he assumed he would surely die or suffer from a lingering sickness, he was prudent in his straitened circumstances and thought to himself that it was better to make his way back home, even if laboriously, and there near his blessed nurse await death or be afflicted with weakness, rather than to be finished by death or be detained by a lingering illness in a foreign land without any comfort from his mother. As he thought this out to himself, he supported himself by leaning on a walking stick. Although he made it with hard effort and the skimpiest of treatment, he did finish his difficult journey. When he had found the handmaid of Christ at Oignies and told her of his illness and the reason for his coming, the spirit moved him interiorly and he begged the holy woman of God to give him some remnants from her hair. He was confident beyond doubt that they would cure him of his sickness. She immediately put her hand in her hair and with surprising ease pulled out a big bunch of hair as though it were a leaf. When he saw this, he was aghast at what she had done, lest the holy woman of God suffer some wound from doing this. She replied to what he was thinking: 'Don't worry, I am not wounded.' As she said this, she got up and left the man alone. When he found himself alone, he rubbed the place of his sickness with the relics. Immediately, in an instant, all the pain was gone. The man was dumbstruck by this. He accepted his health with a genuflection. Since he felt no ill effects, he proceeded to resume his customary penance of saying the Hail Mary with frequent genuflections. Because of his illness, he had abandoned the practice for eight days. Just as he completed the last genuflection, she entered and congratulated the cured man. In the spirit of prophecy, she added, 'I went away from here for a while and left you alone so that you could be cured and recommence your customary penance which you were constrained to abandon by your sickness.' The faithful man was completely astonished at her words. He was frightened not only by the speedy cure of his illness, but also that she could know immediately when it happened and what he had done in the meantime.

V. How the same man's son, gravely injured, received his health through the same strands of hair
VI. A miraculous vision of the same strands of hair

7. After these things had occurred, the healthy man returned home. When he arrived there, he found that his little son had received a serious head wound. But the man could not be enkindled by the fire of frenzy, for he had just left the holy woman of God and was still aglow with the fire of the divine spirit. In fact, certain that he would find here the occasion for a greater miracle, he turned with trust to God and said, 'O wonderful God, now again in this misfortune make known the merits of your handmaid.' Then, calling his wife and companion, he ordered her to wash the wound on the boy's head that was putrefied with blood. But when she took the boy and began to wash away the blood with water, she saw the horrible, gaping wound. She could not stand it and went away leaving the boy behind. His father, full of faith, approached him and pushed all the relics of the already tested hair of the holy woman of God into the open wound. An astounding thing happened! While the father was praying and watching for the outcome, his gaze faltered for an instant. Looking again [because he wanted] to see what had happened, he observed that the wound had been reduced to a scar and that the blood that had been flowing was now absorbed. He saw that instead of crimson gore, there lay in the opening of the wound something like a dewdrop. The boy is alive to this day. He has grown to manhood. We can see

the place of the wound that has so receded and faded that, although there is still a long scar running down, it looks like a needle line.

The same man referred to a very great miracle of Mary's relics. One day, while he, as was his wont, held these same relics of the hair of the handmaid of Christ on a silken cloth on his lap and prayed to the Lord, he glanced at them, and behold, the hairs came alive and insofar as such things could, they rejoiced together. This wondrous sight did not just last for a short time, but for almost a whole hour. Thus was the bunch of hair reposing with dormant power.

Chapter II

Miracles performed during her life, revelations

VII. How, while on a journey, the handmaid of Christ was saved from a threatening downpour by blessed John the Evangelist

8. The same religious man related another miracle widely known in his homeland. It happened that he and another man of faith were travelling on a pilgrimage with Mary and her handmaid. While they were travelling, a great rainfall threatened to pour down from a heavy cloud into the water. The sky was covered with a hideous storm cloud. The others were fearful because they were travelling far from human habitation. The handmaid of Christ raised her eyes to heaven and asked something of God with a wonderfully beautiful expression on her face. No one heard what she asked since they only saw her praying: but anyone can guess from the result that her soul obtained by asking with fitting merits. It happened that, although heavy rains fell so that the land practically frothed, the road on which the holy woman travelled with her companions stayed so dry for some cubits on each side, right and left, that not a drop fell on them. Her travelling companions looked at each other but for a while they were too dumbfounded by the divine miracle to say anything. When the inundation ceased, only that faithful man about whom we have said so much asked the servant of God, at the request of those who were going with him, why and whence came the miracle manifest in what had happened. She then replied, 'Please keep this a secret. I saw John, the evangelist of Christ, in the air. By the command of almighty God, he protected us from the great downpour of rain.' So let no one be moved by any scruple of unbelief against the man who reported to us so many miracles about the handmaid of Christ.

VIII. How she miraculously crossed a wide stream without a boat
IX. How, without any human intervention, a ship located far away came miraculously to convey her across

9. The Sambre is a very wide river in Lotharingia, about eighteen strides across. It flows by one side of the town of Oignies in a wide expanse. Because of the width of the river in that area, there is no bridge by which passage across is offered to travellers. It happened one day that the servant of Christ wished to go to a certain oratory where she dearly liked to pray. The oratory was located across the river. She began journeying towards the river on the proper path. When a certain man happened to see this, he was amazed that the woman would direct her step towards the uncrossable waters, especially since there was no bridge and he saw no boat at hand by which she might cross. He looked around to see if there were a boat and when he saw none, he looked back at her as she went along. He was about to conclude that she was crazy. Lo and behold, in an instant the handmaid of Christ was transported across the river and continued her journey. When he saw this, the man was amazed and frightened. We, too, are amazed when we hear that a woman walked dry-shod across the unstable water as though she were on dry land.

To make my readers fully confident, right now I will add to this chapter a miracle involving very similar events. Brother Andrew is a lay brother in the monastery of Oignies. Although he is a layman, he is tested in religion. At a time when he had not yet become a religious and at almost the same time as the events just reported, he was standing by the bank of the same river and saw the handmaid of Christ returning from the same oratory across the river. When she arrived at the bank of the river, she saw the man standing across on the other bank and called to him, 'How shall I cross?' He replied, 'There is no boat on this side of the river. I see one on the side you are standing on, but I don't see any way for me to get it here.' As the man said this, he looked around in case he might spot a boat on his side. Seeing nothing, he turned back his gaze. Before his eyes, the boat that he had just seen on the other bank of the river moved across instantly by the divine will and stopped before his feet so it could convey the handmaid of Christ across. The man almost fainted in amazement at this event. When, with some confusion, he had thought about the woman for whom these things had happened, he became confident. Entering the boat, he first went across to the handmaid of Christ; then he took her into the boat and transported her across the river.

X. How on the day of the Holy Trinity the servant of Christ obtained from God through her prayers the mass for herself and those dwelling with her

10. When the venerable prior of Oignies heard that his blood sister was gravely ill about four kilometres away,[10] he hurried there. On the second day, however, when the prior had not returned for terce, the handmaid of Christ began to fear that on that solemnity (the Feast of the Trinity had dawned)[11] the celebration of mass would be impeded. By the order of the then bishop of Liège, the other brethren who were priests travelled to different parishes of the region. So the devout lady was troubled and implored the Lord with tears to send back the prior so that he could celebrate. As soon as it was approaching noon, she arose from prayer and went to the mother of the prior and the other religious women who served the Lord there. They were already settling themselves at the table to eat. She said to them, 'Don't sit down at the table to eat. The prior is coming to celebrate.' After she said this, she returned to the church. Then the mother of the prior, an elderly woman almost one hundred years old, was furious at the words of the handmaid of Christ and said to the rest, 'Sit down now and let us eat. Is my son going to celebrate mass at this hour when he comes back tired out from travelling?' The sisters said to her, 'Mistress, Mary said he was coming and we don't believe that she would lightly tell a lie.' She was highly indignant and replied to them, 'Has your mistress Mary never lied? Sit down, I say, and eat.' Since the sisters believed the words of the handmaid of Christ, they kept waiting. The old woman sat down again at the table and began to eat. She had scarcely eaten four bites of food when the servant of God sensed that the prior was coming. She grabbed the rope and rang the bell. The prior came in right away and, without asking any questions, celebrated mass. Then the old lady arose from the table and after mass, much abashed, asked and received from the handmaid of Christ pardon for her derogatory remarks.

11. The blessed woman so believed that Christ was faithful that never did she doubt his answers in the spirit or in revelations — and rightly so. The reverend Bishop James has given true testimony about her to the effect that, in all her

[10] McDonnell, *The Beguines and Beghards*, pp. 59–62, describes the beguinage of Oignies to which he believes Giles's sister and mother both belonged. It is a common beguinal meal that Mary disrupts in this story. Simons, *Cities of Ladies*, speaks of the Oignies beguinage on pp. 45–46, and App. I, 83.

[11] The feast of Holy Trinity was a new feast, invented in the Liège area and particularly popular among the religious women. See Boespflug, 'Le dogme trinitaire'.

revelations, she had discernment of spirits so that, in such matters, she was never once, deceived by the enemy of the human race. This was a great thing. Indeed, we think it especially great, even the greatest of all her miraculous deeds. I have seen and known many religious men and women in Lotharingia where there is a great abundance of holiness. As a man brought up in that region, I have accepted their visions and secret visitations, but I have not known anyone among them, except Mary, who never was deceived. What, then? Are the revelations of God to be considered insignificant in all? Certainly not. Surely they are to be much venerated. He who spurns them despises Christ who is revealing. However, when we expose the deceits of the enemy, we forewarn the hearts of their listeners in such matters, and we gloriously exalt the servant of Christ who was exempt from such deceits.

XI. How her dead mother appeared to her and informed her of her damnation

12. She was extremely compassionate towards the souls in purgatory. She was very concerned in spirit about the soul of her mother who was deceased but, as will be seen, this had a carnal basis. She had hoped that her mother could be saved, as though by fire (cf. 1 Corinthians 3. 15), because of the alms she frequently gave to the poor and because of her honest way of life by which she lived in the world among those of the world. Sometimes she was troubled by doubts about this because many judgements of God are unfathomable (cf. Romans 11. 33). So she asked the Lord to give her certainty about what [state] of damnation or salvation the soul of her mother had entered from this world. When she had poured out many tears over this, it happened one day that venerable Giles, the prior of Oignies, was celebrating mass. Mary was sitting next to the altar as though at the feet of the Lord. While mass was going on, the handmaid of Christ was struck with horror by what she saw: a dark spirit sat near her. As soon as her fear had been dispelled by the sign of the cross, she boldly asked who this was. The spirit answered, 'I am your mother for whom you prayed.' Her daughter said to her, 'How is it with you, mother?' She replied, 'Bad. Your prayers cannot help me at all since the gates of hell hold me perpetually damned.' At this the daughter, uttering a loud groan, said, 'Alas, mother, what is the cause of your damnation?' She replied, 'I was brought up and I lived on what had been acquired by usury and unjust commerce.[12]

---

[12] How, in the early thirteenth century the fear of usury obsessed religious women, can also be seen in the case of Yvette, who had invested her children's property with traders in the city:

Although I was aware of the evil, I didn't take care to restore what had been taken, nor did I notice what was against God's commandments. Having entered the crooked ways of the world, I reckoned it intolerable to leave the wretched paths of my ancestors. I was not sorry about these things but, exchanging a fruitless life for death, I was lost to the future life of the world [to come].' As she said these things, she suddenly disappeared. When the handmaid of Christ had pondered all these things in an orderly way, she blessed God's just judgement, even in regard to her mother's damnation. Nor did she weep any more about her through whom she had received the beginnings of the flesh, who had now been handed over to everlasting death. The intellectual reason of her soul, which only the Almighty created, was in harmony with God, the judge of all to whom it was subject. Meanwhile Prior Giles heard her asking and answering, but he did not see the spirit with whom she spoke.[13]

XII. How, by the spirit of prophecy, she predicted that an accident to some ornamental material would be repaired in an incomparable way

13. The solemn feast day of some saint was at hand. The relics of the saints and the silk vestments (those which this house had were still inexpensive and poor) had been brought out. The aforesaid prior of Oignies was preparing the altar in the way customary for solemn days. When vespers for the day were finished, the prior was going to put away the silk vestments with the relics; he set them down on the altar. Since the hour for supper was already pressing, the prior set the folded silk vestments next to the altar and put a burning candle in front of the relics of the saints. Then he hurried to supper with the brothers. While they were eating, a burning candle fell among the vestments and burned them up. The smell of them prompted the concerned handmaid of Christ to look through the window opening that adjoined the altar to see what it was. Then she ran to the prior in the refectory to tell him of the mishap she had seen. He immediately rose from supper and when he found the damage caused by the

usury. See *VIH* 9, 25–32.

[13] Another account of this story appears in *BUA* 2, 54, 18: 529–30. The account is almost exactly the same except for the following. In the *Bonum universale* account, Thomas says that he heard the story from Master John of Nivelle who heard it directly from Mary. He does not mention that it was Prior Giles who was celebrating mass. Mary's mother specifies her offence somewhat: 'I did not wish to notice what was done against God['s commands] under my roof and by those subject to me [...].' Finally, she says that she 'spurned Mary's admonitions about these and my other evils'. A similar concern about benefitting from ill-gotten goods is prominent in *VMO* 2, 44; 2, 52.

fire, he poured out tears about it and was immeasurably sad. When the devout handmaid of Christ saw him weeping, she moaned with compassion for his sorrow. She prostrated on the ground, and then rose in tears. She said to the prior with great confidence, 'Be consoled, dearest father, be consoled. Within ten years, God will make unparalleled restitution to you for this damage. You will rejoice four times as much over acquiring those adornments than now you are saddened over these that have been lost. Poor me! I won't be there to see them.'

God did not deceive her by his promise. For later, when the venerable James was chosen bishop of Acre across the sea, he sent to the same prior every episcopal vestment, with many other garments of fine linen, as well as all the altar vessels, with the diverse utensils of its ministers, all crafted of gold and silver.[14] The bearer of all these crossed the sea so fast, within fifteen days in fact, that it seemed incredible to many. It is no wonder that it happened by a divine miracle, since it was near the end of the ten years when the handmaid of Christ had predicted these things would be fulfilled. It is not easy to describe how that same prior danced for joy at the arrival of those gifts. He had forgotten the words of the handmaid of Christ. He spent the whole day rejoicing and did not seem to quiet down even for an hour. Then in the evening he began to reproach himself for having rejoiced immoderately over passing things. Suddenly it was as if he wished to cover with the bitterness of sorrow the guilt he had contracted because of his immoderate joy. At that moment he remembered what the holy woman of God had predicted to him ten years before, when he had been saddened by the burning of the vestments; namely, that when the damage had been made up beyond compare, he would rejoice four times as much over the ornaments he acquired than he had been saddened over those which were lost. When he remembered these things, he immediately looked at the calendar. He found that it was twenty days beyond the ten years that she had predicted would pass. When the prior was certain of this, he rejoiced over the fact with trembling and was afraid.

---

[14] See the contribution of Bolton to this volume.

Chapter III

Miracles after her death, especially the expulsion of a spirit of blasphemy

XIII. How she predicted that after her death, her mouth would close tight.
XIV. How she predicted that after her death, she would not allow the teeth of her mouth to be removed unless prayers had been offered beforehand

14. When the time was approaching when the blessed woman would migrate from the world, it happened that a certain religious and genuinely holy man called John of Pomerania passed from this world. The prior, who was well aware of this man's holiness, was taking the teeth out of his mouth with pliers. When the handmaid of God heard the grating of the pliers from her place of prayer, she looked through the window that adjoined the place. With a woman's fear she was horrified at what was happening. Meekly she rebuked the prior: 'O Lord prior, why are you behaving so cruelly towards a lifeless corpse? I didn't think you were such a hard man.' The prior answered, 'My lady, know that should it happen that you die before me, I am not doing anything with this corpse which I will not also do to you after you are dead.' She replied to him, 'No, you certainly won't do that to me. I would close my mouth and clench my teeth so that you couldn't.' Then the prior laughingly said, 'How will you be able to do this when you are dead?' She added nothing to these words but, after the window was closed, she retired to her place.

Not much time had passed after this when she left the world and travelled to the God of life. The prior of Oignies with some friends and fellow thieves transferred the body of the dead woman to a hidden place. He lay the head down on his knee and grasped the chin with his right hand while he pushed down hard on the forehead with his left hand. However, in accord with the words of the prediction she made while she was alive, he was unable to open her teeth or even her lips. Then he tried a knife and other iron tools to no avail so, frustrated, he arranged to put the body back on the bier. Suddenly and unexpectedly there came to his mind what the handmaid of Christ had predicted to him when she was alive and also what he had replied to her as though he were laughing at her. He immediately prostrated on the ground and with suppliant prayer addressed the sacred body: 'Truly, my lady, I wanted to act stupidly when I tried to annul your words. I really didn't remember them and, even if I had remembered, I believed that the words that you spoke were idle and silly. But now I see that none of your words will pass in vain. Therefore I ask and implore your gentle charity that you kindly allow me to receive some of your teeth as solace for my sorrow. You know, too, and it is really true, that what I wished to do (although not in the proper way because, as is now clear, such violence does not befit your dignity) I arranged to do for your honour and glory. So now allow what is asked of you.'

A wondrous thing! Scarcely had the prior closed his mouth on these words than the lifeless corpse, as though it were pleased with these words of the suppliant, opened its mouth and, of its own accord, shook out seven teeth into the hand of the prior. What could be more glorious than these wonders? Many who were present are still alive and have testified to this miracle. It would not be easy for an incredulous person to doubt their credibility.

XV. How Lord Hugolino, cardinal bishop of Ostia, was freed from a spirit of blasphemy by the relic of Christ's handmaid

15. In the time of Pope Honorius III,[15] venerable James, who was still bishop of Acre, went to Rome.[16] He was most solicitously received by Pope Honorius himself, by his brothers the cardinals and, above all, by Hugolino[17] who was then bishop of Ostia and cardinal of the Roman curia, a man most renowned for every kind of holiness. This venerable bishop of Ostia had been wanting to see James for a long time.

It should not be left unmentioned that when the bishop of Acre sent that same bishop of Ostia a precious gift, beautiful to behold, namely a heavy silver cup full of nutmeg, the latter, who firmly refused all gifts, immediately sent the cup back to the bishop of Acre. However, he did keep the nutmeg, saying, 'This nutmeg is the fruit of the Orient, but the silver cup is the fruit of the city of Rome.' He spoke eloquently and truly.

So, later, when they were able to hold a private conversation together, the bishop of Ostia said to the bishop of Acre, 'I am very pleased that you have come to these parts. For a long time I have desired to converse with you and reveal the secrets of my heart, which I have scarcely ever been disposed to reveal to anyone else. Would that by your counsel and the help of your prayers, some favour

[15] Honorius III, the successor of Innocent III, was pope from 1216 to 1227.

[16] The events described in this paragraph probably occurred in 1227/1228.

[17] Hugolino of Segni, the nephew of Innocent III and friend of St Francis, became bishop of Ostia in 1206 and later Pope Gregory IX (1227–41). It was this same Hugolino who interrupted St Francis in Florence on the founder's journey to visit these *mulieres sanctae* in 1217. See Callebaut 'Autour de la rencontre à Florence de S. François', and Mens, 'L'Ombrie italienne et l'Ombrie brabançonne'.

might be granted me by almighty God. I will pour out to you all the secrets of my heart. Diligently ponder what I say to you. Know that with blessed Job, I have received from the Lord a goad of the enemy (cf. Job 2. 2; II Corinthians 12. 7). Mine is all the more severe since while his was in the body, mine is in the soul. A spirit of blasphemy troubles my soul and submerges it with waves of temptations. Almost every day I am driven to desperation.[18] I only receive respite, and little enough at that, when I sit with my brother cardinals in the consistory to consider legal cases. Then for a while the suffering by which I am troubled ceases. But, alas, when I return to my normal activities, the immense, tortuous sting returns to me again. It does not allow me to be refreshed and rested by food, drink or sleep. When my spirit has been worn out by countless thoughts, it drives my nearly exhausted body to destruction. Finally, so that nothing within me will remain undisclosed to you, I am as fearful as I can be that I will be unable to carry such a burden and will be completely dislodged from the holy faith.'

16. While the bishop of Ostia accompanied these and similar topics with heavy sighing, the bishop of Acre (since he is a man of kindly disposition) mixed his own deep sighs with those of the blessed man. Having entered the treasures of divine mercy in the Scriptures, he proclaimed (to one who was not ignorant of such matters) the things that seemed to be apt and suitable for temptations of this kind. However, the bishop of Acre, a prudent and experienced man, knew that in such cases it often happens that a mind overwhelmed by precisely this kind of temptation does not grasp such reasoning easily unless it is buttressed with the most telling examples. So he immediately added the following.

'In Lotharingia, before I was a bishop, I had a most dear friend of God who by the prerogative of her sanctity and merit, which were without equal in her time, had obtained from God a special grace of expelling blasphemous spirits. In the book of her life, which I wrote, there are many examples of this. This grace was not just for those who invoked her while she was dwelling in this life; she also kept it after her death. So take the book about her way of life with you and read it. With all my heart and with confidence in the mercy of God and the

---

[18] Gregory IX also wrote about his despair to his spiritual friend Clare of Assisi and asked her prayers: 'You are our consolation among the innumerable, bitter, and endless trials by which we are constantly being afflicted,' see *Clare of Assisi: Early Documents*, trans. by Regis J. Armstrong (Saint Bonaventure, NY: Franciscan Institute Publications, 1993), pp. 103–04.

holiness of his handmaid, I anticipate that shortly you will sense that you have been relieved of the temptation which keeps you in turmoil.'

The cardinal of Ostia received these words with a joyful heart. He said to the bishop of Acre, 'Dearest brother, I have heard many wondrous things about this woman. If you have any relics of her, I ask that you lend them to me so that, because of my veneration of them, I will be all the more pleased to invoke that saint just as if she were present.' Then the bishop of Acre smiled happily at his request, saying, 'There is a finger of hers enclosed in a silver case which is constantly hanging from my neck. It has always kept me safe in various dangers and during crises at sea. Take it with you if you insist.'[19]

17. After the bishop of Ostia had gratefully received the items offered him, he first devoted himself to a vigilant reading of the *Life* of the handmaid of Christ. He found in it wondrous hope and peace for himself. From the relic that remained with him he derived great mental confidence. Shortly afterwards he was praying alone at night before an altar which he had in a secret place. The lethargy of his familiar temptation began to flood his mind. He immediately rose from the ground and grasped the finger of the handmaid of Christ in his devout hands. Clasping it tightly to his breast, he suppliantly invoked the handmaid of God and the support of her prayers. Instantly the spirit of blasphemy and his mental torpor were completely dispelled and he was illumined with the heavenly light of interior grace. With the palate of his heart he tasted how sweet is the Lord (cf. Psalm 34. 8). Through the prayers of the handmaid of the Lord he received from the hand of God a shield of inviolable protection and security against the spirits of iniquity. If at that time he perceived anything further in his spirit, if he received any secret revelation, he knows, not I (cf. II Corinthians 12. 2). His secret is his (cf. Isaiah 24. 16). My task is limited to informing my readers about things which I know for certain.

At this point, however, one should consider why this man about whom we have reported these things, a man of eminent sanctity, a man whom (as we will say in what follows) almighty God raised to such heights, should have been handed over to the spirit of blasphemy to be tortured by such cruel temptations. The reason will be clear enough, if we call attention to his predecessor Peter the Apostle, whom Satan asked to sift like wheat (Luke 22. 31). If the Son had not

---

[19] See, in addition to the incident mentioned in paragraph 20 below, another which occurred as James was fording a river in Lombardy: *Lettres de Jacques de Vitry*, ed. by Huygens, p. 72. Thomas refers to this episode in his *Life of Lutgard*, in *VLA* 3, 19.

prayed to the Father (cf. John 14. 16) on his behalf, his faith would have failed after the triple denial (Mark 14. 66–72). But he was to be taught by this temptation, so that he would know how to be compassionate towards the weaknesses (cf. Hebrews 4. 15) of his subjects, for he was to be established as the head of all Christians.

XVI. About another holy woman, tempted by the spirit of blasphemy and freed by the Lord

18. In Lotharingia I saw another most noblewoman who took the cross with wondrous ardour of spirit; belted with an iron chain, she walked barefoot without any conveyance all the way to the holy land of Jerusalem. And you, O venerable James, were then bishop of Acre. You forced her to return home on a horse and with shoes. As soon as she returned home, she joined the Cistercian order, leaving behind her home, countless possessions and her children. After she had done these things so bravely for love of Christ, she was troubled and stung by the spirit of blasphemy. As she informed me with great sorrow, she felt more torment from that powerful temptation than she had ever suffered before. But was this to her damnation or to the destruction of her virtue? Not at all. Virtue is perfected by weakness (II Corinthians 12. 9). Not long afterwards, she was freed by the Lord almighty and fared with such a fullness of grace that wherever she was in the precincts of the monastery, she knew without any hesitation the time of the coming of Christ on the altar through the ministry of the priest, however secretly it came about. Each time it happened, the cooing of a dove echoed in her throat with such a sound that no mortal could imitate it.

I am a witness of these things. While I was celebrating in that place, I heard that dove-like voice and saw something exceedingly wonderful in her. She was about to receive communion in the Body and Blood of the Lord. She was led forward on the arms of those who supported her. She danced with all her limbs and her face was replete with graces. While she danced, she uttered cries of such sweetness that there could be no doubt that she was being called to the wedding banquet of the Lamb (cf. Revelations 19. 9) in which, with invisible power, the almighty Father joins the heavenly to the earthly, the lowest to the highest.

But why do I prolong my words? I have seen many, I have had personal experience of many, who were troubled by the spirit of blasphemy. I have never found even one who was not freed or who was not favoured with greater grace after the temptation. Few indeed are those who are worthy to see the secrets of heaven (cf. Mark 4. 11) without having previously been purified and tested by this temptation. There is a most fitting reason for this. For now, though, let the foregoing examples suffice. For we have a pontiff who can be compassionate towards our weaknesses, one tempted in everything in which we are tempted (Hebrews 4. 15).[20]

Chapter IV

Helps bestowed on a certain bishop, James of Vitry

XVII. How the handmaid of Christ was seen to pray for a bishop who was visiting her tomb

19. At almost the same time, a certain bishop[21] whose name we do not dare record since he forbids that he be named, came suppliantly and devoutly from Italy to Mary's tomb. During her life he had had a great love for that blessed woman who was so deserving of God. One night he stayed awake to pray at her tomb. Suddenly he was rapt in spirit and saw the venerable Mary, risen from her place of rest, praying with extended hands and bended knees opposite the holy altar, interceding to the Lord on his behalf. The manner of his exceptional vision gave the bishop great joy. For about two hours that night he remained stationary. The next day, while he was saying goodbye to the brothers of Oignies, the bishop secretly disclosed to the prior what had happened as he prayed at the tomb of venerable Mary. We heard about this from the trustworthy report of the same prior and so reckoned it worthy to be included in this work.

XVIII. How, in freeing her fifth confessor, venerable Master James of Vitry from the danger of death, she revealed some future events

20. When venerable James, the bishop of Acre, had returned from the city of Rome to the Holy Land, matters came up which required him to sail back to Rome on the great sea. Suddenly a storm blew up so that all who were with him utterly despaired of their lives. Then the venerable bishop took off his clothes and wrapped himself in nothing but a sackcloth so that, if the ship were battered

---

[20] Here Thomas refers the Scripture text to Hugolino of Ostia who had become Pope Gregory IX by the time Thomas wrote the Supplement. Thomas may have felt the need to compliment the pope after having divulged the pope's bout with temptation. At the same time, he draws a pastoral lesson for any of his readers who may have been troubled by similar temptations.

[21] From *BUA* 1, 9, 2–8: 37–40 we know that this bishop was Conrad, a former canon of St Lambert of Liège who became abbot of Villers and finally a cardinal.

on the rocks, he could jump into the sea and maybe swim to land. All those who were on the boat were in the same straits so each of them, as his or her devotion suggested, invoked the saints to help them. Some prayed to St Nicholas, others to St Clement, and others to other saints.[22]

The bishop of Acre remembered the relics of the handmaid of Christ, Mary of Oignies, which he always was careful to have hanging from his neck. He began to importune her patronage, saying, 'O venerable mother and lady, while you were on earth you loved me with a special love. I loved you in return, not as much as I should have, but as much as I could according to the measure of my imperfection. Since I am caught in this threatening situation, in my prayers I call upon the privileged support of your merits. I am disposed to arrange my life quite differently, and so I am afraid to die now the death which threatens me.'[23]

While the bishop prayed these and similar things with anxious mind and trembling lips, he was overcome by a sudden swoon and saw the handmaid of Christ speaking to him. 'Behold, I, your protector, am here because you called me. I did really love you in life and since my life ended, I have been ceaselessly praying for your salvation.'

XIX. How the same venerable James consecrated the church at Oignies in accordance with a vision shown earlier by the handmaid of Christ

21. 'Don't be afraid; this will not be the end of your life.' As she said these things, the bishop had a vision of the handmaid of Christ leading him into the

[22] Both St Clement and St Nicholas were patrons to be evoked in maritime disasters. According to Jacobus de Voragine's *Legenda aurea*, Nicholas rescued some sailors far away at sea at the same time that the bishop was attending the Council of Nicaea: *Legenda aurea*, ed. by T. Graesse (Leipzig: Arnold, 1850), 6 December, pp. 22–29; English translation, *The Golden Legend: Reading on the Saints*, trans. by William Granger Ryan, 2 vols (Princeton: Princeton University Press, 1993), I, 21–27. Another time the son of a pilgrim going to Nicholas's shrine fell overboard. He was found to have been miraculously transported to Nicholas's altar. Similarly, according to the *Legenda aurea*, St Clement was martyred by having an anchor tied to his neck and being thrown into the sea (pp. 777–78; English trans. pp. 323–30). Each year on the octave of his death, the sea receded so pilgrims could visit the miraculous shrine in which his body was preserved. The patronage of Nicholas and Clement for those in danger at sea was a prominent feature in their iconography. See *Lexikon der christlichen Ikonographie*, ed. by Engelbert Kirschbaum and Wolfgang Braunfels (Freiburg im Breisgau: Herder, 1968-), VII (1974), pp. 319–23; VIII (1976), pp. 45–58. It was probably for boatmen that the original chapel to St Nicholas was constructed along the bank of the Sambre at Oignies.

[23] Thomas tells of a similar instance in Chapter 7 of his *Life of John of Cantimpré*, ed. by Godding, pp. 282–83.

church of Oignies. As he climbed a lofty vault, she showed him five altars located throughout the church. She said, 'You will consecrate four of these in honour of the saints designated by the prior of this place, but the fifth, at my admonition, you will consecrate in honour of the holy and undivided Trinity.'[24] Pointing to the place with her finger, she said, 'If you wish, before this altar Christ will give you the peace you have sought. There you will be able to find what you have sought with great effort. But you are a man with a will of your own, and you have never wanted to accede to my counsels and the counsels of those who loved you spiritually. You have always walked according to your own judgements, rather than the judgements of others.' After she had added this rebuke, she disappeared immediately.

When the bishop returned his attention to exterior things, he found the sea most quiet and tranquil. Then, immediately, totally poured out in praise of Christ and his handmaid, he told no one what had been revealed to him. He wished to test whether the things that he had seen revealed beforehand were going to happen. He reached Rome not long afterwards and asked Pope Honorius III to release him from the episcopate. The pope was overcome by his many insistent pleadings and released him.

So, released from the episcopate, he came to Oignies. But he found that the fabric of the church, which had been shown him in spirit from the stone vault of the church, was not yet completed. However, he had no doubts, but quietly awaited what would happen. While the bishop was visiting widely in surrounding areas of Lotharingia to preach zealously there, venerable Prior Giles of Oignies was hurrying to finish the building of the church. By divine providence he distributed five altars throughout the structure, just as the reverend bishop had seen them in the spirit. When it was finished, the prior asked Bishop James to come and consecrate the now completed church of Oignies with its altars.[25]

The bishop came without delay and with the prior and the brothers went up through the church he had first seen in the spirit from the vault. He found five altars arranged in the order foretold. Pleased at this, with exultant heart, he asked

[24] See above *VMO-S* 10 and note 11.

[25] James of Vitry, now auxiliary bishop of Liège, consecrated the church of Oignies between 1227 and 1229. A first church had been consecrated in 1204 by Bishop Hugh of Pierrepont (1200–29), and an altar by Fulk, bishop of Toulouse, when he visited Mary on her deathbed in 1213. The new church at Oignies was begun about 1220. See also Bolton''s contribution to this volume.

the prior, 'Whose will be the altar placed in the middle?' The prior answered, 'For the past year I laboured under a quartan fever. I vowed to the supreme majesty that if I recovered my health, I would make this altar in honour of the holy and undivided Trinity. I regained what I asked and I ask that my promise be kept.' When the bishop heard this in great wonderment, he was filled with inestimable joy. He was frightened and wondrously venerated the outcome of divine revelation manifest in all things. As soon as the altars were consecrated, he told the prior and the brothers what had happened to him.

XX. How the handmaid of Christ appeared to the venerable James in a dream and tried to dissuade him from a plan he had formed

22. When Pope Honorius III died, the reverend fathers, the cardinals of the Roman curia, by divine guidance fittingly elected Bishop Hugolino of Ostia, mentioned above, to be Pope Gregory IX. He was a man particularly outstanding in every virtue. When this happened, venerable Bishop James who, as we said earlier, was well known to this supreme pontiff and on very friendly terms with him, arranged to go to see him. At this the prior and brothers were not a little saddened. They began to be very much afraid that (as, sadly, it turned out) this pope would keep him with him by entangling him in some dignity.

So the day arrived when Bishop James would travel to Rome. After lauds, while he dozed a little, the handmaid of Christ, venerable Mary, appeared like a sick person to the bishop in a dream. It seemed to the bishop that he was very solicitously anointing her with oil, just as if she had been gravely ill. As he was busy at this task, she looked at him with a stern face, as though indignant, and said, 'Since your book of rites does not contain my kind of anointing, you certainly can't anoint me. But anoint our prior and the brothers since, like me, they are gravely weakened by your departure.' Immediately the bishop woke up and called the prior and brothers and told them what the handmaid of Christ had said him in the dream. However, he was not turned back from his plan, but made all the arrangements to begin his journey.

XXI. How the same James made a journey to the curia despite warnings to the contrary from the handmaid of Christ

23. When Prior Giles saw this, he was unbearably saddened. He approached the handmaid of Christ to pray to her about blocking the bishop's journey. The blessed woman appeared to him in a vision and said to him, 'You needn't doubt that I am just as opposed as you are to the bishop's journey. Hence, I will not accompany him as he goes; rather, three women will accompany him. He won't escape their hands. So let him do what he wants; you can't turn him from his purpose now.'

Just as the handmaid of Christ spoke these words to the prior, the bishop suddenly came up. The bishop's voice called the prior back from his ecstasy. He told the bishop what Lady Mary, who had just then appeared to him in a vision, had foretold about his departure. Be stunned, reader! Gaze on a miracle! The bishop was not impressed by these words. He laughingly rejoined to the prior, 'Lady Mary said the same thing to me. I am not moved by such things. There is room in the doorways: I will return faster than you expect. Don't be upset, dearest brother. Truthfully, love, it would be hard for me, and even harder for him, if I didn't visit and see such a good friend in such circumstances. Beside, I don't believe it: indeed I certainly presume that, contrary to your fears, the pope will not detain me with him if I am unwilling.' He tried, as best he could, to console the prior and the brothers with these words; then he set out for Rome. As God revealed to the prior through his handmaid, James was grabbed there by two women, Episcopate and Cardinalate. Who the third woman could be, we cannot clearly know at present.

XX. A complaint for the return of James of Vitry, and how dangerous it is to follow one's own will.

24. So now I must turn to you, bishop of Tusculum and cardinal of the Roman curia. Anyone can see that the handmaid of God spoke most truly when she said you are a man with your own will. You were so obstinate in the face of the clear revelation of the handmaid of Christ that there was no way you could be turned from your own will. Brothers, let the bishop of Tusculum look and see if he has gained through his own will, if he has incurred damage from this, if he has omitted things which could have promoted the honour of Christ and the salvation of abandoned souls. Jesus, the author of our salvation (cf. Hebrews 5. 9), redeemed these souls with his own blood and a disgraceful death on the cross. Let him look to his profit, let him consider in his mind his advantage! He occupies a see in the Roman curia as a bishop and cardinal. He studies the Scriptures, so I heard. He is soothed with quiet. Meanwhile, in Lotharingia (to which, as we surely believe, he was sent back from the East as legate by Christ, the supreme pontiff) souls without counsel or help are headed towards hell. The greatest glory in the Church is to have a place among the cardinals in Rome. But to what purpose is that glory? When Christ was made the reproach of men and the object of people's aversion, he left us an example so we might follow in his footsteps. If, indeed, he strives for glory, which is scarcely believable, what glory is greater than to discard glory and find such glory that no other glory can compare to it? Let no one think of a parable and its interpretation, and conclude I speak here of the glory to come after this life. Not at all. Let him believe in that glory to be possessed afterwards in the future world; now I wish to speak of the glory that is included in this world.

25. Let that bishop of Tusculum and cardinal of the Roman curia answer me now. Let him compare the glory he now has in the bridal chamber with that which previously he had when he was still a poor and private person in Lotharingia. I said poor, but I put it badly. He was, in fact, exceedingly rich. He is no richer now than he ever was. What did he ever need that was missing there? If there was a hint of some lack in the abundant provisions that rightly flowed his way, surely there was no want of hands that would have competed to try to make it good. And no wonder! Why? The world was astonished at an unprecedented wonder. The bishop of the most frequented of cities across the sea renounced his lordship of his own free will. Having exchanged oriental goods for poverty, he chose quiet in the humble place of Oignies among the flocks of beguines whom the Egyptians abominate. The world has many bishops in abundant supply. All of France with its abundance scarcely suffices for the annual taxes of cardinals. But the world [does not] often [see] pontiffs without sees who imitate Christ, who emptied himself and took the form of a servant. France never merited to have such an inglorious cardinal devoid of pomp; Spain, I hear, did merit one and this as recently as three years ago.[26] But by the authority of Christ and through the prayers of his handmaid Mary, Lotharingia had the first one.

I said 'through the prayers of his handmaid', but I confess I spoke in doubt. For I do not know if she still holds back her prayers in anger because she foretold that the journey of the bishop would be made in spite of her opposition. Nevertheless, I believe that even if she has angrily withheld her prayers up to now, perhaps [because of] the most devout and urgent prayers to the Lord of religious men and women in our land, the handmaid of Christ has changed her pronouncement and prays to the almighty Lord for his return. By her intervention may he free him from the hands of the two women, Episcopate and Cardinalate, and send him back to France. The third woman, a certain one of us explained, is the church of Lotharingia. As the first to be united with him by

---

[26] According to the AASS editor of the Supplement, this was St Raymond Nonnatus (1204–40), a Mercedarian.

devotion, she will possess him in marital union until old age. For it would not be shocking, but very consonant with divine law, if he repudiated those two which he added to the first, and sought the first one again and clung to her all the more devoutly, just as he had separated from her so unsuitably.

XXIII. Another admonishing complaint by the author of this little work about the situation of Master James

26. O most honourable bishop, this is what you saw by divine revelation when you were located in our land. Long before that venerable and most worthy lord, Hugolino, the bishop of Ostia, was raised to the apostolic dignity, you testified that you saw in a divine revelation that blessed Gregory (whom he who is now the pope represents both by his name and by his activity) gave you two very beautiful, but dead, birds. Bishop Lambert, the martyr and bishop of Liège, gave you one, but much prettier and alive. This is also what the most blessed woman Mary of Oignies, a prophetess without deceit, once foretold to you when she was alive: the blessed Lambert himself put a mitre on your head.[27] Doubtlessly we saw this happen, since the care of the whole diocese of Liège was fully entrusted to you like a mitre of power and administration. This was the gift of St Lambert. The ruling power of temporal administration did not pertain to him; it was in the giving of the earthly *imperium*. Nevertheless, even from the latter, temporal support was provided you, because no one fights for his own pay.[28] The holy martyr Lambert, bishop of Liège, through the holy prayers of saintly men and women, does not cease offering you each day this bird of spiritual administration, stretched forth on the wings of contemplation, bright with the feathers of virtues, live with holy action. What prudent person, who of your spiritual friends, would bear it quietly if so great a martyr with so great a gift were confounded by you? The birds which blessed Pope Gregory gave you, although they are worthy of being looked upon with great honour, are dead nevertheless. Indeed, you testified that they were dead when they were given to you. Yes, dead! You yourself said those birds were really dead; I remember them as dead. How are they dead? Why are they not alive? If you shake them, you will

---

[27] The episcopal see was vacant after the death of Bishop John of Eppes in 1238, the next bishop died (by poisoning?) in 1239. Rome intervened the year after by appointing a strong bishop, Robert of Thourotte in 1240.

[28] Compare *Lateinische Sprichworter und Sentenzen des Mittelalters*, ed. by Hans Walther, 9 vols (Gottingen: Vandenhoeck und Ruprecht, 1963-86), III: 102 (no. 16478): 'Nemo tenetur militare propriis stipendis'.

understand me better. Then you may say, where is their life? Where is the vigour of living action? Where is the fervour of conscientious preaching? Where is that copious, most efficacious and holy fruit of hearing confessions? Where the zeal and skilful care in rooting out vices? Rumour has it in our part of the world that there you give little or no thought to these things now.

27. O man especially chosen by the Lord from among mortals, and yet remiss in such things, we are confident that you still burn inside with the divine fire, yet you are not put on a candle stand to give light to all (Matthew 5. 16). O beautiful and dead birds! The birds, I repeat, are dead. How are they dead? Those birds have mouths, even though they are dead, but they do not speak through you, because you do not know the language of the country. They have eyes, but they do not see through you in deciding legal cases; for your eyes are pools in Hesebon, which are at the gate of the daughter of the multitude (Song of Songs 7. 4). They have ears, but they do not hear through you, because your ears are open, not to the exactors of dignities, for the sake of which they oppress the poor sons of the Church, but to hear the cries of the poor and to reconcile to Christ those children of wrath who are headed towards hell.

So if those birds which have been given to you neither see, nor hear, nor speak, what has one to think of them except that they are dead? If they are dead, why are they favoured in place of the living one? Take care holy father, take care most reverend bishop, lest the dead birds provide you with stench rather than honour. The nature of things is known to be such that however pretty the birds are dead, when they are dead, they cannot last without decaying. You certainly know that in our French tongue nothing is more reproachful than the proverbial dead hen.

So, I pray you, holy father, and I ask with copious tears, do not be angry with me for saying these things. God and his holy angels are my witness that no cause concerning you, except great charity, moves me to these words, even though they are somewhat harsh. With what charity I love you, with what sincere love I embrace you, he knows who knows all things. When I was not yet fifteen years old and you were not a bishop, I heard you preaching in Lotharingia. I loved you with such veneration that I was happy just at the sound of your name. From then on a special love for you stayed with me. It is no wonder; the things we learn as children take firm root in us. So, holy father, forgive me, especially since I have only recalled to your mind things you saw revealed long ago. I wish that if, by reason of these things which are enumerated about you, my love is able to obtain your return, which is the goal of its desire, I will not be charged a large penalty for my foolishness, because I have presumed to provoke you, a venerable cardinal and bishop of the holy catholic Church, with rather rude, if loving, words.

History of the Foundation of the Venerable Church of Blessed Nicholas of Oignies and the Handmaid of Christ Mary of Oignies

Translated by Hugh Feiss OSB

1. It was the time[1] when God permitted the kingdom of Jerusalem, with the Christians living there, to be subdued and slaughtered with cruelty and hostility by the impious Saracen king, Saladin, a cruel tyrant.[2] This their countless sins required. It was the year 1187 AD. The most humble and holy man, Br Francis, founder and patron of the Minor Order was reigning with Christ and preaching.[3] Our most reverend father and lord, James of Vitry, the confessor of Louis, the king of France,[4] was studying sacred theology in Paris.

2. At this same time there was a certain venerable man named John in the castle of Walcourt.[5] He was adequately endowed with temporal and spiritual riches. By his own wife he begat four sons. In the course of time all but one of them became priests. The names of the priests were Giles, Robert and John. The

---

[1] The *Historia fundationis Venerabilis Ecclesiae Beati Nicolai Oigniacensis ac ancillae Christi Mariae Oigniacensis* was published in *Veterum scriptorum et monumentorum historicorum, dogmaticorum, moralium amplissima collectio*, ed. by Edmond Martène and Ursinus Durand, 9 vols (Paris: Montalant, 1724–33), VI, cols. 327–30, and from a copy annotated by Jean-François Foppens around 1720, and ed. by Edmond Reusens in *Analecta pour servir à l'histoire ecclésiastique de la Belgique*, 10 (1873), 100–07. Discrepancies between these texts are noted in the footnotes to the translation. Eva Maria Link gives the Latin text and a German translation in an appendix to her thesis, 'Hugo von Oignies' (Inaugural-Dissertation, Albert-Ludwigs-Universität zu Freiburg im Breisgau, 1964), pp. 244–52 (Yale University Library has a copy). For the founding of St Nicholas of Oignies, see MB I, II, 450–60; McDonnell, *Beguines and Beghards*, pp. 8–19; Link, 'Hugo of Oignies', pp. 27–36.

[2] Martène–Durand: have 'the impious Saladin, a cruel, Saracen tyrant of the realm'. Saladin captured Jerusalem from the Latins in 1187. The third crusade of 1189–92 recovered considerable territory, but not Jerusalem..

[3] St Francis of Assisi (1181/1182–1226) did not start preaching before the first decade of the thirteenth century. Foppens adds a reference to St Bernard (d. 1153): 'St Bernard, the abbot of Clairvaux, a most holy and venerable worshipper of God, was reigning with Christ; also reigning and preaching was the most humble [...].'

[4] See for this Jean Longère in his Introduction to *Hist. Occ.*, pp. 9–10. If James was born in *c.* 1165, as most scholars hold, and ordained in 1210, as Thomas of Cantimpré writes in his *VMO-S*, he would have been forty-five years old at his ordination. This is not impossible, but an earlier ordination would better explain why he was commissioned with important preaching missions in 1211. Moreover, Vincent of Beauvais, in his *Speculum historiale*, calls him parish priest of Argenteuil near Paris, in *Annales aevi Suevici*, ed. by Georg Waitz, Monumenta Germaniae Historica, Scriptores XXIV (Hannover: Hahn, 1879), p. 166.

[5] Walcourt was a lordship with a famous collegiate church, Notre Dame de Walcourt, see MB I, I: 77–81.

other, who was called Hugh, was renowned for his goldsmith's art.[6] God, the most kindly lover of human beings, knew the thoughts of these brothers who from their youth were diligently and devoutly instructed[7] by their father and mother in the fear of the Lord. So, from the abundance of his love and the depth of his mercy and by the grace of his spirit, he deigned to inspire them so that they were united in fraternal love from the time they were growing up and always cherished the bond of mutual charity.

3. After the death of their father,[8] Giles, the oldest of them, out of great devotion and of his own free will, without any care of ecclesiastical benefice, often celebrated mass in the household chapel of Wéry,[9] the lord of Walcourt, the father of Thierry, a famous knight. Thus did Giles use his patrimony to fight for the Lord. Once he had gained entry,[10] he often went to the chapel. Some of the household of the knight thought to ingratiate themselves in their lord's favour. They were anyway wickedly envious of Giles's pious deeds. So they deceitfully reported that the priest of God had hidden no small treasure in a certain chest in the chapel, to which the priest had the key. By an irreverent impulse,[11] the avarice of the lord proved the servants' accusation was false. When the chest had been broken open, all that was found in it were a missal, a chalice for the altar,[12] priestly vestments, other ornaments for the altar, a sackcloth, and two disciplines. When he saw this, the knight was very embarrassed, and rightly so.

[6] Martène–Durand: 'in the city as a goldsmith'. Much of Hugh's exquisite work is still preserved in the trésor of the priory of Oignies. See for this Bolton's contribution to this volume.

[7] Foppens notes that some witnesses have 'raised' instead of 'instructed'.

[8] Martène–Durand: 'father and mother'. This must be faulty, since their mother is clearly alive in the rest of the account of the foundation. She appears in *VMO* 2, 54 and *VMO-S* 10 as a very elderly woman, much involved in the life at Oignies.

[9] Wéry III, 1165–1206.

[10] Foppens reads *fauto* and suggests the emendation *fausto*: 'once this entry had been favoured'.

[11] Foppens: 'at this irreverent prompting'.

[12] Foppens: 'a chalice, priestly vestments for the altar'.

4. Because of this, the true Israelite, unwilling to stay in the oppressive court of Pharaoh[13] could not see any place for himself among the Egyptians, nor did he see how to make provision for divine worship. So by divine providence he decided to leave there. With the help of his brothers, he determined he would serve God more securely under the profession and in the habit of a religious rule, rather than being worn out by secular troubles. So he did it. He sold everything which by hereditary right belonged to him in Walcourt and the surrounding area. He took with him his mother and brothers; his father was already dead. In this he employed the counsel of the Lord who says 'If you wish to be perfect, go and sell all that you possess, and give it to the poor, and come follow me' (Mark 10. 21). When he reached the area along the Sambre River, he stopped in a place that was then deserted and is now called Oignies.[14] It was a spacious place to stay, the sort of place we read Jacob the patriarch wanted (Genesis 24. 23–25); it provided water, meadows and woods. With his companions he pitched his tent there; then they built a house for God as best they could. He found there a chapel built of wood, established in honour of blessed Nicholas, and endowed with a rent of three hens.

5. According to Gregory in the *Moralia*, possessions are likely to be the cause of grave fault among brothers.[15] Thus we read that when their possessions became many, Abraham and Lot could not live together (Genesis 13. 2–11). It was different when these brothers were supported by adequate possessions. They made the oldest of them, Giles, their prior. They were joined by a number of the faithful whom the Lord inspired with the Holy Spirit. They placed what was common before what was their own, rather than preferring what was private to what was common. They made their profession according to the rule for clerics of blessed Augustine. They began to be much distinguished by their religious title and to be wondrously showered with God's grace.

6. As a result, many distinguished and important people renounced the world and came to them from different parts of the world to which the reputation of

---

[13] Martène–Durand: 'the man of Israel, harried by the aggressive court of Pharaoh'. Foppens notes another variant: 'harried by the oppressive deputyship'. 'True Israelite' recalls John 1. 47.

[14] For Oignies, see Bolton's contribution to this volume and the literature listed there.

[15] Gregory the Great, *Moralia in Iob*, ed. by Adriaen, XXIX, 2–3: 'Solet inter fratres maior substantia discordiae fieri gravioris causa.'

their religious life spread. These people chose to be humbled with the meek rather than to divide spoils with the proud. Among these was the outstanding and venerable man, Master John of Nivelle.[16] We read that he was distinguished by so many virtues and miracles: for example, he nobly uprooted vices, he devoutly converted souls, and he was an outstanding preacher of God's word. In those days there flourished at Oignies that most precious pearl of Christ, Mary of Nivelles. Those who enjoyed her patronage have transmitted to posterity the story of her life, which was endowed with the virtue of many miracles. In God's name she cured the sick, cleansed lepers, and drove out demons from possessed bodies and, what is more, raised the dead.[17] Her very clothing is in our reverent possession still. When women in labour are wrapped in it, they are freed from the danger of death and rejoice in a happy birth.[18]

7. Hastening here from a remote region in the odour of the good name of God's children, the venerable and reverend father of good repute, James of Vitry, bishop of Tusculum and Acre and cardinal of the apostolic see, came to find out if what he had heard about the devotion of our earliest days was evident in deeds. He did not trust our reputation, since reputation sometimes lies, until he saw with his own eyes and found that not even a half of it had been told him. In this he was like the queen of Saba who wondered at Solomon's magnificence (III Kings 10. 1, 7). He was taken up from the womb of our church by the grace of God and the support of his own merits to the summit of dignity. By a special graciousness of his, and because of the affection which stemmed from the veneration he owed her, to whom he knew himself bound by divine precept[19] as a son is bound to his mother, he aided our church with many temporal and spiritual blessings. First, there was his bodily presence when he gave himself to

---

[16] John of Nivelle became a *magister* at Paris late in the twelfth century. He had returned to his homeland by 1202, where he engaged in pastoral work. Some fifteen years later he joined the community of Oignies, where he remained until his death in 1233. For details of his life, see McDonnell, *Beguines and Beghards*, pp. 40–45; Simons, *Cities of Ladies*, pp. 41, 46, 126–27.

[17] Martène–Durand omit 'and, what is more, raised the dead'.

[18] This type of miracle was not described by Thomas in his Supplement. It may be compared to the miracles of Gertrude of Nivelles in her abbey near Mary's parental home. See Binnie Effros, 'Symbolic Expressions of Sanctity: Gertrude of Nivelles in the Context of Merovingian Mortuary Custom', *Viator*, 27 (1996), 1–10, who considers the curative power of textiles 'a survival of pre-Christian belief in the power [...] inherent in the tasks of weaving and binding' (p. 5).

[19] Foppens: 'by the obligation of divine precept'.

our church. He was already consecrated a doctor in sacred theology, but he disdained worldly riches and preferred the company of poverty. Later, when he advanced to a worthier lot, he endowed our church with linen vestments, the relics of the saints, and other church ornaments, books, and many privileges of the apostolic see. Finally, when he was dying in Rome, he determined that his body was to be buried in the church of Oignies. Thus, once more, he spurned the world's vanities, enticements and honours.[20]

8. Giles, the first prior, who was mentioned earlier was the head of the church of Oignies for many years. With his brothers he devoutly served God according to the rule for canons of our blessed father Augustine, whose rules and statutes they followed. Even in their lifetime they acquired many goods[21] and did good work. They laid the foundations of a church constructed in a way that suited us, and left it to their posterity to complete it with much splendid work. After he had lived for a long time in the fervour of religion, he slept with his fathers, full of days in ripe old age, 5 January 1233 AD.[22]

---

[20] Some of the legacy of James of Vitry to the community is still preserved: see Bolton's contribution to this volume.

[21] The early charters are discussed by Edouard Poncelet, 'Chartes du Prieuré d'Oignies de l'ordre de Saint Augustin', *Annales de la Société archéologique de Namur*, 31 (1913), 1–104, and McDonnell, *Beguines and Beghards*, pp. 11–15.

[22] Giles was succeeded as prior by his nephew Baldwin of Barbençon. Baldwin had been chaplain at the abbey of Lutgard of Tongeren in Aywières and was a well-known preacher. Such is the report of Thomas of Cantimpré in *VLA* 3, 8: 'Balduinus, dictus de Barbenzon, Prior de Oignies, quandam in Aquiria annis pluribus capellanus, verbi Dei solemnissimus praedicator, contra consilium amicorum suorum rebus temporalibus se immiscuit minus digne.' Baldouin died in 1242 and was succeeded by Siger. The difficulties the priory experienced in the years after Giles's death can probably be understood as those common in religious communities that are making the transition from an enthusiastic, charismatic foundation to an established community. There was a visitation the next year under the auspices of Robert de Thourotte, bishop of Liège. A second papal visitation took place in 1250. The papal visitors confirmed Bishop Robert's earlier statutes, ordered the demolition of the nearby houses of beguines, and reiterated the need for a customary. For the texts of his early legislation, see Edmond Martène, *De antiquis ecclesiae ritibus*, 4 vols (Antwerp: Novelli, 1763-64), III, 339–47.

THE LITURGICAL OFFICE OF MARY OF OIGNIES
BY GOSWIN OF BOSSUT

Translated by Hugh Feiss OSB

Introduction to the Texts for the Mass and Divine Office in Honour of Mary of Oignies

The Manuscript and its Author

The liturgical Office of Mary of Oignies[1] formed part of a manuscript that contained in addition the Office for Blessed Arnulf Cornibout (d. 1228), a monk of Villers, and the Lives of both Mary and Arnulf. The Offices for the two saints, which evidently were in the middle of the original manuscript, now constitute Brussels, Bibliothèque royale, MS II 1658, which consists of fourteen leaves. They are written in an early thirteenth-century hand. The ornamentation and the musical notation in neums resemble that of a thirteenth century antiphonal from Villers (Brussels, BR, MS 6436).

The manuscript provides what was necessary to celebrate Mary with a special Mass and in the eight offices of the liturgy of the hours, as celebrated in a medieval Cistercian monastery. The structure of the Office follows the monastic practice. In the monastic night office, there were three parts, called nocturns. In the Office for Mary, as in any festive monastic office, there were six psalms with the antiphons said before and after each psalm in each of the first two nocturns and twelve readings. The long responsory at vespers is typical of Cistercian offices.

G.-M. Dreves, SJ, who edited the three hymns for this Office of Mary of Oignies, thought that the same person wrote the six hymns for the Offices of Mary and Arnulf. Since Goswin of Bossut identified himself as the author of the

---

[1] The Office was edited for the first time by Daniel Misonne, 'Office liturgique neumé de la bienheureuse Marie d'Oignies à l'abbaye de Villers au xiiiᵉ siècle', *Revue bénédictine*, III (2001), 267–73, which is reprinted from *Album J. Balon* (Namur: Godenne, 1968), pp. 170–89.

Life of Arnulf, Dreves thought he was also the author of the hymns and probably of the entire Offices. Goswin was the cantor at Villers and knew Arnulf personally. Misonne, who recently edited the Office for Mary of Oignies, concurs with this attribution.[2]

Mary of Oignies and the Cistercians

The rubrics and annotations in the Office for Mary of Oignies are evidence that this Office was written and used for public liturgy by the Cistercian monks of Villers. Mary had some connections with the Cistercian Order. When she was a young girl some Cistercian monks passed by her parents' house, and, entranced by their religious habits, she followed them for a while.[3] She was once gifted with a vision of St. Bernard.[4] A Cistercian abbot, who was a friend of hers, asked her to help one of his monks.[5] Before she went to Oignies, she may have established connections with Villers, which is located not far from Willambroux and Nivelles. The Office mentions Nivelles specifically, but apart from the title there is no mention of Oignies. Goswin seems to have been well acquainted with Nivelles.

Benigna beguina

In the Office Mary is styled blessed, *beata*, the handmaid, *ancilla, domestica*, of Christ, and more often the 'bride of Christ', a title used often by James of Vitry in his *Life of Mary*. More strikingly and more often, the Office calls her *benigna*, which literally means 'kind', but served the author of the Office as a Latin code word for 'beguine'. Mary is the most precious flower in the mystical garden of a new form of religious living. The Office declares that at Nivelles (*Nivella*) Mary founded the beguines' new way of life, distinguished by the white (*niveo*) garments. It is quite possible that that is how the beguines of the Holy Sepulchre may have regarded Mary. Her brother-in-law Guido, a priest who was her

---

[2] In his insightful introduction to the edition, see 'Office liturgique', ed. by Misonne, p. 273. In a private communication to Anneke Mulder-Bakker, Martinus Cawley, ocso, indicated that he did not recognize Goswin's style and *ductus* in the offices for Mary of Oignies.

[3] *VMO* 1, 11a.

[4] *VMO* 2, 90.

[5] *VMO* 2, 62–63.

spiritual director at Willambroux, was a leader among the beguines of Nivelles
for the ten years preceding his death in 1227, and he may have been instrumental
in keeping Mary of Oignies's memory alive among them.[6]

Mary Magdalen

Many of the texts for the Mass and offices for Mary of Oignies were taken over
from the feast of Mary Magdalen as that was celebrated at Villers. Why the
author did that is not clear. For some reason he did not have time or inclination
to create a completely new Office. His decision to borrow parts of the Office of
Mary Magdalen is puzzling. The two saints shared the same name, but the
author does not make that connection; instead, he mentions that Mary of
Oignies shared the same name as Mary, the mother of Jesus. Mary of Oignies
died on June 23, one month before the feast of Mary Magdalen (July 22), but
that does not seem to be enough to connect them. Mary of Oignies was not a
repentant sinner, as Mary Magdalen was thought to be. The connection seems
to be their great love for Christ (Mary Magdalen was thought to be the woman
whose many sins were forgiven because she loved much) and their tasks as
apostles, with Mary Magdalen as apostle of the apostles, *apostola apostolorum*,
and Mary of Oignies, as leader of the beguines.[7]

The Mass Texts

In the Mass, some texts remained the same every day, while others changed
according to the season and the feast. The manuscript gives the changeable parts,
proper to the celebration of the feast of Mary of Oignies. These consisted of the
Introit antiphon, three prayers said by the priest (Collect, Secret, and Post-
Communion), and the Epistle and Gospel with the Alleluia, which was sung
between them. As a rubric indicates, all the other changeable parts were to be
taken straight from the Mass for Mary Magdalen. Even the Gospel reading tells
of Christ's appearance to Mary Magdalen after the Resurrection. The Introit
antiphon given was one that could be sung on any saint's feast day: 'Let us all

---

[6] 'Office liturgique', ed. by Misonne, pp. 273–78; for Guido, see *VMO* 2, 93 and notes 106,
129 there.

[7] Lauwers, '*Noli me tangere*', was not available to me [editor's note: Lauwers did not know
the Office].

rejoice in the Lord, celebrating a feast day in honour of (name) on whose
solemnity the angels rejoice and praise the Son of God.'[8] The three prayers are
specific to Mary of Oignies and tell something of how she was regarded by the
author and the community for whom he produced the texts: she was a beguine
and brought a new harvest of holiness to the church, and by the merits of her
holiness is an intercessor for the believers, living and dead.

The Divine Office

The monastic office consisted of the night office (vigils or matins), and seven day
offices, lauds, prime, terce, sext, none, vespers, and compline. These offices
consisted primarily of psalms. The psalms were preceded and followed by
antiphons. If these were very well known, they were not written out entirely, but
just indicated by the first words of the antiphon.

Vespers. The author gives the text for vespers first, because on important feast
days, the vespers of the night before also was devoted to the saint. Vespers began
with four psalms. Each of these psalms was preceded and followed by its own
antiphon. It is these antiphons that are given first (10–14). They are proper to
Mary of Oignies. The first one announces who she was: the next four outline her
life. These were followed by a short reading from the Bible (Capitulum, 15) to
which a response (16) was sung. This response connects her with Mary, the
Mother of Christ, and reiterates her role among the beguines. Then came a
Gospel canticle, the Magnificat, which also was preceded and followed by an
antiphon (17), which again praises Mary of Oignies's role among the beguines.

Night Office. We have already mentioned that the night office was divided
into three nocturns. These were preceded by an invitatory psalm that had its own
antiphon that was repeated as a refrain (19). These antiphons for the six psalms
of the first nocturn (20) where taken from the existing Office for Mary
Magdalen, and are indicated by just the first words of each. These six psalms
with their antiphons were followed by four readings. For those readings, the
author of the Office takes over a commentary on the Gospel that was used from
Mary Magdalen's feast. The four responses to the readings weave together
various biblical texts and allusions. They emphasize Mary's union with Christ

---

[8] For example, *Graduale romanum* (Paris: Desclée, 1952), p. 647: 'Gaudeamus omnes in
Domino, diem festum celebrantes sub honore Sanctorum omnium, de quorum solemnitate
gaudent angeli, et collaudant Filium Dei.'

(23–25) and her service to him as heroic warrior and athlete (23, 26). The second nocturn is like the first. The antiphons are again taken from the feast of Mary Magdalen; five of them refer to Gospel parables (27). The responsories praise Mary of Oignies's beauty and closeness to Christ, using texts drawn primarily from the Song of Songs. Again, Mary flowers and bears fruit in the garden of the beguines (29–32). The third nocturn consisted of canticles (instead of psalms) and a reading from the Gospel. The first three responses are lyrical praises (36–38); the final response (39) gives two biographical details, neither of which seems to be literally true: Mary became connected with beguines at Nivelles; and she died in the hands of her brothers. As we shall see, at the end of the manuscript the author presents an alternative set of twelve antiphons for the first two nocturns. Those alternative antiphons are proper to Mary of Oignies. He evidently wrote them later, when he had more time or inspiration.

Lauds and the Other Hours of the Day. The antiphons for these hours are mostly drawn from the Bible and sing Mary's praises in a general way. The antiphon for none does suggest that the beguines whom Mary gathered together were joined as a tenth order to the nine orders (choirs) of angels (46).

Hymns. At this point the text places all the hymns for the hours of the divine office. The hymns are replete with scriptural allusions and lavish praise, but they are not verbose, and they make some explicit references to Mary of Oignies. The eight stanzas of the hymn used for both vespers and for lauds (51) (and probably for matins as well) mentions that Mary of Oignies shares the same name as the mother of Christ, and that she came from Nivelles. Christ's 'benign' spirit anointed his 'benign' daughter, who was outstanding among the beguines. The last stanza cites James of Vitry's *Life*. In the Prologue, James tells about a monk of the Cistercian monastery of Aulne, who asked in prayer what he should think about the beguines. He was answered: 'They will be found firm in the faith and effective in action.'[9] The hymns for terce (52) and compline (53) are devoid of explicit reference to Mary.

Second Set of Antiphons for the Night Office. These antiphons are meant to replace the more generic ones given earlier, which were taken from the feast of Mary Magdalen (20, 27). Although the rubric (54) says 'for the first nocturn', there are twelve of them so they must be intended for both the first and second nocturns. These antiphons are closely connected to the second book of James of Vitry's *Life*, which is structured around the seven gifts of the Holy Spirit. Mary

[9] *VMO* Prologue, 4. The monk was told: 'Invenientur in fide stabiles et in opere efficaces'. The hymn has 'In vera fide stabiles, / In opere efficaces'.

had a multitude of virtues, and rather than discuss them all, James writes that he organized the second book of his *Life* around these seven gifts, from which all her virtues flowed out.[10] This is precisely the message of the first two antiphons (55, 56). The next antiphons deal with the gifts in order:

Antiphons	=	*VMO*
fear (57–58)	=	43–49
piety, mercy (59–60)	=	50–63
knowledge (61)	=	64–72
fortitude (62)	=	73–75
counsel (63)	=	76–80
understanding (64)	=	81–86
wisdom (65)	=	87–92

The author of the antiphons derives each one of them almost verbatim from James of Vitry's *Life*. He usually finds the quotation he wants right at the beginning of the sections devoted to that particular gift. The antiphons on fear of the Lord are derived from two passages: 'she conceived such a great love of poverty through the spirit of fear that she hardly even wanted to possess the bare necessities of life' (45), and 'she always had the Lord in her sight and she always thought on him in all her ways' (43). The antiphons on piety are from a single paragraph in the *Life*: 'she regularly kindled the fire of charity in the lamp of her heart with the oil of mercy' (50), and 'from the abundant piety of her heart she therefore busied herself as far as she was able in the external works of mercy' (50). The other five gifts of the Holy Spirit each have one antiphon devoted to them: knowledge: 'the Father of Light [...] illumined his daughter with the spirit of knowledge so that she knew when and in what manner something should be done and avoided and thus she seasoned every sacrifice with the salt of knowledge' (64); fortitude: 'thus did her Father open his treasure chest and adorn his daughter with the spirit of fortitude and thus was she forearmed against all adversity' (73); counsel: 'In all her ways her eyes preceded her steps and she did everything with foresight lest she might repent even a little after the deed' (76); understanding: 'the daughter of Jerusalem, adorned with ornaments, shining with the lights of the aforesaid gifts of the Holy Spirit, turned to heavenly things with a purified heart by the spirit of understanding' (81);

---

[10] *VMO* 2, 42. See also on these gifts, the General Introduction.

wisdom: 'her heart was affected in its innermost parts with a gift of honey-dripping wisdom: her words were made sweet [...]' (87). The final antiphon is cited from a passage describing the heaven-sent song she uttered just before the onset of her final illness: God 'shook every tear from the eyes of his handmaid and filled her heart with exultation and her lips with harmony' (98).

These texts for the Mass and offices for Mary of Oignies tell us almost nothing about Mary that we did not know from James of Vitry's *Life*. They leave us with some puzzles. Why did the author of these liturgical texts choose to make use of the existing Mass and Office texts used at Villers? Why did he then change his mind and compose the second set of antiphons for the night office, using statements found in James of Vitry's *Life*? The offices do provide us with some nice hymns, and they remind us of James's artistry in placing his stories about Mary within the framework of the seven gifts of the Holy Spirit. Most of all, the Mass and offices show us that the monks of an important Cistercian monastery had particular veneration for Mary of Oignies and regarded her as a saint.

1. In the year of the Lord 1213 on the vigil of St. John the Baptist, on the Lord's Day, there died at Oignies the spouse of Christ, Mary of Nivelles.

[MASS]

2. *Introit at Mass.* Let us all rejoice, etc., in honour of Mary the beguine[1] of Christ, at whose solemnity, etc.[2]

3. *Collect.* Almighty, eternal.[3]

4. *Epistle.* A valiant woman.[4]

5. *Alleluia.* The Lord arose, and hastening to meet.

6. *Gospel.* Mary stood etc.[5]

7. *Secret.* Most loving[6] God, sanctify this sacrifice in view of the grace of blessed Mary, your beguine, and by the mighty power of your love assign it to all the faithful living and dead for the enlivening of their souls. You who live.

8. *Post-Communion.* O God, may the sacraments of your goodness, through the intercession of blessed Mary, your beguine, purify us from all that is old,[7] and bestow on all the faithful living and dead the saving effect of your perpetual redemption.

9. *All the rest is as on the feast of blessed Mary Magdalen.*

---

[1] As Misonne explains in his introduction to his edition of these texts, the author of the texts regularly uses the word 'benigna' (kind, good, friendly, favourable, mild) to mean 'beguine' (*beguina*). It will be here translated as 'beguine'. The texts honour Mary as the founder or author of the beguine way of life, although it was only some years after her death that there were those formally designated as beguines. Most of the notes that follow are based on Misonne's introduction and his notes to the texts.

[2] The mass formulary is that of the feast of Mary Magdalen, 22 July, as found in an eighteenth-century missal from Villers (Brussels, BR, MS 3223, fols 125–26).

[3] The full text of the collect is given at para. 18 below.

[4] Proverbs 31. 10–31.

[5] John 20. 11–18 (see para. 40).

[6] 'Benignissime' the superlative form of 'benigna'.

[7] See para. 13.

[AT VESPERS]

10. *For the psalms. Antiphon.* This great feast is held in memory of Mary, the beguine of Christ.

11. *A.* She came from Nivelles, where by her parents she was joined in chaste marriage to John.

12. *A.* When she pursued heavenly concerns more devoutly, she joined her husband John to the grace of God.

13. *A.* Both of them laid aside the old man with all his acts and followed the way of life of one who has been created, as God would have it, in justice and holiness of truth.[8]

14. *A.* The Lord joined his spouse to himself by the privilege of a special grace, and he nurtured her more diligently with greater delights.[9]

15. *Capitulum.* Whoever glories.[10]

16. *At First Vespers. Resp.* Rejoice, daughter Mary.[11]

17. *At the Magnificat. A.* God was magnified in the works of his daughter, who was marked by the light of his countenance and so was radiant with a special seal of his likeness, and like a new star of the sea illumined the paradise of the beguines.[12]

18. *Collect.* Almighty, eternal God, as you continually fructify your Church with the fruit of a new blessing, you awakened your more abundant grace in

---

[8] See Colossians 3. 9; Ephesians 4. 24.

[9] Antiphons are read as introductions to the psalms. Because there are only four psalms at the monastic office, this fifth antiphon is not needed. Below it is used at para. 33 for the canticle in the third nocturn.

[10] II Corinthians 10. 17–18.

[11] For the full text see para. 23.

[12] Compare Psalm 4. 7; Song of Songs 8. 6. According to St Jerome, the etymology of the name 'Mary' was 'star of the sea'.

blessed Mary, your beguine. We ask that you grant that we who celebrate her birthday may also experience more efficaciously in your loving-kindness the support of her merits. Through.

NOCTURNS

19. *Invitatory.* Behold the spouse comes, go out to meet him. * He led his bride into the wedding supper of the Lamb of God. Come.

IN THE FIRST NOCTURN

20. *Antiphons as for Blessed Mary Magdalen. A.* Come, bride. ***A.*** I am dark. ***A.*** You are beautiful. ***A.*** By your appearance. ***A.*** He will help. ***A.*** Return.[13]

21. *V.* By your appearance.[14]

22. *Eight Lessons. From the Exposition of Origen on the Gospel, 'Mary Stood'.*[15]

23. *R.* Rejoice, Mary, daughter of Sion, rejoice, you who share by an intimate grace of union both the name and the virtues of the mother of Christ and, anointed with the ointment of the loving spirit of the Lord, appeared as a burning and bright lamp in the garden of the beguines. * Intercede for us. ***V.*** In

---

[13] The night office had three nocturns. In the first two nocturns there were six psalms with antiphons followed by four lessons, each of which was followed by a responsory. Each of these four responsories consisted of a two-part 'response', followed by a verse, followed by the repetition of the second part of the 'response'. The fourth response was lengthened by the addition of a 'Glory be'.

[14] The versicle and response indicated here are drawn from Psalm 44. 5 (Vulgate): 'By your appearance and your beauty. Go forward, proceed successively and reign'.

[15] John 20. 11–18. The exposition of the Gospel attributed to Origen has been identified and translated by Chrysogonus Waddell, 'Pseudo-Origen's Homily on Mary Magdalen at the Tomb of Jesus', *Liturgy: Cistercians of the Strict Observance*, 23 (1989), 45–64. It pertains to the Gospel account of Mary's presence at the tomb on Easter morning. That Gospel, used on Mary of Oignies's feast, was taken over from the feast of Mary Magdalen.

the splendours of the saints you are now united to Christ, in whose service you faithfully persevered. Intercede.[16]

24. R. Your youth is renewed like an eagle's, for with dove-like simplicity you found joy in ever new loving pursuits of the heavenly spouse. * In fringes of gold, surrounded with variety. **V.** Ears for God's word, the work of your beauty, from the day of your calling.[17] In fringes.

25. R. O blessed heroine, on the way of your virtues with the soldier's lance of love you opened the side of the heavenly spouse, where, incorporated into your original principle, you slept peacefully in the same spirit. * Wisdom you drew out from a secret place; you were tenderly nurtured with heavenly delights. **V.** You have wounded my heart, my sister, my bride, you have wounded my heart. Wisdom.[18]

26. R. Dry bones, heed the word of Mary, the athlete of Christ, for the [...] of the Lord on the fortieth day of your slumber according to the prophecy of the Holy Spirit, through you calling a year a day, and manifest the strength of God's virtues in yourselves. * And the abyss coughed up the dove over against Nineveh on the fortieth day of its overthrow. **V.** The Lord called forth the dry land, and he named the gatherings of the waters seas. And the abyss coughed up. Glory be to the Father and to the Son and to the Holy Spirit. And the abyss coughed up.[19]

IN THE SECOND NOCTURN

27. A. The kingdom of heaven is like a businessman. **A.** Having found a fine pearl. **A.** The kingdom of heaven is like a net. **A.** Come, my chosen. **A.** In the middle of the night. **A.** When the king was.[20]

---

[16] This verse and response, in which as was customary the second member after the asterisk was repeated, contains reminiscences of Lamentations 4. 21; Joel 5. 35; Psalm 1099. 3.

[17] See Psalm 102. 3; Psalm 44. 14; Ezekiel 28. 13. One could more easily translate the first phrase after the asterisk as 'the gold of the word of God'.

[18] See Genesis 2. 23; Joel 19. 35; Song of Songs 4. 9.

[19] There is an illegible word indicated at the ellipse. There are allusions to Ezekiel 37. 4; Numbers 14. 34; Ezekiel 4. 6; Jonah 2. 11, and Genesis 1. 9.

[20] These antiphons were used at Villers for the feast of St. Mary Magdalen.

28. *V.* God will help her.[21]

29. *R.* How great is the expanse of your sweetness, O Lord! How you have perfected Mary, your spouse, hiding her in the hidden place of your countenance away from the disturbance of the sons of men; now you have glorified her. * In the sight of your sons. ***V.*** Blessed be your glory, Lord, in your holy place. In the sight.[22]

30. *R.* How beautiful you are, spouse of Christ, and how comely in the delights of Christ. Your hair is like the purple garment of a king bound into folds. You ascended into the triumphant glory of the Lord, and you took hold of his richest fruit. ***V.*** Your breasts are like grapes, and the scent of your mouth like that of apples. You ascended.[23]

31. *R.* Come, my spouse, you who live in the gardens, my dove in the clefts of the rock in the cave in the wall, and you will be crowned. * From the fruits of your works. ***V.*** I will water the garden plantings and I will drench the fruits of my meadow. From the fruits.[24]

32. R. The pomegranates of the paradise garden have sprouted the bud of a new devotion by the spirit of the mouth of our God Christ. * In whose ardour, once their enemies have been conquered, the young women seize the kingdom of God with violent love. ***V.*** From you emanates, O Christ, a paradise garden of pomegranates.[25] In whose. Glory be to the Father and to the Son and to the Holy Spirit. In whose.

AT THE CANTICLES

33. *Look for the Antiphon in First Vespers,* The Lord joined to himself.[26]

---

[21] Psalm 45. 6.

[22] See Psalm 30. 20–21; Ezekiel 3. 12.

[23] Song of Songs 7. 5, 6, 8.

[24] Song of Songs 8. 13; 2. 14; 4. 8; Sirach 24. 29.

[25] Song of Songs 4. 13. Misonne, the editor of the Latin text, has corrected the Latin in this responsory.

[26] See para. 14. above.

34. *V.* He chose her.[27]

35. *Gospel.* Mary stood. ***Homily of Origen.*** We heard, etc.[28]

36. *R.* The Lord watered your region with the streams of paradise and it grew lush with the sweetness of your spirit. * He multiplied her offspring, and in her mists he fructified the celestial seeds. *V.* With daily wine he inebriated her and with the new wine of his pomegranates. He multiplied.[29]

37. *R.* Thanks be to you, O Lord, for through your spirit you revealed to your little ones, so that they might know what is the hope of Christ's call, what are the riches of the glory of his inheritance in his saints, and what is * the surpassing greatness of his love in him. *V.* The brightness of eternal life and the spotless mirror of God's majesty. Surpassing.[30]

38. *R.* There were given her two wings of a great eagle, and she flew into the arms of her spouse, where she was absorbed by the immense sea of God's delight. * As though into the abyss, she was transformed into the same image by the spirit of the Lord. *V.* Your eyes, dove of Christ, are washed with milk; you now reside near most plentiful waters. As though.[31]

39. *R.* Let us rejoice, exult, and give glory to God, who for the dedication of the new religious life of his beguines, initiated his daughter, Mary, at Nivelles, to make her choice for the snowny white [garment] of her religious way of life. * She died in peace, anointed with heavenly balsam, in the hands of her brothers in the house of anointing. *V.* Christ, you will bless the circle of the year of your kindness, and let your beguines be filled with the richness of your sprit. She. Glory be to the Father and to the Son and to the Holy Spirit. She. [32]

---

[27] This antiphon ('The Lord chose her and favoured her. He made her to dwell in his tent') was used for the Common of Virgins. It does not have a precise scriptural basis.

[28] See note 15.

[29] Compare Psalm 64. 11, 1; Song of Songs 8. 2.

[30] Compare Matthew 11. 25; Ephesians 1, 18, 19; Wisdom 7. 26.

[31] Compare Apocalypse 12. 13; II Corinthians 3. 18; Song of Songs 5. 12. Misonne has altered the verse slightly.

[32] Compare Psalm 64. 12. Misonne has altered the text somewhat.

40. *The Gospel According to John.* Mary stood at the tomb.

AT LAUDS

41. *Antiphon.* In the spirit of the fear of the Lord, the bride of Christ zealously put to flight the works of darkness, and constantly ground down the foul head of the ancient serpent.[33]

42. *Benedictus Antiphon.* Seeking to please only her heavenly spouse, the handmaid of Christ crucified her flesh with its vices and unruly desires. He will reform the body of her lowliness to be configured to the body of his splendour.[34]

AT PRIME

43. A. This is the spouse of Christ, who used the two-sided blade of the sword of humility to conquer enemies on either side.

AT TERCE

44. A. She put her Christ as a seal on her heart and her arm, and clothed her servants twice over.[35]

AT SEXT

45. A. In the warmth of the midday light the bride of Christ melted, and she was completely rapt into God and configured to the splendour of his glory.[36]

AT NONE

46. A. The servant of Christ, burning with zeal for souls, diligently collected a tenth order for him as an addition to the nine orders of angels.

---

[33] Compare Isaiah 11. 2; Romans 13. 12; Apocalypse 12. 9; Genesis 3. 15.

[34] Compare Galatians 5. 24; Philippians 3. 21.

[35] Compare Song of Songs 8. 6; Proverbs 31. 21.

[36] Compare Hebrews 1. 3.

AT VESPERS

47. *For the Psalms.* Come, bride of Christ. I am black. You are beautiful.
Return.[37]

48. *V.* By your beauty. **Hymn.** The glory of the king's daughter.[38]

49. *V.* Spread.[39]

50. *At the Magnificat Antiphon. A.* As she reached the evening of her life,
the bride of Christ was visited more often by the Lord. No longer able to bear
a further expansion of heavenly desire from this very power impulse, ignited with
the ardour of a most fervent charity, and with the chains of death fettered, she
commended her friends most devoutly to the Lord and consummated her
evening holocaust in peace.[40]

51. *Hymn for both Vespers and at Lauds.*[41]

The generation of the just
Now remembers with joy
The glory of the king's daughter
Who was equally the mother of Christ.[42]

2. This Mary of Nivelles,
Star shining from star,
Following the footsteps of his
Virtues from her infancy.

---

[37] Compare Song of Songs 1. 4; 6. 3; 6. 12. The second and fourth antiphons were taken
from the matins for the Common of Virgins.

[38] Psalm 44. 5: 'By your beauty and your comeliness. Stretch forward, proceed with ease
and reign.' The text of the hymn occurs at 51.

[39] Psalm 44. 3: 'Spread over lips is grace. For God has blessed you forever.'

[40] Compare Psalm 140. 2; *VMO* 2, 97–108.

[41] The first four strophes were also for use at matins.

[42] Compare Psalm 44. 14.

3. The spirit of the Lord
Taught her from the start
With all the levels of virtues
As a model for her contemporaries.

4. A love strong as death
Pierced her soul,
And the fire of charity
With the sweet sword of love.[43]

Division

5. The benign spirit of Christ
Anointed his beguine in a heavenly way
With divine nectar
Flowing down from her head.

6. Exquisite relief carved
For the adornment of the beguines,
Who are enflamed with the fire
Of God's love from heaven.

7. Youth with virgins,
Old people with the younger,
Treading down temporal things
Sigh after heavenly things.[44]

8. Standing firm in truth faith,
Effective in action
The divine beehives
Follow the Lord's lamb.[45]

---

[43] Compare Luke 2. 35; Song of Songs 8. 6.

[44] Compare Psalm 148. 12.

[45] Compare Colossians 1. 23; Apocalypse 14. 4. See, *VMO* Prologue, 3; this strophe echoes the response given by the Holy Spirit to a monk of Aulne who prayed to know what to think of beguines.

9. Glory to you, O Lord.

52. *Hymn at Terce.*

1. Let the young women,
Images of heavenly beings,
Nailed to the cross of the Lord,
Exalt the Lord's name with drums;[46]

2. The community of unity,
The breath of the Trinity,
The race of divine majesty,
Examples of virtues.

3. The little flock is instructed
In the art of wisdom,
With heavenly delights,
By the teaching of love.

4. O all-conquering love
You have now revealed to the little ones
The treasures of heavenly
Wisdom and knowledge.[47]

5. Let us now humbly ask for
The clemency of the supreme spouse,
That he may save us from dangers
By the merits of his bride.

Grant, most loving Father.

53. *Hymn for Compline.*

1. O paradise of the Lord,
Where a variety of flowers

---

[46] Compare Psalm 67. 26.
[47] Compare Sirach 1. 26; Matthew 11. 25.

Blooms, flowers, breathes, gives off scent,
And heavenly fruit satisfies.

2. There one finds gentle behaviour,
Voluntary poverty,
Sobriety, satisfaction,
Exertion of labour.

3. Here are faith, hope and charity,
Heavenly meditation,
Zeal for virtue,
Outstanding humility,

4. Chastity, patience,
True obedience,
Clemency and purity,
Peaceful discretion.

5. Piety, worship of the Lord,
Fervent zeal for souls,
Distribution of gifts,
Harmonize in the greatest peace.

Glory to you Lord.

54. *Antiphons for the First Nocturn*[48]

55. *[A.]* Christ conserved for Mary, his spouse, a mind in bloom, bedecked with every kind of virtues and adorned with all garden flowers.

56. *A.* The Lord filled her with the sevenfold gifts of the Holy Spirit, from which, as from springs, all her good flowed out.

57. *A.* By the spirit of fear had she conceived so great a love of poverty that she barely kept necessities for herself, while she disbursed everything on the poor.

---

[48] This rubric was written in another, contemporary hand. There are twelve antiphons, so they were probably meant for both the first and second nocturns of the night office.

58. *A.* She did all her actions while always keeping the Lord in sight, and the thought about him on all her ways.

59. *A.* This outstanding spouse of Christ continually lit the fire of charity in the lamp of her heart with the oil of mercy.[49]

60. *A.* As much as she could, the daughter of the king strove to fulfil exteriorly all the works mercy from the abundant piety of her heart.

61. *A.* God the father of lights illumined his daughter Mary with the spirit of knowledge, so that she would know, for example, what was to be done or avoided, and how to season her every sacrifice with salt.[50]

62. *A.* The heavenly Father opened his treasures and adorned his handmaid Mary with the spirit of fortitude, and fortified her against all adversities.[51]

63. *A.* In all her ways her eyes anticipated her footsteps, and she did everything with the spirit of counsel so that afterwards she would not be sorry about anything even a little.[52]

64. *A.* Mary, the daughter of Jerusalem, was enlightened with charismatic gifts as though with lamps, and she dwelt with purified heart on heavenly things through the spirit of understanding.[53]

65. *A.* The heart of the daughter of the king was so moved by the honeyed gift of wisdom that all her deeds were imbued with spiritual unction.[54]

66. *A.* God dried every tear from the eyes of his daughter and filled her heart with exultation and her lips with melody.

---

[49] Compare Matthew 25. 4.

[50] Compare James 1. 17; Isaiah 11. 2.

[51] Compare Matthew 2. 11; Isaiah 11. 2.

[52] Compare Proverbs 3. 6; Isaiah. 11. 2.

[53] Compare Isaiah 37. 22; Isaiah. 11. 2.

[54] Compare Psalm 44. 14.

Part Three: Studies

MARY OF OIGNIES: A FRIEND TO THE SAINTS

Brenda M. Bolton

For historians of the *Frauenfrage*, Oignies-sur-Sambre in the duchy of Brabant is synonymous with the figure of Mary (d. 1213),[1] 'new' saint of the diocese of Liège and 'precious pearl of Christ',[2] a short-term model for those religious women who became known as beguines. In the first half of the thirteenth century, Oignies had already achieved international renown for the quality of its spiritual life.[3] In this small village, a dependency of the lordship of Aisneau and under the protection of the duke of Lotharingia,[4] was a modest Augustinian priory which soon surpassed and outshone its greater neighbours near at hand: the abbey of St Gerard de Brogne, the Premonstratensian houses

[1] Based on Brenda Bolton, 'Spiegels van Vroomheid: Relieken van Maria van Oignies', in *Dynamiek van Religie en Cultuur: Geschiedenis van het Nederlands katholicisme*, ed. by Marit Monteiro, Gerard Rooijakkers, and Joost Rosendaal, 2 vols (Kampen: Kok, 1993), I, pp. 125–37. I am most grateful to Professor Sharon Farmer for generously allowing me to see her article, 'Low Country Ascetics and Oriental Luxury: James of Vitry, Mary of Oignies and the Treasures of Oignies' (forthcoming). Her focus is not only on Mary but also on the highly significant aspect of James of Vitry's relations with the East and the symbolism of gemstones. On Mary, see now the General Introduction to this volume and the valuable Select Bibliography.

[2] *VMO* 1, 29: 'pretiosa Christi margarita'; *VMO* 2, 109; *Hist. fund.* 6.

[3] F. Moschus, *Coenobarchia Ogniacensis sive Antistitum qui Ogniacensi ad Sabim Monasterio hactenus praefugere numero undetriginta catalogus, cum eulogiis et anagrammatis* (Douai: [n. pub.], 1598); Poncelet, 'Chartes du Prieuré d'Oignies', introduction, p. xxiii, and charters, pp. 1–104; McDonnell, *Beguines and Beghards*; Simons, *Cities of Ladies*, pp. 35–48.

[4] Poncelet, 'Chartes du Prieuré d'Oignies', p. xlix; no. 6 (1210), p. 7; no. 25 (1216), pp. 23–24. In *c.* 1240, Oignies passed into the County of Namur: 'villa de Ongnies (sic) translata est dudum ad dominum Comitis Namurcensis', dated 17 October 1243.

of Floreffe and Fosses, and the collegiate churches of Saint Aubain at Namur and Notre Dame de Walcourt. This was partly the result of a surprising accumulation of relics. Some forty of these precious items still exist to this day with most of them being securely dated to the period *c.* 1200–*c.* 1240.[5]

The attraction of Oignies had begun some years earlier with the establishment of a formidable example of spirituality, a *pauper schola*. As reported in the *History of the Foundation of the Venerable Church of Blessed Nicholas*, in *c.* 1187, Giles of Walcourt, chaplain to the lord of Walcourt, together with two of his brothers, Robert and John, had renounced their hereditary possessions, preferring to hold all things in common according to the New Testament example.[6] At Oignies, the brothers found already in existence a tiny wooden chapel dedicated to St Nicholas with an endowment of three hens a year. There, with proceeds from the sale of their father's estate, they established a small priory in which they could observe the Rule of St Augustine. Giles of Walcourt (d. 5 January 1234) became its first prior, with the bishop of Liège, Hugh of Pierrepont (1200–29), dedicating the rebuilt church on 24 July 1204.[7] A fourth Walcourt brother, Hugh, was a highly distinguished goldsmith of exceptional skill and talent who, whilst never becoming a priest, created works of art which he dedicated to the greater glory of God at Oignies and elsewhere.[8] As their elderly mother had accompanied them to Oignies, some provision needed to be made

---

[5] Suzanne Vandecan, 'L'histoire du Trésor d'Oignies', in *Autour de Hugo d'Oignies*, ed. by Robert Didier and Jacques Toussaint, Musée des Arts anciens du Namurois, 25 (Namur: Société archéologique de Namur, 2003), pp. 47–57 [subsequent references = *Autour de Hugo d'Oignies*]. Other churches in the region also possessed precious relics: Manasses de Hierges (*c.* 1177), Constable of Jerusalem, bequeathed a relic of the True Cross to Brogne, see Ferdinand Courtoy, *Le Trésor du Prieuré d'Oignies aux soeurs de Notre Dame à Namur et l'Oeuvre du Frère Hugo* (Brussels: Editions de la Librairie Encyclopédique, 1953), p. 11, note 3 [subsequent references = Courtoy, *Le Trésor*]. The church of Saint-Aubain received a relic of the True Cross, sent in 1205 by Henry, Regent of the Latin kingdom of Constantinople, to his brother, Philip the Noble, marquis of Namur, see Courtoy, *Le Trésor*, p. 11, note 3; Cécile Douxchamps-Lefèvre, 'Le monde du frère Hugo', in *Autour de Hugo d'Oignies*, pp. 11–19. For Notre Dame de Walcourt see *Recueil des Historiens des Gaules et de la France*, 18, ed. by M. Bouquet (Paris: Palmé, 1880), p. 723; Robert Didier, 'Oeuvres de l'atelier d'Oignies et d'autres ateliers', in *Autour de Hugo d'Oignies*, pp. 320–36.

[6] See *Hist. fund.* 4–5.

[7] Poncelet, 'Chartes du Prieuré d'Oignies', no. 3 (1204), pp. 4–5.

[8] Link, 'Hugo von Oignies'; S. Collon-Gevaert, R. Lejeune, and J. Stiennon, *Art Mosan dans la Vallée de la Meuse aux XIe, XIIe, et XIIIe siècles*, 4th edn (Brussels: Cultura, 1966); Robert Didier, 'Hugo d'Oignies: Prolégomènes', in *Autour de Hugo d'Oignies*, pp. 59–64.

for a female community, however rudimentary.[9] The reputation of Oignies soon spread far and wide and the brothers' exemplary practice of renunciation, poverty, and sacrifice caught the imagination of a flood of visitors, at first from nearby but increasingly from further afield. Amongst these were many ecclesiastics renowned for their knowledge and their talents. Most important of all was a local woman, Mary, from nearby Nivelles, whose presence and guardianship of the relics was to bring a whole new spiritual dimension to this already respected place.

In 1207, Mary came to Oignies after serving devotedly with her husband John at the leper–colony of Willambroux, with the intention of escaping from the pressure of her many followers.[10] At Oignies, between the priory and the River Sambre, were grouped some simple dwellings for the mother of Giles and other close female relatives of the Walcourts; and these women Mary joined. They lived in common for the greater part of the time, taking their meals together. These were presided over by the prior's mother, then almost a hundred.[11] From 1207 until her death six years later, Mary chose to live in a small cell adjacent to the newly consecrated conventual church where, by looking through the window adjoining the altar, she could share not only the canons' communal offices but also their zeal for the cure of souls and the apostolic mission.[12] The eloquence of local preachers such as John of Liroux and John of Nivelle, combined with Mary's presence and her reputation for sanctity acquired at Willambroux, attracted even more visitors to the priory.[13]

---

[9] On the beguines in Oignies see Simons, *Cities of Ladies*, App. 1, 83, p. 293. For valuable comparative insights see Luigi Pellegrini, 'Female Religious Experience and Society in Thirteenth-Century Italy', in *Monks and Nuns, Saints and Outcasts*, ed. by Sharon Farmer and Barbara Rosenwein (Ithaca: Cornell University Press, 2000), pp. 97–122; Jean-Baptiste Lefèvre, 'Le cadre religieux', in *Autour de Hugo d'Oignies*, pp. 21–45.

[10] *VMO* 2, 93: 'frequentiam hominium ad eam ex devotione concurrentium'; Poncelet, 'Chartes du Prieuré d'Oignies', p. vii, note 1.

[11] *VMO* 2, 54: 'mater fratrum de Oignies'; *VMO-S* 10: 'mater prioris'; Poncelet, 'Chartes du Prieuré d'Oignies', pp. lx–lxi.

[12] *VMO-S* 13.

[13] John of Nivelle (died 1233), dean of the cathedral of Saint Lambert in Liège, entered the priory of Oignies after 1211, and was instrumental in supporting the beguines of the diocese: *Hist. Occ.* IX: 103; McDonnell, *Beguines and Beghards*, pp. 40–45. John of Liroux, close friend of James of Vitry and Lutgard of Tongeren, died in the Alps in the winter of 1215 or 1216 while travelling to Rome to seek papal approval for the pious women of the diocese of Liège. See *Hist. Occ.* 'John de Liro', App. C, pp. 285–86; *VLA* 2, 8; Simons, *Cities of Ladies*, pp. 173–74,

One of these was the distinguished Paris-trained doctor of theology, James of Vitry (1160/1170–1240).[14] In 1210 or 1211, he specifically abandoned his studies and all worldly pursuits to follow the example of renunciation, poverty, and sacrifice for which Oignies was justly famous, remaining there until 1216. Under Prior Giles and with the interaction of the unique personalities of Mary and James of Vitry, the whole community became known as a quite extraordinary centre of religious virtue and spirituality. Mary and James were strongly drawn to each other. He regarded her as his 'spiritual mother', seeing Christ anew through her example.[15] Indeed, it was Mary's influence which helped James to overcome the disorganized nature of his sermons so that he developed into a highly effective preacher.[16] Their lives and beliefs remained so closely entwined at all levels that, following Mary's death in 1213, and at the request of his friend and fellow preacher, Fulk, bishop of Toulouse, James readily agreed to compose her *Life*.[17] He did this not only to commemorate her sanctity but also to reveal to the Christians of the beleaguered southern France and elsewhere that they would do well to emulate the northern example of Mary of Oignies, both in faith and lifestyle, as the religious women of Brabant had been encouraged so to do.[18]

note 36.

[14] For James of Vitry see Margot King in the introduction to *VMO*; Maurice Coens, 'Jacques de Vitry', in *Bibliographie nationale de Belgique*, Académie Royale des sciences, des lettres et des beaux-arts de Belgique, 31, supplément 3 (Brussels: Académie Royale, 1962), cols 465–47. For a complete bibliography and excellent summary of the career and writings of this popular preacher see *Hist. Occ.*, pp. x–xiii, 3–15; *Lettres de Jacques de Vitry*, ed. by Huygens, pp. 491–657; James of Vitry, *Lettres de la cinquième croisade*, trans. by G. Duchet-Suchaux, Sous la Règle de Saint-Augustin (Turnhout: Brepols, 1998); Bolton, 'Faithful to Whom?'; Jessalyn Bird, 'Heresy, Crusade and Reform in the Circle of Peter the Chanter' (unpublished doctoral thesis, University of Oxford, 2001).

[15] *Lettres de Jacques de Vitry*, ed. by Huygens, I, p. 550, lines 44–45.

[16] *VMO* I, 17; 2, 79.

[17] Brenda M. Bolton, '*Vitae Matrum*', p. 255; Lejeune, 'L'évêque de Toulouse'; Bolton, 'Fulk of Toulouse'.

[18] *VMO* I, 2–3; Carol Neel, 'The Origins of the Beguines', *Signs: The Journal of Women in Culture and Society*, 14 (1989), 321–41.

Relic Veneration

One way by which James of Vitry sought to encourage the imitation of Mary's example was to develop that passionate interest in relics, those tokens of faith, which they had both shared.[19] Several recent studies have highlighted the religious significance given to relics — as if they were the saints themselves — and the psychological need that people felt for them.[20] Body relics were always regarded as sacred, worthy even of theft, but at various times the ecclesiastical authorities acted firmly to require their strict enclosure in reliquaries so that they would be safe. The associative relic or *brandeum* then became a substitute — almost as good as the original.[21]

In Brabant in general and at Oignies in particular, emphasis was placed on whatever religious significance could be linked to every aspect of the body, living and dead, real or associative. Bynum demonstrates that the body acquired a new religious significance at precisely this period and that this could be linked to a heightened female spirituality.[22] Mary of Oignies epitomized this bodily aspect of spirituality. In the *Life* that he wrote of her, James of Vitry describes the terrible self-inflicted immolations inspired by her contemplation of Christ's sufferings.[23] Her loathing of her body even led her to cut out a piece of her own flesh. So inflamed was she by an all-consuming fire of love that she was able to rise above the pain of her wound.[24] Her desire for poverty was so great that she

---

[19] Eduardo Formigoni, 'Jacques de Vitry et le prieuré d'Oignies', in *Autour de Hugo d'Oignies*, pp. 37–45.

[20] Patrick J. Geary, *Furta Sacra: Thefts of Relics in the Central Middle Ages* (Princeton: Princeton University Press, 1978); Peter Brown, *The Body and Society: Men, Women and Sexual Renunciation in Early Christianity* (New York: Columbia University Press, 1988); Caroline Walker Bynum, 'The Female Body and Religious Practice in the Later Middle Ages', in her *Fragmentation and Redemption*, pp. 181–238, especially p. 183.

[21] For a discussion of the term *brandeum*, see John M. McCulloh, 'The Cult of Relics in the Letters and "Dialogues" of Pope Gregory the Great: A Lexicographical Study', *Traditio*, 32 (1976), 145–84; John M. McCulloh, 'From Antiquity to the Middle Ages: Continuity and Change in Papal Relic Policy from the Sixth to the Eighth Century', in *Pietas: Festschrift für Bernhard Kötting*, ed. by Ernst Dassmann and K. Suso Frank, Jahrbuch für Antike und Christentum Ergänzungsband, 8 (Munster: Aschendorffsche Verlagsbuchhandlung, 1980), pp. 313–24.

[22] Bynum, 'The Female Body and Religious Practice', p. 183.

[23] *VMO* I, 21–22.

[24] *VMO* I, 22.

nearly starved herself to death on several occasions. She longed to live by begging and, dressed in old woollen garments, she would set out with her scrip or pouch and the little wooden cup from which she could both eat and drink.[25]

Her particular ecstatic veneration of Christ's body was expressed through her reception of the Eucharist. This was the only comfort she could not bear to be without. To receive Christ's body was to die and in dying, she was with the Lord himself.[26] James of Vitry recounts how, with the help of her priest, he tried to see if she could be made to take a small portion of an unconsecrated host. So nauseated was she by it that she spat it out and cried aloud in disgust.[27] Mary's veneration for the Eucharist was only matched by the stress she placed on the Trinity. Even on her deathbed, she sang about the holy Trinity, the Trinity in unity, and the unity in Trinity.[28]

Mary's self-appointed function in the priory of Oignies had been to guard the relics of the saints during the night. It was, says James of Vitry, 'as if the relics were applauding her guardianship'.[29] When some new relics had been brought to the priory, she sensed their arrival in the spirit and, according to James, 'for a whole night she exulted with the holy relics and saw Christ rejoice and the other relics received the new relics with exultation and joy'.[30] Most interestingly too, her spirit perceived whether or not they were true relics.[31] Her ability to authenticate relics was amply tested by a mutual friend of James and herself. Bringing a bone for her verification, a saint appeared. Instead of identifying

[25] *VMO* 2, 45; *Autour de Hugo d'Oignies*, pp. 236–37.

[26] For an illuminating insight into the celebration of the Eucharist see Gary Macy, *The Theologies of the Eucharist in the Early Scholastic Period: A Study of the Salvific Function of the Sacrament according to Theologians c. 1080–c. 1220* (Oxford: Clarendon Press, 1984); Gary Macy, *Treasures from the Storeroom: Medieval Religion and the Eucharist* (Collegeville MN: The Liturgical Press, 1984), especially pp. 36–38; Bernard Cooke and Gary Macy, *Christian Symbol and Ritual: An Introduction* (Oxford: Oxford University Press, 2005), especially pp. 87–107.

[27] *VMO* 2, 105. James of Vitry cites this event in *Hist. Occ.* XXXIX: 277.

[28] *VMO* 2, 99. See Boespflug, 'Le dogme trinitaire'; Piotr Skubiszewski, 'L'iconographie de la patène et du calice du frère Hugo', in *Autour de Hugo d'Oignies*, pp. 99–131.

[29] *VMO* 1, 34.

[30] *VMO* 1, 34: 'Et quoniam pretiosas sanctorum reliquias, quibus copiose munita est et ornata ecclesia de Oignies, nocturnis custodiebat excubiis; eadem reliquiae noctem festam cum ea ducentes, et custodi suae quasi applaudentes, mirabili solatio spiritum ejus laetificabant'.

[31] *VMO* 2, 91: 'et alias reliquias, quasi cum exultatione et veneratione novas reliquias suscipientes videbat'.

himself orally, he wrote down four letters, 'A. I. O. L.'.[32] This may have been either Aigulf, abbot of Lérins, who verified and translated the bodies of St Benedict of Nursia and his sister from Monte Cassino to Fleury c. 690–707, or perhaps Aigulf, a recluse from near Bourges.[33]

When he was called to be an active preacher, both against the heretics in Languedoc and for the taking of the cross in a Fifth Crusade throughout France and Brabant, James of Vitry was forced to be absent from the priory for much of the period between 1212 and 1216.[34] When he subsequently became bishop of Acre (1216–27) and cardinal bishop of Tusculum (1229–40), he was only able to return on two or three occasions.[35] On one of these, arriving from Acre sometime between 1220 and 1226, he was honoured with the invitation to consecrate the new priory church.[36] Later, he spent the intervening period of two years, between his resignation from the See of Acre and elevation as cardinal bishop of Tusculum, in Brabant acting as auxiliary (1227–29) to the ageing bishop of Liège and performing some religious functions at Oignies.[37] Whilst there, he took the opportunity to attempt to repay the debt which he owed to Mary by influencing the commissioning of works of art for the church which she had so loved at Oignies.[38] Some of these early commissions went to Hugh, the goldsmith, whose specifically dated works fell within two periods, the first between 1228 and 1230, while James was in the Liège area for some of the time, and the second from 1238 to 1240, when, from Rome and approaching the end of his life, the cardinal

---

[32] *VMO* 2, 91.

[33] For abbot Aigulf see Geary, *Furta Sacra*, pp. 147–49; for the recluse Aigulf see 'S. Agiulfus', in *Gallia Christiana*, II, ed. by Dionysius Sammarthan (Paris: Typographia Regia, 1720), cols 21–23.

[34] *VMO-S* 3; Petrus de Vaux de Cernay, *Historia Albigensium*, in PL 213, cols 545–712, especially cols 654 and 658.

[35] P. Funk, *Jakob von Vitry: Leben und Werke*, Beiträge zur Kulturgeschichte des Mittelalters und der Renaissance, 3 (Berlin: Teubner, 1909), pp. 51–59 suggests that his first journey took place between 1222–23 and a second in 1225–26. See also Bernard Hamilton, *The Latin Church in the Crusader States: The Secular Church* (London: Ashgate, 1980), pp. 253–57; *Lettres de Jacques de Vitry*, ed. by Huygens, App., pp. 651–52.

[36] Courtoy, *Le Trésor*, p. 11. On 4 October 1226, he consecrated a chapel at the abbey of Brogne.

[37] Ursmer Berlière, 'Les évêques auxiliaires de Liège', *Revue Bénédictine*, 29 (1912), 60–81; Poncelet, 'Chartes du Prieuré d'Oignies', p. vii; Funk, *Jakob von Vitry*, pp. 54–55, 57–60; *Hist. Occ.*, p. 7, note 1.

[38] Douxchamps-Lefèvre, 'Le monde du frère Hugo', pp. 11–19.

directed a last bequest to help Oignies. This represented a significant part of the final disposition of his goods.[39]

James of Vitry's Own Contribution

In spite of all this, James of Vitry was still unable to venerate Mary as he would have wished, and as her importance as 'a precious pearl of Christ' merited.[40] This was certainly not the result of a lack of effort on his part. With the changing times came the wider spread of an enhanced spirituality emanating from elsewhere, in particular, his admiration for the friars and other religious groups.[41] However, even when he was far removed from Brabant, whether in Palestine or in Rome, and right up to the end of his life, James was never to forget the community where his career had received such impetus. In a detailed attestation of the late cardinal's will dated 16 October 1243–46, Siger, third prior of Oignies (1243–53 and 1255–58) made known the extent of these spiritual and temporal benefactions.[42] Siger described in detail how, during his lifetime, James of Vitry had whenever possible enhanced the community with his physical presence. Then, as he rose through the ecclesiastical hierarchy, from the episcopate to the cardinalate, gifts of silk cloths, relics, church ornaments, and innumerable volumes of books had exemplified his commitment.[43] For example, in March 1220, James of Vitry informed his friend, John of Nivelle, that he was sending back to Oignies all sorts of oriental silks and precious vestments captured by the

---

[39] Courtoy, *Le Trésor*, pp. 12–117.

[40] *VMO* I, 29.

[41] *Lettres de Jacques de Vitry*, ed. by Huygens, I, pp. 551–56, lines 54–149 for his encounters with the Humiliati of Lombardy and the *fratres minores et sorores* of Umbria and the Valle Spoletana.

[42] Poncelet, 'Chartes du Prieuré d'Oignies', pp. 101–03 (no. 114), dated to *c.* 1244; Agostino Paravicini Bagliani, *I Testamenti dei cardinale del duecento*, Miscellanea della Società Romana di Storia Patria, 25 (Rome: Biblioteca Vallicelliana, 1980), p. 8.

[43] In 1718, when Dom Martène visited, he greatly admired, amongst other things, a sacramentary and the works of St Bernard: Ursmer Berlière, *Correspondences littéraires du XVIII* *siècle* (Liège: [n. pub], 1913), pp. 24–26; Poncelet, 'Les Chartes du Prieuré d'Oignies', p. xxii; Xavier Hermand, 'L'évangélaire d'Oignies (Namur, Trésor des Soeurs de Notre Dame), vers 1230', in *Autour de Hugo d'Oignies*, pp. 165–79.

crusaders at Damietta.[44] The anonymous late thirteenth-century *History of the Foundation* draws heavily on Prior Siger's account and refers to James of Vitry's actual presence in the *pauper schola*.[45] All this culminated in the cardinal's determination as he lay dying in Rome that his body should be returned to Oignies for burial and that his final bequests should accompany it.[46] Siger attributed to him not only the significant privileges granted to Oignies but also a series of most generous gifts of money and possessions by which he raised the community from poverty. His deathbed gift of 1500 pounds *alborum* enabled the community to buy wine for the sick and for guests of the priory.[47] The grateful canons readily undertook to commemorate their benefactor by holding a special daily mass at his tomb. In all these gifts, it was always the intention and purpose of James of Vitry that Mary should be remembered.[48]

The visible witness of the spiritual relationship between James and Mary of Oignies still exists today in the unique relic collection entrusted, after the many vicissitudes of centuries of invasion and revolution, to the Sisters of Notre Dame at Namur.[49] James of Vitry not only collected relics, which he knew that Mary

---

[44] *Lettres de Jacques de Vitry*, ed. by Huygens, VI, p. 615, lines 128–30: 'Invenimus autem in civitate pauca valde victualia, aurum vero et argentum et pannos sericos cum vestibus preciosis et aliam multam supellectilem reperimus in civitate'; p. 623, lines 280–84: 'Missimus vobis duos parvulos de incendis Babylonis extractos, cum quibus pannis sericis et litteris aliis'. The crusaders entered Damietta on 2 February, the Feast of the Purification, and witnessed the dedication of the basilica to the Virgin Mary.

[45] Appendix to *VMO-S*: *De Jacobo a Vitriaco scriptore, ex Ms Rubeae-vallis*, 4, in AASS, 23 June, XXV, p. 582.

[46] *Hist. fund.* 7.

[47] Bagliani, *I Testamenti*, p. 8.

[48] Appendix to *VMO-S*, 4, p. 582: 'Tandem vir Dei Jacobus venerandus quamvis auctoritate apostolica ad episcopatum et cardinalatum sublimatus esset, pauperem tamen scholam, quam in Oignies, reliquerat, non est oblitus; quin potius, ejus inopiam Romanis opibus supplere curans, multa pondera auri ab urbe Roma illuc destinavit, ut fratribus et hospitibus vini copia usquequaque non deesset ad necessitatem. Quinimo etsi propter officia et ecclesiasticas dignitates, quibus invite implicabatur, absentare se haberet corporaliter ab eis, dum ad viveret; tamen ex vita praesenti migraturus, fecit corpus suum post mortem Oignies deferri, et in eadem ecclesia sepeliri'.

[49] I am most grateful to Soeur Suzanne Vandecan of the Sisters of Notre Dame, 17 rue Julie Biliard, Namur, for allowing me to see the treasure at such close quarters in April 1992. See now *Autour de Hugo d'Oignies*, the catalogue of the exhibition held at the Musée des arts anciens du Namurois between 29 May and 30 November 2003, especially Vandecan, 'L'histoire', pp. 47–57.

would have been eager to have for use in the church but also relics of Mary herself.[50] The treasure falls into three distinct categories: relics and reliquaries; liturgical artefacts; and those personal objects such as rings and mitres connected with the performance of James of Vitry's high status clerical office as bishop and as cardinal. The purpose was the same for all three categories, namely, the veneration of Mary of Oignies, the faith she displayed, and the enhancement of Oignies, the place which had become the focus of her spiritual life.

Thomas of Cantimpré (*c.* 1200–70) whose Supplement to James of Vitry's *Life of Mary of Oignies*, written *c.* 1230, was dedicated to Giles of Walcourt, founder and prior of St Nicholas, Oignies, further develops the understanding of James's purpose. Thomas had been greatly moved by James of Vitry, whose preaching he must have heard before 1216, and he remained his spiritual disciple for the rest of his life.[51] Thomas provides corroborative evidence to that in the *History of the Foundation of Oignies* of James's part in this wonderful relic collection which he began to collect first at Mary's own request and then later in her memory. One further source is of vital importance, linking even more closely Thomas to James. Thomas's *Life* of Lutgard of Tongeren (d. 1246), the Cistercian nun with whom James had corresponded and who later became Cantimpré's spiritual guide, reveals vital evidence of the thirteenth-century preoccupation with body relics.[52] Thomas corroborates the information given by his other mentor, James of Vitry, whose memory of Mary was kept alive, not merely by meditation or by prayer but also through his relic of her, the finger which must have come into his possession shortly after her death in 1213 and which can be attested from as early as 1216.[53] James venerated this precious reminder and always kept it close to him, suspended around his neck in a small silver case. This was in addition to the phylactery which Hugh had made to contain what must have been a second finger amputated later from Mary's corpse. One was for the safe keeping of the relic while the other served as an additional and constant reminder of the spiritual debt which James owed to

---

[50] Courtoy, *Le Trésor*, pp. 17–109.

[51] For Thomas of Cantimpré (*c.* 1200–*c.* 1270) see Hugh Feiss in his Introduction to *VMO-S*; Thomas de Cantimpré, *Les Exemples du livre des abeilles*, ed. and trans. by Henri Platelle (Turnhout: Brepols, 1997), pp. 11–17; as disciple of James: Appendix to *VMO-S*, pp. 581–82; Bolton, 'Faithful to Whom?', p. 60.

[52] *VLA* 3, 19; Bolton, '*Vitae Matrum*', pp. 259–60.

[53] *Lettres de Jacques de Vitry*, ed. by Huygens, I, p. 550, lines 44–45: 'in quo matris mee Marie de Oegnis digitum reposueram'; Poncelet, 'Chartes du Prieuré d'Oignies', pp. lxiv–lxv.

Mary.[54] After Lutgard's death at Aywières, Thomas had requested both her head and her hand as personal relics but, following an unseemly dispute, the abbess, Hawide, disappointed him by declaring that a single finger would have to suffice.[55]

James of Vitry was neither exceptional nor perverted in his attachment to Mary's finger.[56] There is evidence at that time of what might be considered by some to be the brutal treatment of corpses in Brabant in general and at Oignies in particular. In his desire to augment his priory's relic collection, Giles of Oignies was ready to go to considerable — some might say extreme — lengths. On one such occasion, possibly in early 1213, just before Mary's death, John of Pomerania, a member of the community, had died.[57] The prior began immediately to remove John's teeth with pliers knowing that his holiness would make the man's relics collectable. Mary, horrified, rebuked him and Giles replied that he was doing nothing to the corpse that he would not do to her after her death. She replied defiantly that she would clench her teeth to prevent his assault. Following her death, the prior and some of the brothers took her body to a secret place and tried to prise open her mouth by pushing at the forehead and pulling on her chin. When this did not work the prior tried a knife and other iron tools, but to no avail.[58] Then, it seems, he remembered her words and fell down before the corpse to pray and supplicate. Immediately, Mary's mouth opened and, of her own accord, she spat out seven teeth into the prior's hand.

Mary's tomb itself exercised a beneficial effect and for some years became the object of frequent pilgrimage.[59] She was first buried in the common cemetery at Oignies but then, on 4 October 1226, following the consecration of the new collegiate church, James of Vitry had proceeded with the exhumation and

---

[54] Courtoy, Le Trésor, p. 11; Robert Didier and Jacques Toussaint, 'Oeuvres dispersées du Trésor d'Oignies', in Autour de Hugo d'Oignies, pp. 295–96 (p. 295), for inscription and identification of the relic: HIC: EST: IVNCTVRA: BEATE: MARIE: DE: OIGNIES.

[55] VLA 3, 19.

[56] Nicole Herrmann-Mascard, Les Reliques des saints: formation coutoumière d'un droit. Société d'histoire du droit, Collection d'histoire institutionelle et sociale, 6 (Paris: Éditions Klincksieck, 1975), pp. 26–32; David Rollason, Saints and Relics in Anglo-Saxon England (Oxford: Blackwell, 1989), especially pp. 34–42.

[57] VMO-S 14.

[58] VMO-S 14.

[59] Poncelet, 'Chartes du Prieuré d'Oignies', pp. lxiv–lxv.

translation of her body.[60] Some of her relics were placed in reliquaries: a phylactery contained one of her fingers and another her jawbone, while the remainder of her corpse was placed in a stone sarcophagus.[61] Conrad, abbot of the Cistercian house of Villers and former canon of Liège, had once come to pray all night at her tomb.[62] When she appeared in a vision, she interceded with the Lord on the abbot's behalf. As he left the next day, Abbot Conrad revealed to the prior what had occurred at the tomb, thus adding to the holy status of the place.

Much of Thomas of Cantimpré's evidence illuminates still further the progress of the building campaign at Oignies and the accumulation of its treasures. One example is the account where, just before Mary's death in 1213, the rather poor and inexpensive relics and vestments at Oignies had been laid out while the prior, Brother Giles, was preparing the altar to honour the feast of a saint. Absent-mindedly he left the folded silk vestments next to the altar but placed a lighted candle before the relics. While the community was at supper a fire broke out and destroyed the vestments. Mary, looking into the church through the window adjoining the altar, saw what had happened. The prior was inconsolable but Mary comforted him by prophesying that God himself would make unparalleled restitution for the damage. Within ten years the prior would have acquired new ornaments and rejoice fourfold over them. The fulfilment of Mary's prophecy did indeed occur approximately within the specified time. James of Vitry had meanwhile caused to be sent from Acre episcopal and other vestments of fine linen together with mass vessels for the altar, all crafted in gold and silver.[63] The bearer of these rich gifts crossed the sea so fast, within fifteen

---

[60] Poncelet, 'Chartes du Prieuré d'Oignies', p. lxv; *VMO*, p. 631. Further translations occurred in 1333, 1400, and 1608.

[61] Didier and Toussaint, 'Oeuvres dispersées du Trésor d'Oignies', pp. 303–04, for the reliquary containing Mary's jawbone, which seems to have been specially made for the translation of 1608. See also Michel Lauwers, *La Mémoire des ancêtres, le souci des morts: morts, rites et société au moyen âge: Diocèse de Liège, IXᵉ–XIIIᵉ siècles* (Paris: Beauchesne, 1997), pp. 410–13.

[62] *VMO-S*.19.

[63] *Lettres de Jacques de Vitry*, ed. by Huygens, VI, p. 623: 'Misimus vobis duos parvulos de incendio Babylonis extractos cum quibusdam pannis sericis et litteris aliis'; *VMO-S* 13: 'Venerabilis Jacobus [...] transmisit dicto priori omnem infulam Episcopalem, cum aliis multis vestibus bissinis et universa altaris vasa, cum diversa utensilibus ministrorum ejus ex auro et argento omnia fabricata'.

days in fact, that his speed seemed incredible.[64] Just twenty days beyond the ten-year period that Mary had predicted (c. 1222–23), the lost vestments of Oignies had been replaced and the prior literally danced with joy at their receipt.[65]

Thomas of Cantimpré also describes the manner in which James of Vitry, whilst auxiliary of Liège, had visited Rome, perhaps in 1227, being received there by Honorius III (1216–27) and Hugolino, cardinal bishop of Ostia, later Pope Gregory IX (1227–41).[66] After the visit, James sent Hugolino a precious and beautiful gift, a silver cup containing nutmegs.[67] Hugolino returned the cup but kept the nutmegs on the grounds that the cup was the fruit of his own city of Rome, whereas the nutmegs were the fruits of the East. At the time that he rejected this gift, Hugolino revealed to James his own lack of faith and the strong temptation he often felt to succumb to blasphemy. He feared that he would be unable to bear the burden of sin and guilt and that his faith would fail completely. In response, James of Vitry told the cardinal to take the *Life of Mary of Oignies*, which he had written and which, if he were to read, would surely free him from this temptation. Hugolino received the news joyfully and further asked if he had any relics of Mary which he could borrow so that when his own veneration of her increased, he would feel all the more able to invoke her just as if she were present.[68] James in reply explained that he had a finger of Mary of Oignies, in a silver case, hanging constantly around his neck.[69] It had already kept him safe in various dangers and crises, whilst crossing rivers in flood in Lombardy and whilst at sea. The cardinal was most welcome to have it. Once he had received this relic, Hugolino read Mary's *Life* most carefully, deriving great

---

[64] *VMO-S* 13: 'Portitor autem horum omnium, tanta velocitate mare transivit, infra dies videlicet quindecim, ut multis hoc incredibile videretur'. Professor J. S. C. Riley-Smith has confirmed that the contrary winds and tides of the eastern Mediterranean would ensure that such a journey might require three times as long if the weather was unfavourable.

[65] *VMO-S* 13: 'dictus prior tripudiaverit gaudio'.

[66] Hugolino, cardinal deacon of S. Eustachio (1198–1206), cardinal bishop of Ostia (1206–27), Pope Gregory IX (1227–41). See Werner Maleczek, *Papst und Kardinalskolleg von 1191 bis 1216: die Kardinäle unter Coelestin III und Innocenz III* (Vienna: Verlag der Österreichischen Akademie der Wissenschaften, 1984), pp. 126–33.

[67] *VMO-S* 15: 'Cuppam, scilicet argenteam pondere gravidam, plenam muscatis nucibus transmisisset'.

[68] *VMO-S* 16: 'Sed quaeso, si ullae sunt tibi de hac Reliquiae, mihi eas accomoda'.

[69] *VMO-S* 16: 'Est, inquit, digitus ejus argenteo locello reconditus, assidue mihi suspensus ad collum qui me utique in diversis periculis et inter marina discrimina semper tutavit illaesum. Hunc ergo si praecipis, tecum assume.'

mental confidence, both from what he was reading and from the relic. At one stage, whilst at prayer and as his attention began to wander, he grasped the finger relic and found his mental torpor completely dispelled.[70]

Elaborating on the efficacy of this relic of Mary, Thomas of Cantimpré recounts further exploits of James of Vitry. Returning from Acre on another occasion, a great storm blew up at sea. The whole crew invoked the saints, some St Nicholas, others St Clement, whilst the remainder turned to their own particular saints. James of Vitry invoked Mary whose finger was hanging around his neck.[71] She appeared as his protector in response to his call and assured him of her ceaseless prayers for his salvation. Telling him that he would not lose his life at sea, she led him, in a vision, into the church at Oignies. From a high vantage point, she showed him five altars located throughout the church. She instructed him to consecrate four of these altars in honour of the saints designated by the prior, but the fifth, on her instruction, was to be consecrated in honour of the holy and undivided Trinity. That altar would give him the peace of Christ and enable him to find that which he was seeking. As she disappeared, the sea became quiet. When James reached Rome, he requested Honorius III to relieve him of his episcopal duties so that he could return to Oignies.[72] On completion of the new church, it did indeed contain the promised five altars and James was invited by Prior Giles to perform their consecration in January 1228 or 1229.[73] With some trepidation, James asked to know to whom the central altar was to be dedicated. His fears were removed when the prior replied that it would be to the holy and undivided Trinity and, in this way, Mary's vision was happily fulfilled.

The Treasure of Oignies Now

Many of these interesting accounts with accompanying local details were neglected over the years and it was not until 1628 at Douai that Arnold de Raisse compiled the first inventory of the Treasure of Oignies, twenty years after the

---

[70] *VMO-S* 17: 'Qui [...] digitum Ancillae Christi piis in manibus apprehendit.'

[71] *VMO-S* 20: 'Acconensis Episcopus, Reliquarum Ancillae Christi Mariae de Oignies quas ad collum semper suspensas habebat sedule recordatus.'

[72] 6 March 1224, *Lettres de Jacques de Vitry*, ed. by Huygens, pp. 651–52; Pietro Pressutti, *Regesta Honorii papae III*, 2 vols (Rome: Loescher, 1888-95), I, no. 4839.

[73] *VMO-S* 21; Poncelet, 'Chartes du Prieuré d'Oignies', p. ix.

translation of Mary's remains.[74] This inventory provides the basis against which to indicate what has survived to the present day.[75] Associative relics of Mary of Oignies included her woollen clothing, said to bring special relief in childbirth, her knife, and the walking stick she used to support herself.[76] Relics said to belong to James of Vitry were the flail with which he punished himself, two double mitres, one in parchment, the other in silk;[77] two rings of office, a missal, an ebony foot reliquary, a portable altar which opens and contains relics of the wood of the cross, the holy lance, and assorted relics of SS Peter, Andrew, Bartholomew, the martyrs Laurence and Vincent, Nicholas, Joseph of Arimathea, St Bernard, and St Cecilia. In addition, there were two exceptional pieces specific to Oignies itself: a silver-gilt chalice and paten and a Gospel lectionary, both said to have been made for the founder and first prior of Oignies, Giles of Walcourt (d. 1234) by his natural brother, Hugh the Goldsmith.

James of Vitry's contribution to the collection of relics to demonstrate the value of Mary's spirituality was both massive and unique, while the survival of the treasures provides an insight into both their lives of faith. From Acre and Rome, the gifts heaped by James on his companions at Oignies played the foremost role in forming the genesis of the treasures. His position in Acre enabled him to be the great provider to the monastery of relics from the East. He either sent or had them carried in Arab or Fatimid glasses,[78] mounted later as reliquaries, and in the little Siculo-Arabic ivory boxes still amongst the treasures of Oignies.[79] He even managed to find a substantial piece of the true cross, much coveted in Brabant, where the abbeys of Brogne and Floreffe already possessed

---

[74] 'Historia translationis in novam arcam factae anno 1608', in AASS, 23 June, XXV, 583–88.

[75] Arnoldus Rayssius, *Hierogazophylacium Belgicum sive Thesaurus sacrarum reliquarum Belgii* (Douai: Pinchon, 1628), pp. 386–87; Courtoy, *Le Trésor*, p. 136; 'Inventaire de 1628', in *Autour de Hugo d'Oignies*, Annexes, pp. 401–02.

[76] *Commentarius Praevius II. 9–12: 'De B. Mariae imaginibus, reliquiis et professione'*, in AASS, 23 June, XXV, 545–46.

[77] Appendix to *VMO-S* 5, p. 582; J. Greven, 'Die Mitra des Jakob von Vitry und ihre Herkunft', *Zeitschrift für Christliche Kunst*, 20 (1907), cols 217–22; Courtoy, *Le Trésor*, pp. 100–05; *Autour de Hugo d'Oignies*, pp. 272–77.

[78] Courtoy, *Le Trésor*, pp. 64–67.

[79] R. H. Pinder-Wilson and C. N. L. Brooke, 'The Reliquary of St Petroc and the Ivories of Norman Sicily', *Archaelogia*, 104 (1973), 261–305; *Autour de Hugo d'Oignies*, pp. 258–59.

other fragments.[80] With all these relics, the modest priory of Oignies soon became as favoured as those nearby abbeys and the collegiate churches of Namur and Walcourt.

The dedication of the monastery church, the consecration of its five new altars, and the three exquisite small works by Hugh the Goldsmith, all raised further the standing of this holy place. Hugh's works were the double-sided cover of an Evangelistary or Gospel book, a chalice and paten, and a jewelled reliquary containing St Peter's rib and embellished with an ancient intaglio.[81] These magnificent pieces are all signed and can be securely dated to between 1228 and 1230. The Evangelistary depicts Christ in Majesty and is decorated with six niello plates with representations of angels, dragons, St Nicholas, and Hugh himself.[82] Hugh himself signed the chalice which is said to have been made for Giles of Walcourt.[83] The niello decoration of the paten represents the holy Trinity. God the Father is seated upon an altar-like throne decorated with foliated capitals while God the Son hangs from the cross. The dove of the Holy Spirit with a halo passes between them, its wings just touching the mouths of both.[84]

Mary's influence and interest were clearly at work. The reliquary obtained in her memory by James of Vitry shows evidence of this. St Peter had appeared to her in a vision and the reliquary of his rib, dated to 1228, has niello decorations of a seated bishop blessing, together with Saints Nicholas, Augustine, and Lambert, patron of the diocese of Liège. Once more, an incised inscription identifies the work as emanating from the hand of Hugh, supported by an authentication on parchment.[85] James of Vitry must have been pleased with the result of his commissions for the dedication ceremony of the priory, and so

[80] Courtoy, *Le Trésor*, p. 11, note 3.

[81] Laurent Wilmet, 'Les intailles et le camée des orfèvreries du Trésor d'Oignies', in *Autour de Hugo d'Oignies*, pp. 153–63 (p. 160), pp. 204–10.

[82] Courtoy, *Le Trésor*, p. 18; *Autour de Hugo d'Oignies*, p. 193.

[83] Courtoy, *Le Trésor*, pp. 17–24 (p. 20); *Autour de Hugo d'Oignies*, pp. 193–98 (p. 195): + LIBER SCRIPTVS INTVS EST FORIS HVGO SCRIPSIT: INTVS: QVESTV FORIS MANV + ORATE PRO EO. + ORE CANVNT ALII CHRISTVM CANIT ARTE FABRILE HVGO SVI QVESTV SCRIPTA LABORIS ARANS.

[84] Courtoy, *Le Trésor*, p. 28, fig. 10; Skubiszewski, 'L'iconographie de la patène'.

[85] Courtoy, *Le Trésor*, pp. 29–36; *Autour de Hugo d'Oignies*, pp. 204–10. A small strip of parchment in a thirteenth-century cursive hand reads RELIQ(UI)E ISTE FUERU(N)T HIC RECO(N)DITE ANNO DOMINI MCCXXOCT(AVO).

would Mary have been. She would certainly have received these new relics with joy!

Other relics build up the quality of the treasure. A double reliquary cross or *staurotheca*,[86] a little reliquary containing oil from the tomb of St Nicholas at Bari, including some of the Blood of Christ which seems to have been a late substitution, indicates Mary's special relationship with St Nicholas, who appeared to her at Oignies as she saw oil exuding from his bones.[87] The magnificent phylactery of one of Mary's fingers has companions housing relics of SS Margaret, Hubert, Andrew, and Martin,[88] whilst a Fatimid vase-reliquary is likely to be the one brought back from the East by James of Vitry, possibly being carried by him in an ivory casket.[89] A reliquary in the shape of a dove contained what purported to be the Virgin's milk.[90] This may have been galacite, a type of white chalk from the Cave of Milk near Bethlehem where the Holy Family were reputed to have taken refuge.

The relics associated with Mary herself are of interest. The treasure contains her so-called goblet in beechwood and bird's eye maple, in a little cover with alternate spiral bands of niello and gold, its top decorated with griffons.[91] This was not attributed to Mary until an inventory of the treasure in 1648 and may perhaps have been a *pocula* of the sort used by noble knights as travelling cups,[92] while her walking stick, knife, and belt were also all attested.[93]

Items in the possession of James of Vitry are even more indicative of high quality. His ivory crozier volute with painted decoration has been used as

---

[86] Courtoy, *Le Trésor*, pp. 38–45; *Autour de Hugo d'Oignies*, pp. 211–16.

[87] *VMO* 2, 94; Courtoy, *Le Trésor*, pp. 45–47; *Autour de Hugo d'Oignies*, pp. 217–19; Jones, *Saint Nicholas*.

[88] Courtoy, *Le Trésor*, pp. 47–60; *Autour de Hugo d'Oignies*, pp. 220–35. The phylactery of Mary herself is in the Musée Royaux d'art et d'histoire de Bruxelles. See *Autour de Hugo d'Oignies*, pp. 295–96.

[89] Courtoy, *Le Trésor*, pp. 64–67; Ferdinand Courtoy, 'Deux verres arables du trésor d'Oignies à Namur', *Annales de la Société archéologique de Namur*, 36 (1925), 145–57 (p. 153); *Autour de Hugo d'Oignies*, pp. 238–41.

[90] Courtoy, *Le Trésor*, pp. 66–70; *Autour de Hugo d'Oignies*, pp. 222–24.

[91] Courtoy, *Le Trésor*, pp. 61–63; *Autour de Hugo d'Oignies*, pp. 236–37. For the legend of the little cup from which she ate and drank, see *VMO* 2, 45.

[92] Courtoy, *Le Trésor*, p. 63; *Autour de Hugo d'Oignies*, App., pp. 403–04, '26: Item, 'un petit reliquaire de cuivre en forme de poire'.

[93] See note 76.

evidence for dating other relics.[94] He may well have also owned the Byzantine double *staurotheca* with its preparation for the throne of judgement.[95] He certainly used the portable altar of grey-green marble, decorated with enamel champlevé work showing Christ between the Virgin and St John.[96] The relics contained within were of the holy lance and Christ's own fetters, SS Peter, Andrew, and Bartholomew, the wood of the cross, SS Matthew, Laurence, Vincent, Nicholas, Joseph of Arimathea, SS Bernard, and Cecilia. The thirteenth-century triptych shows SS Peter, Paul, Barbara, and Ursula flanking an unnamed saint. It contained relics of the bread from the Last Supper, oil from St Nicholas's tomb, the hair of SS John and Paul, St Agnes, John the Baptist, the clothes of the Virgin, and assorted relics of the eleven-thousand virgins, SS Saturnino, Giles, Pancras, and Cornelius.[97] The mid-thirteenth century foot reliquary of St James Major may also have belonged to James of Vitry, and, if so, it raises an interesting light on the two-way exchange of relics.[98] A charter, dated to *c.* 1224, records that the relics of Mary Salome, the mother of the apostles James and John, which had been discovered at Veroli, south of Rome, in 1209, were sent to James of Vitry in Acre.[99] Several bishops and abbots local to the region had sworn on oath to the authenticity of these relics in a number of complicated procedures, including written attestations. Approved by no less a figure than Innocent III himself, the relics of Veroli generated both a significant local cult and a treasure, today held in the crypt of the cathedral of S. Erasmo, which numbers more than six hundred items.[100]

[94] Pinder-Wilson and Brooke, 'The Reliquary of St Petroc', pp. 284–86; *Autour de Hugo d'Oignies*, pp. 278–79.

[95] Courtoy, *Le Trésor*, pp. 85–95; *Autour de Hugo d'Oignies*, pp. 260–66.

[96] Courtoy, *Le Trésor*, pp. 96–97; *Autour de Hugo d'Oignies*, pp. 267–69.

[97] Courtoy, *Le Trésor*, pp. 98–99; *Autour de Hugo d'Oignies*, pp. 267–69.

[98] Courtoy, *Le Trésor*, pp. 70–72; *Autour de Hugo d'Oignies*, pp. 245–46.

[99] Poncelet, 'Chartes du Prieuré d'Oignies', no. 47 (*c.* 1224), p. 43: 'Litera erga reliquias beate Marie matris apostolorum Joannis et Jacobi, missa ad episcopum Acconensem'. The text is missing.

[100] Federico Farina and Ignio Vona, *L'abate Giraldo di Casamari*, Bibliotheca Casaemariensis, 3 (Casamari: Edizioni Casamari, 1998); Brenda M. Bolton, 'Gerald of Casamari between Joachim of Fiore and Innocent III', *Florensia* 13/14 (1999–2000), 31–43 (pp. 37–38); Brenda M. Bolton, 'Signs, Wonders, Miracles: Supporting the Faith in Medieval Rome', in *Signs, Wonders, Miracles: Representations of Divine Power in the Life of the Church*, ed. by Kate Cooper and Jeremy Gregory, Studies in Church History, 41 (Woodbridge: Boydell and Brewer, 2005), pp. 157–78.

The most evocative relics of the person of James of Vitry are two mitres, one in parchment and one in embroidery.[101] That in parchment is undoubtedly unique. On the horizontal orphrey around the base are twelve Romanesque arcades. The apostles, wearing haloes, are sitting on stone seats, legs crossed, feet bare, blue clothing or the reverse. The only identifiable figure is St Paul carrying his sword. On the *titulus* or vertical orphrey are three medallions. In the first, Christ is seated, blessing and holding a red disc, symbol of the bread of life. There is a half-bust of the Virgin *orante* and a bishop with a mitre, holding a cross. The reverse side has a dragon and Samson fighting a lion. Five unidentified figures decorate the *fanon* or ribbon pendant. The provenance of this mitre has been suggested as northern French.[102] However, a clear parallel would seem to occur in the so-called Lunette of Mentorella,[103] part of the decoration for the door which Innocent III (1198–1216) had made to protect the greatest relic chamber, the *confessio* or tomb of St Peter himself.[104] The cardinal bishop of Tusculum would have been one of the few with privileged access to this doorway. James of Vitry's second mitre is embroidered in silk *examitum* and depicts two scenes of martyrdom: those of Becket and Laurence.[105] The embroidered maniple of English origin shows SS Bartholomew, John, Paul with his sword, Denis the Martyr, Andrew, James, and Peter with the keys, together with Becket.[106] The mitres may well have formed part of the gift of liturgical vestments attested by Prior Siger in *c.* 1244. Four rings, part of the insignia of episcopal office, complete this quite exceptional collection.[107]

[101] Courtoy, *Le Trésor*, pp. 100–02; *Autour de Hugo d'Oignies*, pp. 272–77.

[102] J. Braun, 'Die Paramente im Schatz der Schwestern U. L. Frau zu Namur', *Zeitschrift für Christliche Kunst*, 19 (1906), cols 289–304.

[103] Attested from the seventeenth century at the Convent of S. Maria in Vulturella, at Mentorella (Tivoli) and conserved today in the Museo di Palazzo Venezia in Rome.

[104] M. M. Gautier, 'La clôture emaillée de la confession de Saint Pierre au Vatican hors du Concile de Latran, 1215', in *Synthronon: Art et Archéologie de la Fin de l'Antiquité*, Recueil d'études offertes à M. André Grabar, Bibliothèque des Cahiers Archéologiques, II (Paris: Éditions Klincksieck, 1968), pp. 237–46; Brenda M. Bolton, 'Signposts from the Past: Reflections on Innocent III's Providential Path', in *Innocenzo III: Urbs et Orbis*, ed. by Andrea Sommerlechner, Atti del Congresso Internazionale, Roma, 9–15 settembre 1998, 2 vols (Rome: Biblioteca Vallicelliana, 2003), I, 21–55 (pp. 25–28).

[105] Courtoy, *Le Trésor*, pp. 104–07; *Autour de Hugo d'Oignies*, pp. 274–77.

[106] Courtoy, *Le Trésor*, p. 106; *Autour de Hugo d'Oignies*, pp. 277–78.

[107] Courtoy, *Le Trésor*, pp. 108–09; *Autour de Hugo d'Oignies*, p. 280.

No Cult, No Canonization

As the fame of Oignies spread and its relic collection grew, the question arises as to why the cult of Mary of Oignies should have failed to materialize in accordance with earlier expectations? How was it that she came to be remembered as only a relatively transient model for the beguines? Mary's death in 1213 had dramatically deprived her followers of a figurehead, but negotiations behind the scenes before the Fourth Lateran Council in November 1215 might well have ended in some arrangements similar to the approval given to Clare of Assisi and the community of San Damiano.[108] Indeed, that such attempts were made is clear. John of Liroux's journey to Rome in 1215 to defend the religious women of Brabant against those who were harassing them had ended with his unfortunate death in the Alps.[109] Similarly, in July 1216, James of Vitry, arriving at Perugia to appeal on their behalf in person to Innocent III, found only the pope's despoiled corpse, and succeeded in gaining nothing more substantial from the newly elected pope, Honorius III, than permission for the women of the diocese of Liège to remain together in their houses, urging one another to lead religious lives by mutual exhortation.[110] However, the female community did not flourish as it might reasonably have been expected to. While benefactions continued, typical of that small bequest made on 24 July 1239 by Robert, a priest of Walcourt, to the 'beguinis Walcuria [...] illis de Nivella [...] beguinis de Ognies',[111] the attitude of the local hierarchy grew harsher towards the women. Claiming evidence of indiscipline caused by them, the customs of the priory, confirmed on 6 May 1243 by Robert of Thourote, bishop of Liège, prohibited any canon from hearing the confessions of the beguines, even in the case of urgent necessity, unless specifically permitted to do so by the prior. The fact was that the female followers of Mary of Oignies passed on their simple dwellings and personal possessions from one to the other, and it was this which enabled

---

[108] Pellegrini, 'Female Religious Experience', pp. 98–101.

[109] *VLA* 2, 8; Simons, *Cities of Ladies*, pp. 173–74, notes 36–37.

[110] *Lettres de Jacques de Vitry*, ed. by Huygens, p. 552, lines 85–89: 'Obtinui praeterea ab ipso, et litteras mulieribus religiosis non solum in episcopatu Leodensi, sed tam in regno quam in imperio in eadem domo simul manere et sese invicem mutuis exhortationibus ad bonum invitare'.

[111] C. Roland, 'Les seigneurs et comtes de Rochefort', *Annales de la Société archéologique de Namur*, 20 (1893), 63–144, 329–411 (p. 354, note 2); Poncelet, 'Chartes du Prieuré d'Oignies', p. lxi.

the community to survive for as long as it did. By 1250, the women had been forced to leave their original site close to the River Sambre, and by the early fourteenth century, their community had ceased to exist.

The most important determining factor may have been the attitude of the popes. Both Honorius III and Cardinal Hugolino, later Gregory IX, showered the male community of canons at Oignies with privileges, typical of those granted in 1227 and 1239.[112] Indulgences followed, not only from Gregory but also from Innocent IV, further enhancing the prestige and material condition of the priory, while clerics and laity alike made generous testamentary gifts.[113] However, while the original modest male *cenobium* had been transformed over time by such benefactions,[114] the situation of Mary's female followers, in buildings situated apart from the canons' dwellings and close by the River Sambre, was much less happy. In line with papal thinking, requiring religious dynamism to be directed into deliberately planned and organized channels, rigid claustration was imposed on female religious communities in widely differing areas.[115] St Clare, for example, had no fewer than six rules imposed on her own and her sister communities in Umbria and the Valle Spoletana between 1219 and 1263, but not until the religious revival of the seventeenth century did Mary finally receive something of the recognition merited by the quality of her spiritual life.

By the early thirteenth century, not only had *Audivimus*, the letter by which Alexander III (1159–81) claimed the exclusive right of the pope to canonize, begun to enter canon law collections, but Innocent III had also established clear guidelines, thus bringing canonization under papal control for the first time.[116] Even in the period 1228–35, when Francis (1228) and Dominic (1234) were

[112] Poncelet, 'Chartes du Prieuré d'Oignies', no. 56 (4 August, 1227), pp. 49–52; no. 99 (15 January, 1239), no. 75 (19 April, 1234), pp. 69–70; McDonnell, *Beguines and Beghards*, pp. 11–15.

[113] Poncelet, 'Chartes du Prieuré d'Oignies', no. 75 (19 April, 1234), pp. 69–70; no. 100 (18 March, 1239), pp. 87–88; no. 112 (25 June, 1243–24 June, 1244), pp. 100–01; no. 113 (25 June, 1243–24 June, 1244), p. 101.

[114] Poncelet, 'Chartes du Prieuré d'Oignies', p. xv, lists among the privileges, one from Innocent III (1207), three from Honorius III (1219 and 1223–25), eight from Gregory IX (1227–39), and five from Innocent IV (1244–49), although not all the texts have survived.

[115] Pellegrini, 'Female Religious Experience', p. 113.

[116] Michael Goodich, 'Vision, Dream and Canonization Policy under Pope Innocent III', in *Pope Innocent III and His World*, ed. by John C. Moore (Aldershot: Ashgate, 1999), pp. 151-63 (p. 151).

canonized, Elizabeth of Thuringia (d. 1231) was the sole woman to be named in the catalogue of the saints and, as Goodich has argued, the success of her canonization trial (1234) was substantially enhanced by personal testimonies.[117] James of Vitry's absence, first in the Holy Land and then in Rome, may well have contributed towards the loss of impetus in the creation of a significant cult of Mary. Perhaps the high status that he was to attain and the far distant places to which his duties took him obscured the significance of Mary and Oignies, although these were never far removed from his own thoughts and veneration. His outstanding contributions to the relic collection demonstrated this but back in Brabant, it was otherwise. Thomas of Cantimpré, this most fervent of James of Vitry's disciples took it upon himself to write letters of reproach to one who had been the leading light in the veneration of Mary of Oignies.[118] James not only replied politely and penitently but also ensured that he increased his relic giving and made ample provision for Oignies in his will.[119] After reaching its height in the first three decades of the thirteenth century, the influence of both Mary and Oignies over James of Vitry began to wane as the cardinal remained occupied and far away from Brabant. His death in Rome in 1240 marked a further turning point in the fortunes of the priory. In fulfilment of his final wish, his body was returned for burial in the conventual church at Oignies, *ibique honorifice eius ossa recondita sunt.*[120] Henceforth, those in high places and other locations were to find other examples of faith and dedication. But in Oignies and its environs, the relic collection was to remain as a memorial to the life and work of Mary, its guardian — an example to her followers, the beguines — and supreme tokens of the shared faith between the 'new' saint of the diocese of Liège and the cardinal bishop of Tusculum.

---

[117] Michael Goodich, '"Mirabilis Deus in sanctis suis": Social History and Medieval Miracles', in *Signs, Wonders, Miracles: Representations of Divine Power in the Life of the Church*, ed. by Kate Cooper and Jeremy Gregory, Studies in Church History, 41 (Woodbridge: Boydell and Brewer, 2005), pp. 135–56 (pp. 138–40).

[118] *VMO-S* 24–27.

[119] Bagliani, *I Testamenti*, p. 8; Poncelet, 'Chartes du Prieuré d'Oignies', no. 114 (*c.* 1244), pp. 101–03.

[120] Appendix to *VMO-S* 5.

THE MANUSCRIPT TRANSMISSION OF THE *VITA MARIAE OIGNIACENSIS* IN THE LATER MIDDLE AGES

Suzan Folkerts

The *Life of Mary of Oignies* is now well known amongst scholars. It usually serves as a source for the history of Mary of Oignies, but here the subject is the manuscript transmission of the *Life*. Mary is considered a prototype of the saints of the new spirituality of the later Middle Ages. Her *Life* is studied as the classic exemplary source for the history of the *mulieres religiosae* of the thirteenth-century southern Low Countries. Attention has been given, not only to the role Mary and her *Life* played in the development of the beguine movement, but also to their importance to the adversaries of the Cathars. James of Vitry wrote the *Life* as a testimony to a new and alternative, although orthodox, way of life for women. He wrote it both for the sake of the pious women whom he defended against attacks from within the church, and for the use of Fulk of Toulouse, who fought the Cathars in southern France. André Vauchez, in one of the first studies written on Mary of Oignies, has discussed the intentions of the *Life* with regard to the struggle against Catharism. He concluded that, since no versions of the *Life* exist in Occitan, the *Life* cannot have been very successful.[1] He also argued that the religious model given in the *Life* was probably only able to be appreciated in the fifteenth century, because it was of a too-mystical nature for the contemporary public. Although he was right in that no witnesses (vernacular or Latin) of the *Life* have survived from southern France, copies of the Latin *Life* were already in circulation in other regions in the thirteenth century.

[1] Vauchez, 'Prosélytisme', pp. 104–05.

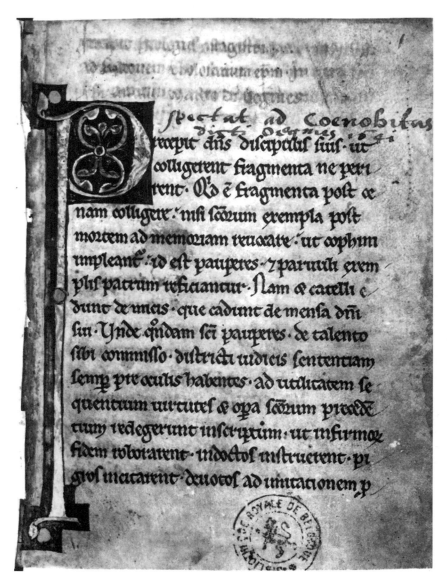

'Beginning of the *Vita Mariae Oigniacensis* with illuminated initial', Brussels, KBR, II 700, fol. 1ʳ, from the convent of Canons Regular of Oignies (thirteenth century). This manuscript was possibly used by the Bollandists for their edition of the *Life* (see note 4). Reproduced with permission of the Bibliothèque royale de Belgique, Brussels.

A few years after Vauchez, Michel Lauwers published two illuminating studies on the hagiography of Mary of Oignies and other beguines. He argued that the *Life* of Mary enjoyed a certain popularity, listing the relevant manuscripts in his footnotes.[2] Although this was not the main topic of his research, he was the first scholar to investigate the manuscript transmission of the *Life*. In all further studies on the *Life* of Mary, however, reference to the manuscript witnesses has been confined to footnotes.[3] These lists of manuscripts have been incomplete and often contained errors. The examination of the public of the *Life* has been restricted to its intended audience. Work on the reception of the *Life* in later centuries has hitherto been lacking (although some research has been carried out into the vernacular versions of the *Life*). The purposes of this chapter, then, are to plot a course for further investigation into the *Nachleben* of the *Life of Mary*, and to provide a list of manuscripts (Latin and vernacular versions), which is as complete as possible, on which the interested researcher can build.

The reasons for directing attention towards the transmission of the *Life*, rather than to the *Life* in its own time, are twofold. The first is that 'the' *Life of Mary of Oignies* does not exist. When we quote the *Life*, we refer to the edition in the *Acta sanctorum*, which was based on three manuscripts, one owned by the Bollandists (now Brussels, Bollandistes, 398), another from Rooklooster (now Vienna, ÖNB, Ser. N. 12707), and a third, belonging to Aubertus Miraeus (signature unknown). The text was collated with a manuscript from the convent of Oignies and some other manuscripts.[4] Because the edition drew from several manuscripts, the text given by the Bollandists does not appear in any manuscript in exactly the same form. All manuscripts give slightly different versions of the text. These differences and variations may be minimal and in most cases not significant, but we should be aware of the relativity of an edition. Let me give one example. The *Acta sanctorum* edition of *VMO* Prologue, 3 has:

---

[2] Lauwers, 'Expérience béguinale', p. 83, notes 99 and 100; idem, 'Entre Béguinisme et Mysticisme', pp. 46–47, note 3.

[3] For example: Geyer, *Maria von Oignies*, p. 45, note 97; Calzà, *Dem Weiblichen*, pp. 48–49, note 121.

[4] Papebroeck in his 'Commentarius praevius' to the edition of *VMO*, p. 546. At first sight, the manuscript from the convent of Oignies could be Brussels, KBR, II 700. This is doubtful, however, because Papebroeck also made use of an Appendix from the same manuscript from Oignies for his edition of the Supplement. MS II 700 does not contain an Appendix (any more?).

> Vidisti enim (et gavisus es) in hortis liliorum Domini multas sanctarum Virginum in diversis locis catervas, quae spretis pro Christo carnalibus illecebris, contemptis etiam amore regni coelestis hujus mundi divitiis, [...]

> You saw many holy virgins in the lily gardens of the Lord and you rejoiced. You saw crowds of them in different places where they scorned carnal enticements for Christ, despised the riches of this world for the love of the heavenly kingdom, [...] (trans. by Margot King)

whereas manuscript Leuven, Maurits Sabbebibliotheek, Collectie Mechelen, 20, fol. 73^v has (abbreviations are resolved; differences in bold):

> Vidisti en*im* et ga*uis*u*s* es in **o**rtis lylior*um* **d**o*m*ini. m*u*ltas s*a*nctarum **u**irginum in diu*e*rsis locis cate*ru*as. q*ue* spretis *pro* **chr**i*s*to [chr was written as 'xp'; deriving from the Greek χρ] carnalib*us* illecebris. co*n*temptis etia*m* **pro** amo*re* regni c*e*lestis hu*ius* mundi diu*i*tijs. [...]

and manuscript Liège, Bu, 135 C, fol. 171^v has:

> Vidisti e*nim* **et gauisus es** [was added in the margin later] i*n* **o**rtis lilior*um* **d**o*m*ini m*u*ltas **sacrarum** v*i*rginu*m* i*n* diversis locis cate*ru*as: [symbol for pause] q*ue* spretis *pro* **chr**i*s*to [written as 'xp'] carnalib*us* illecebris co*n*temptis**que** amore regni c*e*lestis hu*ius* m*u*ndi diu*i*ciis. [...]

Apart from the different spelling (h could be left out, j for i, y for i, u for v, e for ae, and xp for chr in 'christus'), small differences on the word level are traced: 'sacrarum' instead of 'sanctarum', 'contemptisque' instead of 'contemptis etiam', and the addition of 'pro' before 'amore'. To be sure, these differences are not crucial. What is shown here, is that the reader of the *Acta sanctorum* edition gets a somewhat distorted impression of what the medieval *Life* looked like. More importantly, several manuscripts exist that hold compilations or adaptations of the *Life of Mary of Oignies*. For example: manuscript Trier, SB, 1168/470 8° contains a shortened version of the *Life* in which, according to the copyist, 'nothing of the necessary things seems to have been left out'.[5] This text does not correspond to the *Acta sanctorum* edition at all and needs to be studied as such. All in all, lots of authentic texts (originating from the Middle Ages) are found in manuscripts, each in its own individual appearance. In the words of Sylvia Huot: 'each version has its own integrity as a literary text'.[6] Of course we need editions

---

[5] MS Trier, SB, 1168/470 8°, fol. 204^r: 'Incipiu*n*t excerpta ex vita s*a*nct*e* m*a*rie de oegnies ~~brabancie~~ [scored out] In q*ui*b*us* t*ame*n ni*h*il de necessar*ijs* vi*detur* omissum.'

[6] Sylvia Huot, *The Romance of the Rose and its Medieval Readers: Interpretation, Reception, Manuscript Transmission*, Cambridge Studies in Medieval Literature, 16 (Cambridge:

to refer to, but in the meantime we should not forget the real existing material witnesses that have come directly to us via the work of copyists.

The second reason for paying attention to the manuscript transmission of the *Life* has to do with questions on the level of context. The reception context(s) of a text constitute(s) an important aspect of a text and affect(s) its meaning. The author and their intended public form only a small and comparatively 'frozen' part of the history of a text. The later reception history comprises several other histories, that, too, need to be unfolded. Questions that need answers concern the impact of the *Life of Mary of Oignies* on later medieval readers and copyists, who adopted and adapted the *Life*. How was the *Life* understood and used in the fourteenth or fifteenth century, when it was read in a different context, for example compiled in a manuscript with other texts that may have influenced the reading of Mary's own life story? How was it read in a period in which crusades against the Cathars were no longer an issue, and in which the beguine movement had a different character than in the thirteenth century? An example of this kind of research is given in the third paragraph of this chapter.

In this chapter a rough sketch is given of the transmission and the impact of the *Life of Mary*. Firstly, room is made for figures about the spread of the *Life* throughout medieval Europe and the monastic world. The Supplement written by Thomas of Cantimpré, the adaptations of the *Life* in collections of examples, and the vernacular versions can only be treated very briefly. Secondly, a case study on the reception of the *Life* in the context of fifteenth-century Brabant will serve as an example of what an examination of the afterlife of the *Life* can yield. Thirdly, lists of extant manuscripts are presented.

The Diffusion of the Life of Mary of Oignies

Thus far, I have collected from catalogues and footnotes in other literature thirty-nine manuscripts that contain either the complete *Life*, or fragments or shortened adaptations of the *Life*. The *Life of Mary of Oignies* was more successful than any other *Life* of a *mulier religiosa* of the southern Low Countries. For example: the *Life of Elisabeth of Spalbeek* is known in eleven medieval manuscripts, the *Life of Margaret of Ypres* in three, and the *Life of Juliana of Mont-Cornillon* in five.[7] In contrast, thirty-three copies of Mary's *Life* belonged

Cambridge University Press, 1993), p. 4.

[7] MSS with (fragments of) the *Life of Elisabeth of Spalbeek*: Brussels, KBR, 2864–71;

to or were copied in monasteries in northern France, the southern and northern Low Countries, the German Rhine area and central Germany, and England (Table 1). The origin of six other manuscripts is as yet unknown. The *Life* was thus spread in a wide area around Oignies and even crossed the North Sea. As for the vernacular versions, copies originate not only from France, the Low Countries, and England, but also from Scandinavia and Italy (see the last list in this chapter). The Latin *Life* probably circulated there as well.

Table 1: Diffusion of Manuscripts of VMO — Regions (the numbers between parentheses refer to the numbers in the alphabetical list at the end of this chapter)

Northern France: 11 mss	Mons Dei (7); Belval (8); Cîteaux (10); Laon (12); Laon (13); Vauclair (14); Loos (19); Bonport (26); Bourgfontaine (27); Clairvaux (34); Clairvaux (35)
Northern Low Countries: 4	Eastern Netherlands (2); Utrecht (3); Venlo, Hoorn (4); IJsselstein (11)
Southern Low Countries: 11	Oignies (6); Huy (15); Huy (16); Sint-Truiden (17); Bois-Seigneur-Isaac (21); Jardinet (22); Cambron (28); Clairmarais (32); Rooklooster (37); Rooklooster (38); Rooklooster (39)
Germany: 4	Himmerod (1); Echternach (29); Erfurt (30); Beatenberg (33)
England: 3	England (20); Bury (23); England (24)
Unknown: 6	[Brussels] (5); [Coimbra] (9); [Lille] (18); [Paris] (25); [Porto] (31); [Vienna] (36)

Cambridge, Corpus Christi College, 138; Cambridge, Jesus College, 24; Durham, Dean and Chapter Library, B.IV.39; The Hague, KB, 70 H 49; Liège, Bu, 135C; olim Münster, UB, 348 (lost during the Second World War); Oxford, BL, Bodley 240; Oxford, BL, Bodley 694; Oxford, St John's College, 182; Vienna, ÖNB, Ser. N. 12708. MSS with the *Life of Margaret of Ypres*: Brussels, KBR, 3391–99; Brussels, KBR, 4459–70; Brussels, KBR, 8751–60. MSS with (fragments of) the *Life of Juliana of Mont-Cornillon*: Brussels, KBR, 9159–61 (Volume II); Brussels, KBR, II 2759; Cologne, HA, W 172; Paris, Bibliothèque de l'Arsenal, 945; Vienna, ÖNB, Ser. N. 12707.

If we look at the periods from which the manuscripts originate, we see that nineteen manuscripts date from the thirteenth and fourteenth centuries, and seventeen manuscripts date from the fifteenth century (Table 2). We can conclude from this that the *Life* was already well known in the thirteenth century and its popularity continued into the fifteenth century.

Table 2: Diffusion of Manuscripts of VMO — Periods

1215–1300: 12–14 mss	Himmerod (1); Oignies (6); Cîteaux (10); Laon (12); Laon (13); Vauclair (14); Sint-Truiden (17); England (20)?; [Paris] (25); Bonport (26); Cambron (28); Clairmarais (32)?; Clairvaux (35); [Vienna] (36)
1300–1400: 5–7	Mons Dei (7); Belval (8); Loos (19); England (20)?; Bury (23); Erfurt (30); Clairmarais (32)?
1400–1525: 17–18	Eastern Netherlands (2); Utrecht (3); Venlo, Hoorn (4); [Brussels] (5); IJsselstein (11); Huy (15); Huy (16); [Lille]? (18); Bois-Seigneur-Isaac (21); Jardinet (22); England (24); Bourgfontaine (27); Echternach (29); Beatenberg (33); Clairvaux (34); Rooklooster (37); Rooklooster (38); Rooklooster (39)
Unknown: 2–3	[Coimbra] (9); [Lille]? (18); [Porto] (31)

Almost all manuscripts were written in or belonged to monasteries of male monks. One manuscript originated from a house of Brothers of the Common Life (Modern Devout), which was not an enclosed monastery.[8] The origin of eight other manuscripts is unknown. The number of manuscripts from Cistercian monasteries (eleven) is remarkably high, especially in the thirteenth

---

[8] MS Brussels, KBR, 7917 (fifteenth century).

century. The popularity of the *Life of Mary* can be explained by the concern for religious women of Cistercian monasteries like Villers in the thirteenth century, although that concern was decreasing in the second half of the century. Also, the spirituality of Mary's *Life* was connected to Cistercian Christ-centred spirituality and therefore attractive to Cistercian readers. In such a context, anecdotes that tell of Mary's love for the Cistercian way of life are significant. As a child she walked in the footsteps of Cistercian monks. James of Vitry also reports that Mary had a vision in which St Bernard appeared to her.[9] Furthermore, Mary was probably claimed by Cistercians as their own saint. This assumption is supported by the fact that the manuscript of Villers with the Office for Mary also contained the Office for Arnulf of Villers, a lay brother of the Cistercians' own order. The list of Cistercian saints composed by Chrysostomus Henriquez in 1630 points in the same direction.[10] He put Mary in the list as follows: *S. Maria Oegnies soror seu oblata ordinis Cisterciensis in Belgio, 23, Iun.*[11] He called Mary a Cistercian nun or oblate. Perhaps his ignorance stemmed from a tradition in which Mary was considered a Cistercian nun. Not only Cistercians felt the need to copy the *Life of Mary of Oignies*. Other orders are represented in Table 3 as well.

Table 3: Diffusion of Manuscripts of VMO — Institutions

Benedictines: 5 mss	Laon (13); Sint-Truiden (17); Bury (23); Echternach (29); Erfurt (30)
Cistercians: 11	Himmerod (1); Cîteaux (10); IJsselstein (11); Vauclair (14); Loos (19); Jardinet (22); Bonport (26); Cambron (28); Clairmarais (32); Clairvaux (34); Clairvaux (35)

---

[9] *VMO* 2, 90.

[10] Chrysostomus Henriquez, *Quinque prudentes virgines sive B. Beatricis de Nazareth, B. Aleydis de Scharenbecka, B. Idae de Nivellis, B. Idae de Lovanio, B. Idae de Lewis, Ordinis Cisterc. praeclara gesta, ex antiquis M. S. eruta. Accessit catalogus copiosus sanctarum et beatarum maxime illustrium eiusdem instituti* (Antwerp: Joannes Cnobbaert, 1630), p. 459: Catalogus sanctarvm ac beatarum maximè illustrium ordinis Cisterciensis, ex probatis ecclesiae auctoribus collectus.

[11] Henriquez, *Quinque prudentes*, p. 474.

Table 3 cont.

Carthusians: 4	Mons Dei (7); England (24); Bourgfontaine (27); Beatenberg (33)
Canons Regular: 6	Oignies (6); Laon (12); Bois-Seigneur-Isaac (21); Rooklooster (37); Rooklooster (38); Rooklooster (39)
Premonstratensians: 1	Belval (8)
Crutched Friars: 3	Venlo, Hoorn (4); Huy (15); Huy (16)
Brothers of the Common Life: 1	Utrecht (3)
Unknown: 8	East Netherlands (2); [Brussels] (5); [Coimbra] (9); [Lille] (18); England (20); [Paris] (25); [Porto] (31); [Vienna] (36)

The Supplement written by Thomas of Cantimpré was less successful. This text has come to us through six manuscript witnesses, all from the fifteenth century. In five of these manuscripts the Supplement is accompanied by the *Life* by James of Vitry. The sixth manuscript, the *Historiologium* of Johannes Gielemans of Rooklooster, contains some excerpts of the Supplement (number 44 on the list of the Supplement at the end).

Several composers of large collections of exempla made use of the *Life of Mary of Oignies* by James of Vitry. Michel Lauwers named some famous collections, all from the thirteenth century, that contain one or more chapters about Mary of Oignies: the *Speculum historiale* by Vincent of Beauvais (XXX, 10–51), the *Bonum universale de apibus* by Thomas of Cantimpré (II, 53), the *Libri VIII miraculorum* by Caesarius of Heisterbach, and the *Alphabetum narrationum* of Arnold of Liège (several chapters).[12] Another collection is that of Stephen of

---

[12] Lauwers, 'Expérience béguinale', pp. 83–84, note 102. For Mary of Oignies in the *Speculum historiale*, see Monique Paulmier-Foucart, 'Les religieuses dans une encyclopédie du XIIIe siècle: le *Speculum historiale* de Vincent de Beauvais', in *Les Religieuses en France au XIIIe siècle: Table ronde organisée par l'Institut d'Études Médiévales de l'Université de Nancy II et le C.E.R.C.O.M. (25–26 juin 1983)*, ed. by Michel Parisse (Nancy: Presses Universitaires de Nancy, 1989), pp. 199–213 (p. 205).

Bourbon.[13] It would be interesting to examine the connection(s) between the *Life of Mary of Oignies* and the exempla about her. The example that Thomas of Cantimpré gave in the *Bonum universale de apibus* was the same story as told in Chapter 11 of his Supplement.

Vernacular Versions

The *Life of Mary of Oignies* was transmitted in many vernacular languages. French, Dutch, Italian, Norse, and Swedish translations or adaptations are known.[14] No translation has been preserved in more than four copies. These translations were probably meant for a female or lay public. This assumption is supported by the case of the Dutch translations. All three known (but not all three preserved) copies belonged to convents of women. The preserved Dutch text is an abridged version of the *Life of Mary* that holds only about four percent of the Latin original. It was copied in 1491 by Adam Daemsz, a Canon Regular of Gaesdonck (near Goch in the German Rhine area).[15] The language of the translation is a mixture of eastern and western Dutch dialects. Adam Daemsz was not its author. He may have selected parts of an already existing Dutch translation of the *Life*. Adam was the *socius* of rector Johannes van den Haeff of the convent of Canonesses Regular of Neerbosch (near Nijmegen in The Netherlands). According to a colophon on fol. 323[v], Adam wrote the manuscript at the request of Maralde of Sallant, the prioress of Neerbosch. Adam and Johannes possibly used the manuscript for preaching to the women of Neerbosch. The manuscript holds, among other texts, Dutch translations of the exempla collections *Exordium magnum cisterciense sive Narratio de initio cisterciensis ordinis* of Conrad of Eberbach and *Bonum universale de apibus* of Thomas of Cantimpré. The Dutch fragments of the *Life of Mary* probably served as examples too.

---

[13] Calzà, *Dem Weiblichen*, pp. 48–49, note 121.

[14] For the French and Italian versions, see Vauchez, 'Prosélytisme', p. 104; Lauwers, 'Entre Béguinisme et Mysticisme', p. 47, note 5. The Norse and Swedish versions were treated by G. A. van der Toorn-Piebenga, 'De *vita Mariae Oigniacensis* in Scandinavië', *Ons Geestelijk Erf*, 65 (1991) 13–22; for the English translation see 'Prosalegenden: Die Legenden des ms. Douce 114. (Dialekt von Nottinghamshire?)', ed. by C. Horstmann, *Anglia: Zeitschrift für Englische Philologie*, 8 (1885), 102–96.

[15] MS Utrecht, UB, 1016 (5 D 6), fols 307[v]–309[r] (1491). See the list at the end of this chapter for further details.

Two other Dutch versions of the *Life of Mary of Oignies* are known to have existed. The first was copied by Evert Blomendael, a Canon Regular of Ezens in East Friesland. He wrote it for the Sisters of the Common Life of Mariëngaarde in Schuettorf.[16] Given the small number of folios, the translation cannot have covered the whole Latin *Life*. The manuscript was in private possession until 1932, when it disappeared. The second copy was owned by the Canonesses Regular of St Barbara in Delft, as is testified by a fifteenth-century book list that included the titles present in the library of the convent.[17] The *Life of Mary* is mentioned in this list.

One would expect that a *Life* of a lay woman would have been much more interesting to a female or lay public than to a male monastic public, but that is not the case. If we look at the manuscript evidence, we can conclude that the Latin *Life* was far better known than any vernacular version. In my view, Mary was not so much a role model for women as an example for learned men. James of Vitry convinced his colleagues, in his own time as well as centuries later, of the saintliness of women like Mary, who were not learned theologians, but inspired prophetesses. Also, by studying the *Life*, monks were instructed in the seven gifts of the Holy Spirit and other theological themes.

The Afterlife of the Life of Mary of Oignies *in Fifteenth-Century Brabant*

To give an illustration of the research into the reception history of the *Life of Mary of Oignies*, I shall take a closer look at the use of the *Life* in the context of fifteenth-century Brabant.

One of the first questions that leads to a better insight into the function and meaning of the *Life of Mary of Oignies* in different periods and regions, is: in what collections was the *Life* included? What other texts were copied in the same manuscript? Around half of all thirty-nine surviving manuscripts consist of a

---

[16] MS olim Israel (Arnhem), 1, fols 38ᵛ–54ᵛ (1454). See the database of the *Bibliotheca Neerlandica Manuscripta* at the Universiteitsbibliotheek of Leiden (http://www.bnm. leidenuniv.nl).

[17] MS The Hague, KB, 130 E 24 (*c.* 1475). The *Life of Mary of Oignies* is number 71 of the book list. See W. Moll, 'De Boekerij van het St. Barbara-klooster te Delft, in de tweede helft der vijftiende eeuw: Eene bijdrage tot de geschiedenis der middeleeuwsche Letterkunde in Nederland', *Verhandelingen der Koninklijke akademie van Wetenschappen. Afdeeling Letterkunde*, 1 (1858), 1–60 (p. 13).

mixture of genres: hagiographical and theological writings put in one codex. The *Life of Mary* is accompanied by treatises and sermons of Richard of St Victor, Gregory the Great, Bernard of Clairvaux, and others. Remarkably, the manuscripts that contain mixed genres are mostly from the thirteenth and fourteenth centuries. The remaining manuscripts contain only hagiography (*passiones, vitae, miracula*). Almost all manuscripts from the fifteenth century are of this type. These hagiographic collections are never the same: all manuscripts have a unique arrangement, and texts about all kinds of saints are included (martyrs, virgins, abbots and abbesses, bishops, etc). The *Life of Mary of Oignies* was not included in a fixed collection of texts like the *Legenda Aurea*. Nevertheless, we discern some recurring elements in the hagiographic collections. The *Life of Mary* is accompanied several times by Lives of other 'new' saints, belonging to the religious reform movements of the later Middle Ages, like Francis, Dominic, Bernard, and Catherine of Siena. For example: the manuscript Brussels, Bollandistes, 398 (1413; of unknown origin) consists of Lives and accounts of the miracles of Mary of Oignies, Elisabeth of Hungary, Angela of Foligno, Malachy, Francis, and Anthony of Padua. The only 'old' saint represented in this manuscript is Martin of Tours.

Of the seventeen manuscripts from the fifteenth century, four have a provenance from Brabant. If we take a closer look at these manuscripts, we see that Mary of Oignies no longer functions as the prototype of the Liège religious movement, as James had presented her. She is now presented as one of the holy ancestors of the duchy of Brabant. The first manuscript from Brabant is from Bois-Seigneur-Isaac, a monastery of Canons Regular that belonged to the Congregation of Windesheim (Modern Devout). The manuscript was later split up into three parts, whereby some folios have been lost.[18] It contains a mixture of historiographic and hagiographic texts, which are all about the glorious history of Brabant. They include Lives of Gertrude of Nivelles, her mother Yduberga, Berlendis of Meerbeke, Mary of Oignies, and Ida of Nivelles, all from Brabant, and genealogies of Charles the Great, and the dukes of Lotharingia and Brabant. In local historiography, the duchy of Brabant was considered the heir of the old Lotharingian territory of the Carolingians. Genealogical schemes were made to prove the descent of the dukes of Brabant from the Carolingians. Various saints

---

[18] MS Leuven, Katholieke Universiteit Leuven, Maurits Sabbebibliotheek (Faculteit Godgeleerdheid), Collectie Mechelen, Bibliotheek van het Grootseminarie, 19, 20, and 21. The cover photo was taken from this manuscript (fol. 72').

were fitted into the genealogy to give an odour of sanctity to the duchy.[19] In the manuscript of Bois-Seigneur-Isaac such a scheme was included twice, on fol. III[r] and fol. 49[v] (the diagram on fol. III[r] was added later; this folio is of a different size). It includes, among other names, the names of Charles the Great and Gertrude of Nivelles. Exactly the same diagram is found in another manuscript, Brussels, KBR, 8751–60 (written in 1442). This manuscript originated from Rooklooster and contains the *passiones* of many virgin martyrs and the Lives of Brabant saints like Amelberga of Maubeuge, Raineldis and, again, Gertrude of Nivelles. Obviously, the diagram (and the texts) had been exchanged.

The second manuscript from Brabant containing the *Life of Mary of Oignies* is Volume II of a well-known collection, namely the *Hagiologium Brabantinorum* of Johannes Gielemans.[20] This *Hagiologium* holds Lives of saints who were akin to Charles the Great, or who were born in Brabant, or were otherwise connected to Brabant. Johannes Gielemans was a Canon Regular of Rooklooster, just like Bois-Seigneur-Isaac, a monastery of the Congregation of Windesheim. Gielemans had set himself to the task of collecting texts about many saints. He made several collections, the *Hagiologium Brabantinorum* being one of these. His other collections were the *Historiologium Brabantinorum*, the *Novale sanctorum*, and the *Sanctilogium*. Like the *Hagiologium Brabantinorum*, the *Historiologium Brabantinorum* was intended to propagate the gloriousness of Brabant by means of telling stories about Brabant's holy ancestors. It contains historiographic works, including parts of the Supplement by Thomas of Cantimpré.[21] The *Novale sanctorum* is a collection in two volumes of hagiography of saints from the fourteenth and fifteenth centuries.[22] The *Sanctilogium* is a work in four volumes containing short versions of Lives of hundreds of saints.[23] Volume IV of the *Sanctilogium* contains an extract of the *Life of Mary of Oignies*. This is the third manuscript from Brabant of the four I mentioned earlier. The fourth manuscript from Brabant is also from Rooklooster. It includes the Lives of,

---

[19] Robert Stein, *Politiek en historiografie: Het ontstaansmilieu van Brabantse kronieken in de eerste helft van de vijftiende eeuw* (Leuven: Peeters, 1994) pp. 120–21.

[20] MS Vienna, ÖNB, Ser. N. 12707 (1476–84). Volume I of the *Hagiologium Brabantinorum* is Vienna, ÖNB, Ser. N. 12706.

[21] MS Vienna, ÖNB, Ser. N. 12710, fols 190[r]–194[v] (1486–87).

[22] MS Vienna, ÖNB, Ser. N. 12708–12709 (1485–87).

[23] MS Vienna, ÖNB, Ser. N. 12811–12814 (before 1487).

among others, Mary of Oignies, Gudule of Brussels, and Arnulf of Villers. This
manuscript has, again, a 'nationalistic' Brabant character.[24]

The Life of Mary served historiographers of Brabant as well as hagiographers
like Gielemans. The chronicle *De Laude Brabantiae* (1467) by the monk Walter
of Affligem consists of short chapters in which the Lives of Brabant saints were
summarized. One of these chapters is about Mary of Oignies. Walter had used
the *Hagiologium Brabantinorum* as a source.[25] Apparently, in the monasteries
around Brussels much effort was given to the laudation of Brabant. Saints were
employed to serve this purpose. Lives were exchanged, among them the *Life of
Mary of Oignies*. In Brabant monasteries, Mary of Oignies was received as a holy
ancestor of Brabant, and not as the 'precious and surpassingly excellent pearl' of
Liège, as James of Vitry had called her.[26]

List of Extant Manuscripts

In the following lists, manuscripts are arranged according to the places where
they are preserved today. The date and provenance of each manuscript is given,
if known. In most cases we know in which monastery the manuscript was kept,
but we are almost never sure that the manuscript was actually written there.
Therefore, I distinguish between production and possession. Only if the copyist
or the place of production is known for certain, is it put under the heading
'production'. Under the heading 'possession', the names of medieval owners (in
most cases known from notes in the manuscripts) are cited. For all manuscripts
the most important literature (catalogues or other) is mentioned. Occasionally,
I was not able to inspect a library catalogue. If such was the case, the article or
book in which I found the reference is cited.

The *Speculum historiale* of Vincent of Beauvais has been preserved in many
manuscripts. Only the manuscripts in which separate extracts of the *Speculum
historiale* concerning Mary of Oignies were copied, are mentioned below. In the
Bibliotheca hagiographica manuscripta (Internet database) a BHL number was

---

[24] MS Vienna, ÖNB, Ser. N. 12831 (fifteenth century).

[25] A[lbert] Ampe, 'Walter Bosch, monnik van Affligem, en zijn twee bewerkingen van Jan
van Boendales Brabantsche Yeesten', *Bijdragen tot de Geschiedenis*, 60 (1977), 3–84 (p. 43, note
59).

[26] *VMO* Prologue, 9.

reserved for those extracts (Maria 10).[27] All lists, but especially the listing of BHL Maria 10, are probably far from complete. All over Europe (and perhaps other parts of the world) there are manuscripts as yet to be discovered.

(Fragments of) the *Life* by James of Vitry (BHL 5516)

1. Baltimore, Walters Art Museum, W 385, fols 73–97 (thirteenth century). Possession: Cistercians of Himmerod near Trier.
   Seymour De Ricci and W. J. Wilson, *Census of Medieval and Renaissance Manuscripts in the United States and Canada*, I (New York: Wilson, 1935), p. 820.

2. Brussels, Bibliothèque des Bollandistes, 398, fols 1ʳ–27ᵛ (1413). Possession: unknown. Not Aduard, as stated by Coens and Mariani. According to the decoration: possibly eastern Netherlands.
   H. Moretus, 'Catalogus codicum hagiographicorum latinorum bibliothecae Bollandianae', *Analecta Bollandiana*, 24 (1905), 425–72 (p. 453); M. Coens, 'Les manuscrits de Corneille Duyn donnés jadis a Héribert Rosweyde et conservés actuellement a Bruxelles', *Analecta Bollandiana*, 77 (1959), 108–34 (pp. 129–30); Paolo Mariani, 'Liber e Contesto: Codici miscellanei a Confronto', in *Angèle de Foligno: Le dossier*, ed. by Giulia Barone and Jacques Dalarun, Collection d'École Française de Rome, 255 (Rome: École française de Rome, 1999), pp. 71–144 (pp. 103–06).

3. Brussels, Bibliothèque royale de Belgique, 7917 (3189), fols 122ᵛ–142ᵛ (fifteenth century). Possession: Utrecht, Brothers of the Common Life of St Jerome.
   Catalogus codicum hagiographicorum bibliothecae regiae Bruxellensis, I: *Codices latini membrani*, II (Brussels: Polleunis, Ceuterick et De Smet, 1889), pp. 155–61; J. Van Den Gheyn, *Catalogue des manuscrits de la Bibliothèque Royale de Belgique*, V: *Histoire — hagiographie* (Brussels: Henri Lamertin, 1905), pp. 163–65; Albert Ampe, *Jan van Ruusbroec 1293–1381*, Catalogi van tentoonstellingen georganiseerd in de Koninklijke Bibliotheek Albert I, C 182 (Brussels: Koninklijke Bibliotheek Albert I, 1981), pp. 17–18.

4. Brussels, Bibliothèque royale de Belgique, 8629–39 (3209), fols 3ʳ–51ᵛ (1477). Production: Venlo, Crutched Friars. Possession: Venlo, Crutched Friars; later: Hoorn, Crutched Friars of Sint-Pietersdal (Holland).
   Coens, 'Les manuscrits', pp. 124–25; Van Den Gheyn, *Catalogue des manuscrits*, V, pp. 183–84. See also no. 40.

5. Brussels, Bibliothèque royale de Belgique, 20605 (3259), fols 23ʳ–51ᵛ (fifteenth century). Possession: unknown.
   Van Den Gheyn, *Catalogue des manuscrits*, V, p. 257.

6. Brussels, Bibliothèque royale de Belgique, II, 700 (3280), whole manuscript (thirteenth century). Possession: Oignies, Canons Regular of St Nicolas.

---

[27] The BHL number Maria 10 was not included in the paper version of the *Bibliotheca Hagiographica Manuscripta*. It can only be found in the Internet database (http://ß. bhlms.fltr.ucl.ac.be). The number refers to *Speculum historiale*, XXX (abstracts of), 10–51.

Catalogus codicum [...] Bruxellensis, I, p. 436; Van Den Gheyn, *Catalogue des manuscrits*, V, p. 267.

7. Charleville-Mézières, Bibliothèque municipale, 181, fols 224ʳ–251ʳ (fourteenth century). Possession: Carthusians of Mons Dei (Mont-Dieu) near Charleville.

   Catalogue général des manuscrits des bibliothèques publiques des départements, V: *Metz –Verdun – Charleville* (Paris: Imprimerie nationale, 1879), pp. 623–24.

8. Charleville-Mézières, Bibliothèque municipale, 244, fols 177ʳ–190ʳ (1346, this part 1316). Production: Bellevallis; copyist: Johannes de Blegney. Possession: Premonstratensians of Bellevallis (Belval) near Charleville.

   Catalogue général [...] départements, V, pp. 656–57.

9. Coimbra, Biblioteca General da Universidade, XX, Est 15, Caixa 27.

   John Frederick Hinnebusch, 'Extant Manuscripts of the Writings of Jacques de Vitry', *Scriptorium*, 51 (1997), 156–64 (p. 163).

10. Dijon, Bibliothèque municipale, 662 (401), whole manuscript (thirteenth century). Possession: Cistercians of Cîteaux.

    Catalogue général des manuscrits des bibliothèques publiques de France: Départements, V: *Dijon* (Paris: E. Plon, 1889), p. 194.

11. The Hague, Koninklijke Bibliotheek, 70 H 49, fols 34ʳ–57ᵛ (fifteenth century). Possession: Cistercians of IJsselstein near Utrecht.

    'Catalogus codicum hagiographicorum bibliothecae regiae Hagensis', *Analecta Bollandiana*, 6 (1887), 161–208 (p. 203–04); *Catalogus codicum manuscriptorum bibliothecae regiae*, I: *Libri Theologici* (The Hague: [Koninklijke Bibliotheek], 1922), p. 265; *Inventaris van de handschriften van de Koninklijke Bibliotheek: Voorlopige uitgave*, I: *(kastnummers 66–70)* (The Hague: Koninklijke Bibliotheek, 1988), pp. 63, 120.

12. Laon, Bibliothèque municipale, 80 (thirteenth century). Possession: Laon, Canons Regular of Nôtre-Dame.

    Catalogue général [...] départements, I, p. 85.

13. Laon, Bibliothèque municipale, 278 (thirteenth century). Possession: Benedictines of St Vincent near Laon.

    Catalogue général [...] départements, I, pp. 165–66.

14. Laon, Bibliothèque municipale, 345 (thirteenth century). Possession: Cistercians of Vauclair near Laon.

    Catalogue général [...] départements, I, pp. 190–91.

15. Liège, Bibliothèque du Grand Séminaire, 6 L 21, fols 166ᵛ–168ʳ (1479). Fragments. Production: Huy, Crutched Friars of Clairlieu. Possession: Huy, Crutched Friars of Clairlieu.

    Gilbert Tournoy and Jozef IJsewijn, *I codici del Petrarca nel Belgio*, Censimento dei Codici Petrarcheschi, 10 (Padua: Antenore, 1988), pp. 76–79.

16. Liège, Bibliothèque universitaire, 135 C (232), fols 171ʳ–207ʳ (fifteenth century). Possession: Huy, Crutched Friars of Clairlieu.

    Bibliothèque de l'Université de Liège: Catalogue des manuscrits (Liège: H. Vaillant-Carmanne, 1875), p. 174; 'Catalogus codicum hagiographicorum bibliothecae publicae civitatis et academiae Leodiensis', *Analecta Bollandiana*, 5 (1886), 313–64 (pp. 40–42). See also no. 41.

17. Liège, Bibliothèque universitaire, 260 (233), fols 103ᵛ–146ʳ (1213–1300). Possession: Sint-Truiden, Benedictines of Sint-Truiden.

Bibliothèque de l'Université, p. 175; 'Catalogus codicum [...] Leodiensis', pp. 47–48.

18. Lille, Archives départementales du Nord, 239, whole manuscript (sixteenth century).[28]
Catalogue des manuscrits conservés dans les dépots d'archives départementales communales et hospitalières (Paris: E. Plon, 1886), p. 228.

19. Lille, Bibliothèque municipale, 450 (Part II), fols 58ᵛ–59 (fourteenth century). Possession: Cistercians of Loos near Lille.
Catalogue général des manuscrits des bibliothèques publiques de France: Départements, XXVI: *Lille – Dunkerque – Bergues – Roye – Péronne – Ham – La Chatre* (Paris: E. Plon, 1897), pp. 295–303.

20. London, British Library, Harley 4725, fols 157– (thirteenth or fourteenth century). Possession: probably England, 1513: bought by D. T. Walwell.
A Catalogue of the Harleian Manuscripts in the British Museum: With Indexes of Persons, Places, and Matters, III (Hildesheim: Georg Olms, 1973), p. 196.

21. Leuven, Katholieke Universiteit Leuven, Maurits Sabbebibliotheek (Faculteit Godgeleerdheid), Collectie Mechelen, Bibliotheek van het Grootseminarie, 20, fols 73ʳ–118ʳ (fifteenth century). On fol. 72ʳ a woodcut with the depiction of Mary was pasted in the manuscript. Possession: (probably) Canons Regular of Bois-Seigneur-Isaac near Ophain. See also nos 42 and 46.
Carlo De Clercq, *Catalogue général des manuscrits des bibliothèques de Belgique*, IV: *Catalogue des manuscrits du Grand Séminaire de Malines* (Gembloux: Duculot; and Paris: J. Duculot and Société d'Édition Les Belles Lettres, 1937), pp. 58–59.

22. Namur, Musée archéologique de la province de Namur, Fonds de la ville, 49, fols 182ʳ–211ᵛ (1428–29). Possession: Walcourt, Cistercians of Jardinet.
Paul Faider and others, *Catalogue général des manuscrits des bibliothèques de Belgique*, I: *Catalogue des manuscrits conservés a Namur (Musée Archéologique, Évêché, Grand Séminaire, Museum Artium S. J., etc.)* (Gembloux: J. Duculot, 1934), pp. 121–23.

23. Oxford, Bodleian Library, Bodley 240 (1377). Sanctilogium of John of Tynemouth. Production: Bury; copyist: Rogerus de Huntedone. Possession: Bury, Benedictines of St Edmund; sixteenth century: Thomas Prise.
Falconer Madan and H. H. E. Craster, *A Summary Catalogue of Western Manuscripts in the Bodleian Library at Oxford Which Have not Hitherto Been Catalogued in the Quarto Series: With References to the Oriental and Other Manuscripts*, II: I (Oxford: Clarendon Press, 1922), pp. 384–85 (no. 2469); Andrew G. Watson, *Catalogue of Dated and Datable Manuscripts c. 435–1600 in Oxford Libraries*, I: *The Text* and II: *The Plates* (Oxford: Clarendon Press, 1984), p. 13.

24. Oxford, St John's College, 182 (1463–74). Production: copyist: Carthusian John Blacman, confessor of Henry VI.
Patricia Deery Kurtz, 'Mary of Oignies, Christine the Marvelous, and Medieval Heresy', *Mystics Quarterly*, 14 (1988), 186–96 (pp. 186–87).

25. Paris, Bibliothèque nationale de France, lat. 2695, fols 119ʳ–150ʳ (thirteenth century). Possession: unknown. Some parts of the *Life* were left out. In the fourteenth century a miracle was added on fol. 150ᵛ.

---

[28] Margot King kindly provided the reference to this manuscript.

Catalogus codicum hagiographicorum latinorum antiquiorum saeculo XVI qui asservantur in bibliotheca nationali Parisiensi, I, Subsidia hagiographica, 2 (Brussels: Picard and Schepens, 1889), p. 171.

26. Paris, Bibliothèque nationale de France, lat. 2795, fols 124ʳ–176ᵛ (thirteenth century). Possession: Cistercians of Bonport near Rouen.

    Catalogus codicum [...] Parisiensi, I, p. 210.

27. Paris, Bibliothèque nationale de France, lat. 3631, fols 76ʳ–83ʳ (fifteenth century). Shortened version of the *Life*. Possession: Carthusians of domus Fontis Mariae (Bourgfontaine) near Villers-Cotterêts.

    Catalogus codicum [...] Parisiensi, I, p. 236.

28. Paris, Bibliothèque nationale de France, lat. 9743, fols 23ᵛ–53ʳ (thirteenth century). Possession: Cistercians of Cambron near Mons.

    Catalogus codicum [...] Parisiensi, II, Subsidia hagiographica, 2 (Brussels: Picard and Schepens, 1890), p. 592.

29. Paris, Bibliothèque nationale de France, lat. 10870, fols 149ᵛ–153ᵛ (this part: fifteenth century; rest: twelfth/thirteenth century). No prologue. Large parts of the *Life* are missing, because folios were cut out. Possession: Benedictines of Echternach near Trier.

    Catalogus codicum [...] Parisiensi, II, pp. 615–17.

30. Pommersfelden, Graeflich Schönborn'sche Schlossbibliothek, 30/2754, fols 89ʳ–136ʳ (fourteenth century). Parts of the *Life* were left out. Possession: Erfurt, Benedictines of St Peter.

    'Vita venerabilis Lukardis monialis ordinis cisterciensis in superiore Wimaria', *Analecta Bollandiana*, 18 (1899) 305–67 (pp. 305–09).

31. Porto, Biblioteca Pública Municipal, Cat. (1879), 22.

    Hinnebusch, 'Extant Manuscripts', p. 163.

32. Saint-Omer, Bibliothèque municipale, 769, fols 40ʳ–91ʳ (thirteenth and fourteenth century). Production: Clairmarais; copyist: Bernardus de Ypris. Possession: Cistercians of Clairmarais near Saint-Omer.

    Catalogue général [...] départements, III (Paris: Imprimerie impériale, 1861), pp. 348–49.

33. Trier, Stadtbibliothek, 1168/470 8°, fols 204ʳ–221ᵛ (fifteenth century). Excerpts of the *Life* (BHL 5517d). Possession: Carthusians of Beatenberg near Koblenz. See also no. 47.

    M. Coens, 'Catalogus codicum hagiographicorum latinorum bibliothecae civitatis Treverensis', *Analecta Bollandiana*, 52 (1934), 157–285 (pp. 229–31); Max Keuffer and Gottfried Kentenich, *Verzeichnis der Handschriften des historischen Archivs*, Beschreibendes Verzeichnis der Handschriften der Stadtbibliothek zu Trier, 8 (Trier: Fr. Lintzschen, 1914; repr. Wiesbaden: Otto Harrassowitz, 1973), p. 232. See also no. 47.

34. Troyes, Bibliothèque municipale, 401, fols 49ʳ–73ᵛ (this part: end of fifteenth or beginning of sixteenth century; other part: thirteenth century). Possession: Cistercians of Clairvaux.

    Catalogue général [...] départements, II (Paris: Imprimerie impériale, 1855), pp. 179–81.

35. Troyes, Bibliothèque municipale, 1434 (thirteenth century). Production: Clairvaux?; copyist: Martinus van Loesuelt? Possession: Cistercians of Clairvaux.

    Catalogue général [...] départements, II, p. 600.

36. Vienna, Österreichische Nationalbibliothek, Han–488, fols 1ʳ–46ʳ (thirteenth century).

Tabulae codicum manu scriptorum praeter graecos et orientales in bibliotheca Palatina Vindobonensi asservatorum, I (Vienna: Caroli Geroldi filius, 1864; repr. Graz: Akademische Druck- und Verlagsanstalt, 1965), p. 81.

37. Vienna, Österreichische Nationalbibliothek, Ser. N. 12707, fols 126ᵛ–146ʳ (1476–84). Some parts of the *Life* are left out. *Hagiologium Brabantinorum*, II of Johannes Gielemans. Production: Rooklooster; copyist: Johannes Gielemans. Possession: Canons Regular of Rooklooster near Brussels.

    'De codicibus hagiographicis Iohannis Gielemans, canonici regularis in Rubea Valle prope Bruxellas', *Analecta Bollandiana*, 14 (1895), 5–88 (pp. 54–61), (no. 9363, II). See also no. 43.

38. Vienna, Österreichische Nationalbibliothek, Ser. N. 12814, fols 1103ᵛ–1104ʳ (206ᵛ–207) (before 1487). Extract of the *Life*. *Sanctilogium*, IV of Johannes Gielemans. Production: Rooklooster; copyist: Johannes Gielemans. Possession: Canons Regular of Rooklooster near Brussels.

    'De codicibus hagiographicis', pp. 14–42 (no. 9397 a).

39. Vienna, Österreichische Nationalbibliothek, Ser. N. 12831, fols 16ʳ–51ʳ (fifteenth century). Possession: Canons Regular of Rooklooster near Brussels.

    'Catalogus codicum hagiographicorum qui Vindebonae asservantur in bibliotheca privata serenissimi Caesaris Austriaci', *Analecta Bollandiana*, 14 (1895), 231–83 (pp. 237–38), (no. 7909). See also nos 45 and 51.

Supplement by Thomas of Cantimpré (BHL 5517)

40. Brussels, Bibliothèque royale de Belgique, 8629–39 (3209), fols 53ʳ–62ᵛ (1477). Production: Venlo, Crutched Friars. Possession: Venlo, Crutched Friars; later Hoorn, Crutched Friars of Sint-Pietersdal. See also no. 4.

41. Liège, Bibliothèque universitaire, 135 C (234), fols 221ʳ–231ᵛ (fifteenth century). Possession: Huy, Crutched Friars of Clairlieu.

    Bibliothèque de l'Université, p. 175. See also no. 16.

42. Leuven, Katholieke Universiteit Leuven, Maurits Sabbebibliotheek (Faculteit Godgeleerdheid), Collectie Mechelen, Bibliotheek van het Grootseminarie, 20, fols 118ʳ–133ᵛ (fifteenth century). Possession: (probably) Canons Regular of Bois-Seigneur-Isaac near Ophain. See also nos 21 and 46.

43. Vienna, Österreichische Nationalbibliothek, Ser. N. 12707, fols 146ʳ–149ᵛ (1476–84). *Hagiologium Brabantinorum*, II of Johannes Gielemans. Production: Rooklooster; copyist: Johannes Gielemans. Possession: Canons Regular of Rooklooster near Brussels. See also no. 37.

44. Vienna, Österreichische Nationalbibliothek, Ser. N. 12710, fols 190ʳ–194ᵛ (1486–87). Extracts of Supplement. *Historiologium Brabantinorum* of Johannes Gielemans. Production: Rooklooster; copyist: Johannes Gielemans. Possession: Canons Regular of Rooklooster near Brussels.

    'De codicibus hagiographicis', pp. 80–88 (no. 9365).

45. Vienna, Österreichische Nationalbibliothek, Ser. N. 12831, fols 126ʳ–141ᵛ (fifteenth century). Possession: Canons Regular of Rooklooster near Brussels. See also nos 39 and 51.

Excerpts of *Speculum historiale* by Vincent of Beauvais (BHL Maria 10)

46. Leuven, Katholieke Universiteit Leuven, Maurits Sabbebibliotheek (Faculteit Godgeleerdheid), Collectie Mechelen, Bibliotheek van het Grootseminarie, 20, fol. 72ᵛ (fifteenth
century). *Speculum historiale*, XXX, 10. Possession: (probably) Canons Regular of Bois-
Seigneur-Isaac near Ophain. See also nos 21 and 42.

47. Trier, Stadtbibliothek, 1168/470 8°, fols 221ᵛ–222ᵛ (fifteenth century). *Speculum historiale*,
XXX, 10; *Bonum universaleʒe Liber Apum*, I, 22 and II, 53. Possession: Carthusians of
Beatenberg near Koblenz. See also no. 33.

48. Vatican, Biblioteca Apostolica Vaticana, Palatini latini, 866, fols 92ᵛ–100ʳ (fourteenth
century). *Speculum historiale*, XXX, 10–51 (fragments?).
Albertus Poncelet, *Catalogus codicum hagiographicorum latinorum Bibliothecae Vaticanae*,
Subsidia Hagiographica, 11 (Brussels: Socii Bollandiani, 1910), pp. 283–84.

49. Vatican, Biblioteca Apostolica Vaticana, Reginensi latini, 583, fol. 2ᵛ (fifteenth century).
Speculum historiale, XXX, 16.
Poncelet, *Catalogus codicum [...] Vaticanae*, pp. 378–79.

50. Venice, Biblioteca Nazionale Marciana, IX.18, fols 298ʳ–301ᵛ (fourteenth century). *Speculum
historiale*, XXX, 10–51 (abstract). Legendary of the Dominican friar Pierre Calo.
Albertus Poncelet, 'Le légendier de Pierre Calo', *Analecta Bollandiana*, 29 (1910), 5–116 (pp.
45–108), esp. p. 76.

51. Vienna, Österreichische Nationalbibliothek, Ser. N. 12831, fol. 142ʳ (fifteenth century).
Speculum historiale, XXX, 10. Possession: Canons Regular of Rooklooster near Brussels. See
also nos 39 and 45.

Vernacular Versions

French

52. Cambrai, Bibliothèque municipale, 210, fols 125ᵛ–130ᵛ (fifteenth century). Production:
possibly Liège or Tongres. Possession: Cambrai, abbey of St Aubert.
Auguste Molinier, *Catalogue général [...] de France: Départements*, XVII: *Cambrai* (Paris: E.
Plon, 1891), p. 67.

53. Douai, Bibliothèque municipale, 869, fols 89–97 (fifteenth century). Possession:
Franciscans of Douai.
Catalogue général [...] départements, XXV: *Douai* (Paris: Imprimerie nationale, 1878), p.
627–28.

54. Valenciennes, Bibliothèque municipale, 126, fols 291ᵛ–305ᵛ (fifteenth century). Possession:
unknown; later: Maison de Croy.
Catalogue général [...] de France: Départements, XXV: *Poitiers – Valenciennes* (Paris: E. Plon,
1894), p. 240.

Italian

55. Siena, Biblioteca Communale, T. II. 7, fols 181–208 (fifteenth century?).
Vauchez, 'Prosélytisme', p. 110, note 47.

Dutch

56. Utrecht, Universiteitsbibliotheek, 1016 (5 D 6), fols 307^v–309^r (1491). Production: probably Neerbosch; copyist: Adam Daemsz., Canon Regular of Gaesdonck near Goch, *socius* of rector Johan vanden Haeff of Neerbosch. Possession: probably Canonesses Regular of Neerbosch near Nijmegen.
   Wouter Antonie van der Vet, *Het Biënboec van Thomas van Cantimpré en zijn exempelen* (The Hague: Martinus Nijhoff, 1902), pp. 415–17; K[oert] van der Horst and others, *Handschriften en Oude Drukken van de Utrechtse Universiteitsbibliotheek: Samengesteld bij het 400-jarig bestaan van de Bibliotheek der Rijksuniversiteit, 1584–1984*, 2nd edn (Utrecht: Universiteitsbibliotheek, 1984), pp. 230–31.

English

57. Oxford, Bodleian Library, Douce 114, fols 26^v–76^r (fifteenth century). Possession: Carthusians of Belle Vallis near Nottingham.
   'Prosalegenden', ed. by Horstmann, pp. 102–06; Kurtz, 'Mary of Oignies', p. 187.

Swedish

58. Linköping, Cod. XXXIX.2 or 42 fol. (sixteenth century). Possession: Birgittines of Vadstena.
   Van der Toorn-Piebenga, 'De *vita Mariae*', p. 20, note 11; Hinnebusch, 'Extant Manuscripts', p. 163.

Norse

59–62. See Van der Toorn-Piebenga, 'De *vita Mariae*', p. 16, note 8. There are four manuscripts: C. R. Unger, *Maríu Saga* (Christiania: Brögger og Christie, 1871), pp. 917–21.

SELECT BIBLIOGRAPHY

Selected list of primary and secondary sources used in this volume. All works are given full bibliographical reference in the notes at first citation. For an expanded bibliography, see *The 'Mulieres Religiosae' of the Diocese of Liège: A Select Bibliography* ed. by Margot H. King, Peregrina Bibliographies Series (Toronto: Peregrina, 1998).

Primary Sources and Translations

Bernard of Clairvaux, *On the Song of Songs*, trans. by Kilian Walsh and Irene M. Edmonds (Kalamazoo: Cistercian Publications, 1979).

Caesarius of Heisterbach, *Dialogus miraculorum*, ed. by Joseph Strange (Cologne: Heberle, 1851).

——, *The Dialogue on Miracles*, trans. by H. E. von Scott and C. C. Swinton Bland (London: Broadway, 1929).

——, *Libri VIII miraculorum*, in *Die Wundergeschichten des Caesarius von Heisterbach*, ed. by Alfons Hilka, 2 vols (Bonn: Hanstein, 1933–37).

Desert Fathers: The Sayings of the Early Christian Monks, trans. and introd. by Benedicta Ward (London: Penguin, 2003).

Gregory the Great, *Dialogues*, trans. by Odo John Zimmerman (Washington: Catholic University of America Press, 1959).

——, *Moralia in Iob*, ed. by M. Adriaen, CCSL 143 (Turnhout: Brepols, 1979).

Historia fundationis Venerabilis Ecclesiae Beati Nicolai Oigniacensis ac Ancillae Christi Mariae Oigniacensis, in *Veterum scriptorum et monumentorum historicorum, dogmaticorum, moralium amplissima collectio*, ed. by Edmond Martène and Ursinus Durand, 9 vols (Paris: Montalant, 1724–33), VI, cols. 327–30.

Historia fundationis [...], ed. by Edmond Reusens, *Analecta pour servir à l'histoire ecclésiastique de la Belgique*, 10 (1873), 100–07.

History of the Foundation of the Venerable Church of Blessed Nicholas of Oignies and the Handmaid of Christ Mary of Oignies, trans. by Hugh Feiss OSB, in this volume.

James of Vitry, *The Exempla or Illustrative Stories from the 'Sermones Vulgares of Jacques de Vitry'*, ed. by Thomas Frederick Crane (London: Nutt, 1890; repr. New York: Lenox Hill, 1971).

——, *Die Exempla aus den Sermones Feriales et Communes*, ed. by Joseph Greven (Heidelberg: Winter, 1914).

——, *The Historia Occidentalis of Jacques de Vitry: A Critical Edition*, ed. by John Frederick Hinnebusch (Fribourg: Fribourg Presse Universitaire, 1972).

——, *Histoire occidentale*, trans. by Gaston Duchet-Suchaux, introd. and notes by Jean Longère (Paris: Cerf, 1997).

——, *Lettres de Jacques de Vitry (1160/1170–1240) évêque de Saint-Jean-d'Acre: éditions critique*, ed. by R. B. C. Huygens (Leiden: Brill, 1960).

——, *Lettres de la cinquième croisade*, trans. by Gaston Duchet-Suchaux, Sous la Règle de Saint-Augustin (Turnhout: Brepols, 1998).

——, 'Sermones ad status', in *Analecta novissima spicilegii Solesmensis, Altera continuatio*, ed. by J. Pitra, 2 vols (Paris: Typis Tuscolanis, 1885–88; repr. Farnborough: Gregg Press, 1971), pp. 189–93, 344–461 [partial edition].

——, 'Sermo ad virgines et iuvenculas', ed. by Joseph Greven, in 'Ursprung des Beginenwesens', *Historisches Jahrbuch*, 35 (1914), pp. 25–58; 291–318.

——, 'Quatre Sermons *Ad religiosas*', ed. by Jean Longère, in *Les Religieuses en France au xiiiᵉ siècle*, ed. by Michel Parisse (Nancy: Princeton University Press, 1985), pp. 215–300.

——, 'Deux Sermons de Jacques de Vitry (d. 1240): *Ad servos et ancillas*', ed. by Jean Longère, in *La Femme au moyen âge*, ed. by Michel Rouche and Jean Heuclin (Maubeuge-Paris: Touzot, 1990), pp. 261–96.

——, 'Sermo in festo Marie Magdalene', ed. by Michel Lauwers, in '*Noli me tangere*: Marie Madeleine, Marie d'Oignies et les pénitentes de xiiiᵉ siècles', *Mélanges d' École française de Rome: Moyen Age*, 104 (1992), 209–68.

——, *Vita Mariae Oigniacensis*, in AASS, 23 June, XXV, 542–72.

——, *The Life of Mary of Oignies by James of Vitry*, trans by Margot H. King, in this volume.

——, 'The Lyf of Seinte Marye of Oegines', ed. by C. Horstmann, in 'Prosalegende: Legende des ms. Douce 114', *Anglia*, 8 (1885), 134–84 [Middle English translation].

The Liturgical Office of Mary of Oignies by Goswin of Bossut, trans. by Hugh Feiss OSB, in this volume.

Moschus, F., *Coenobarchia Ogniacensis sive Antistitum qui Ogniacensi ad Sabim Monasterio hactenus praefugere numero undetriginta catalogus, cum eulogiis et anagrammatis* (Douai: [n. pub.], 1598).

Officium Mariae Oigniacensis, in 'Office liturgique neumé de la bienheureuse Marie d'Oignies à l'abbaye de Villers au xiiiᵉ siècle', ed. by Daniel Misonne, *Revue bénédictine*, III (2001), 267–73 [reprinted from *Album J. Balon* (Namur: Godenne, 1968), pp. 170–89].

Send me God: The Lives of Ida the Compassionate of Nivelles, Nun of La Ramée, Arnulf, Lay Brother of Villers, and Abundus, Monk of Villers, by Goswin of Bossut, trans. by Martinus Cawley, OCSO, with a preface by Barbara Newman (Turnhout: Brepols, 2003).

Thomas of Cantimpré [Cantipratanus or Cantimpratensis], *Bonum universale de apibus*, ed. by Georgius Colvenerius (Douai: Bellerus, 1627).

——, *Der Byen Boeck: De Middelnederlandse vertalingen van Bonum universale de apibus van Thomas van Cantimpré*, ed. and introd. by Christina M. Stutvoet-Joanknecht (Amsterdam: VU Uitgeverij, 1990).

——, *Les Exemples du livre des abeilles*, ed. and trans. by Henri Platelle (Turnhout: Brepols, 1997).

——, *De natura rerum*, ed. by Helmut Boese (Berlin: De Gruyter, 1973).

——, *De natura rerum: lib. IV–XII: Tacuinum sanitatis*, ed. by Luis García Ballester (Granada: Universidad de Granada, 1973–74).

——, *Vita S. Christinae Mirabilis virginis*, in AASS, 24 July, XXXIII, 637–60.

——, *The Life of Christina Mirabilis by Thomas de Cantimpré*, trans. by Margot H. King (Toronto: Peregrina, 1986).

——, *Vita Ioannis Cantimpratensis*, in 'Une oeuvre inédite de Thomas de Cantimpré: La "Vita Ioannis Cantimpratensis"', ed. by Robert Godding, *Revue d'histoire ecclésiastique*, 76 (1981), 241–316.

——, *Vita Lutgardis*, in AASS, 16 June, XXIV, 187–209.

——, *The Life of Lutgard of Aywières by Thomas de Cantimpré*, trans. by Margot H. King (Toronto: Peregrina, 1987).

——, *Vie de sainte Lutgard*, ed. and trans. by André Wankenne SJ (Namur: Presses Universitaires de Namur, 1991).

——, 'Supplement à l'édition de la Vita Lutgardis', in *Catalogus codicum hagiographicorum Bibliothecae Regiae Bruxellensis*, 2 vols (Brussels: Typis Polleunis, Ceuterick et Lefébure, 1889), II, p. 220.

——, *Vita Margarete de Ypres*, ed. by G. Meerseman in 'Les frères prêcheurs et le mouvement dévot en Flandres au XIIIᵉ siècle', *Archivum fratrum praedicatorum*, 18 (1948), 106–30.

——, *The Life of Margaret of Ypres*, trans. by Margot H. King (Toronto: Peregrina, 1990).

——, *Vita Mariae Oigniacensis, Supplementum*, in AASS, 23 June, XXV, 572–81.

——, *The Supplement to James of Vitry's Life of Mary of Oignies by Thomas of Cantimpré*, trans by Hugh Feiss OSB, in this volume.

——, *La Vie de Marie d'Oignies, par Jacques de Vitry. Supplément, par Thomas de Cantimpré*, trans. by André Wankenne (Namur: Société des études classiques, 1989).

'Vita Idae Nivellensis: Appendix ad cod. 8609–8620: *De beata Ida de Rameia virgine*, in *Catalogus codicum hagiographorum Bibliothecae Regiae Bruxellensis*, II (Brussels: Polleunis, Ceuterick et De Smet, 1889), pp. 222–26.

Vincent of Beauvais, *Speculum historiale* (Douai: Bellerus, 1624, repr. Assen: Gorcun, 1965).

Secondary Sources

Arbesmann, Rudolf, 'The *daemonium meridianum* and Greek and Latin Patristic Exegesis', *Traditio*, 14 (1958), 17–31.

Autour de Hugo d'Oignies, ed. by Robert Didier and Jacques Toussaint (Namur: Société archéologique de Namur, 2003).

Agostino Paravicini Bagliani, *I Testamenti dei cardinale del duecento*, Miscellanea della Società Romana di Storia Patria, 25 (Rome: Biblioteca Vallicelliana, 1980), p. 8.

Baldwin, John W., *Masters, Princes and Merchants: The Social Views of Peter the Chanter and his Circle*, 2 vols (Princeton: Princeton University Press, 1970).

Bauer, Gerhard, *Claustrum animae: Untersuchungen zur Geschichte der Metapher vom Herzen als Kloster* (Munich: Fink, 1973).

Benton, John F., 'Qui étaient les parents de Jacques de Vitry?', *Le Moyen Age*, 19 (1964), 32–43.

Berlière, Ursmer, 'Jacques de Vitry et ses relations avec les abbayes d'Aywières et de Doorezeele', *Revue bénédictine*, 25 (1908), 185–93.

Bériac, Françoise, *Histoire des lépreux au moyen âge: une société d'exclus* (Paris: Éditions Imago, 1988).

Bériou, Nicole, 'La confession dans les écrits théologiques et pastoraux du XIIIe siècle: medication de l'âme ou démarche judiciaire', in *L'Aveu, antiquité et moyen âge: colloque organisé par l'École française de Rome* (Rome: École française de Rome, 1986), pp. 261–82.

——, 'Femmes et prédicateurs: la transmission de la foi aux XIIe et XIIIe siècles', in *La Religion de ma mère: les femmes et la transmission de la foi*, ed. by Jean Delumeau (Paris: Cerf, 1992), pp. 51–70.

——, 'The Right of Women to Give Religious Instruction in the Thirteenth Century', in *Women Preachers and Prophets Through Two Millennia of Christianity*, ed. by Beverly Mayne Kienzle and Pamela J. Walker (Berkeley: University of California Press, 1998), pp. 134–45.

Bird, Jessalynn, 'The Religious's Role in a Post-Fourth-Lateran World: Jacques de Vitry's *Sermones ad Status* and *Historia Occidentalis*', in *Medieval Monastic Preaching*, ed. by Carolyn Muessig (Leiden: Brill, 1998), pp. 209–39.

Boeckl, K., *Die Sieben Gaben des Heiligen Geistes in ihrer Bedeutung für die Mystik nach der Theologie des 13. und 14. Jahrhunderts* (Fribourg im Breisgau: Herder, 1931).

Boespflug, F., 'Le dogme trinitaire et l'essor de son iconographie en Occident de l'époque carolingiennne au IVe Concile de Latran (1215)', *Cahiers de Civilisation Médiévale*, 37 (1994), 181–240.

Bolton, Brenda M., '*Mulieres Sanctae*', in *Sanctity and Secularity, The Church and the World*, ed. by Derek Baker, Studies in Church History, 10 (Oxford: Blackwell, 1973), pp. 77–99.

——, 'Fulk of Toulouse: The Escape that Failed', *Studies in Church History*, 12 (1975), 83–93.

——, '*Vitae Matrum*: A Further Aspect of the *Frauenfrage*', in *Medieval Women*, ed. by Derek Baker, Studies in Church History, Subsidia 1 (Oxford: Blackwell, 1978), pp. 253–73.

——, 'Some Thirteenth Century Women in the Low Countries: A Special Case?', *Nederlands Archief voor Kerkgeschiedenis*, 61 (1981), 7–29.

——, 'Faithful to Whom? Jacques de Vitry and the French Bishops', *Revue Mabillon*, n.s. 9, 70 (1998), pp. 53–72.

——, 'Thirteenth-Century Religious Women: Further Reflections on the Low Countries "Special Case"', in *New Trends in Feminine Spirituality: The Holy Women of Liège and their Impact*, ed. by Juliette Dor, Lesley Johnson, and Jocelyn Wogan-Browne (Turnhout: Brepols, 1999), pp. 129–57.

Bradley, Ritamary, 'The Speculum Image in Medieval Mystical Writers', in *The Medieval Mystical Tradition in England* [...], ed. by Marion Glassoe (Cambridge: Brewer, 1984), pp. 9–27.

Bredero, Adriaan, 'Le Moyen Âge et le Purgatoire', *Revue d'histoire ecclésiastique*, 78 (1983), 429–52.

Bremond, Claude, Jacques Le Goff, and Jean-Claude Schmitt, *L'Exemplum*, Typologie des sources du Moyen Âge occidental, 40 (Turnhout: Brepols, 1982).

Brown, Peter, *The Body and Society: Men, Women and Sexual Renunciation in Early Christianity* (New York: Columbia University Press, 1988).

Bürkle, Susanne, *Literatur im Kloster: Historische Funktion und rhetorische Legitimation frauenmystischer Texte des 14. Jahrhunderts* (Tübingen: Francke, 1999).

Bynum, Caroline Walker, *Jesus as Mother: Studies in the Spirituality of the High Middle Ages* (Berkeley: University of California Press, 1982).

——, 'Women Mystics and Eucharistic Devotion in the Thirteenth Century', *Women's Studies*, 11 (1984), 179–214.

——, *Holy Feast and Holy Fast: The Religious Significance of Food to Medieval Women* (Berkeley: University of California Press, 1987).

——, '"And Woman his Humanity": Female Imagery in the Religious Writing of the Later Middle Ages', in her *Fragmentation and Redemption: Essays on Gender and the Human Body in Medieval Religion* (New York: Zone Books, 1992), pp. 151–79.

——, *The Resurrection of the Body in Western Christianity, 200–1336* (New York: Columbia University Press, 1995).

Calzà, Maria Grazia, *Dem Weiblichen ist das Verstehen des Göttlichen 'Auf den Leib' geschrieben: Die Begine Maria von Oignies (d. 1213) in der hagiographischen Darstellung Jakobs von Vitry (d. 1240)* (Wurzburg: Ergon, 2000).

Carruthers, Mary, *The Book of Memory: A Study of Memory in Medieval Culture* (Cambridge, Cambridge University Press, 1990, repr. 1996).

Carpenter, Jennifer Helen, 'A New Heaven and a New Earth: The *Vitae* of the *Mulieres Religiosae* of Liège', (doctoral dissertation, University of Toronto, 1997).

Chenu, Marie-Dominique, *La Théologie au douzième siècle* (Paris: Vrin, 1957).

——, *Nature, Man, and Society in the Twelfth Century: Essays on New Theological Perspectives in the Latin West*, ed. and trans. by Jerome Taylor and Lester K. Little (Chicago: University of Chicago Press, 1982).

Clark, Anne L., *Elisabeth of Schönau: A Twelfth-Century Visionary* (Philadelphia: University of Pennsylvania Press, 1992).

Coakley, John, 'Gender and the Authority of Friars: The Significance of Holy Women for Thirteenth-Century Franciscans and Dominicans', *Church History*, 60 (1991), 445–60.

——, 'Friars as Confidants of Holy Women in Medieval Dominican Hagiography', in *Images of Sainthood in Medieval Europe* ed. by Renate Blumenfeld-Kosinki and Timea Szell (Ithaca: Cornell University Press, 1991), pp. 222–46.

Constable, Giles, *Attitudes Towards Self-Inflicted Suffering in the Middle Ages* (Brookline, MA: Hellenic College Press, 1982).

——, *Three Studies in Medieval Religious and Social Thought* (Cambridge: Cambridge University Press, 1995).

——, *The Reformation of the Twelfth Century* (Cambridge: Cambridge University Press, 1996).

Courtoy, Ferdinand, 'Inventaire du Musée de Namur 12: Croix reliquaire d'Oignies XIIIᵉ siècle', *Namurcum*, 6 (1929), 1–5.

——, *Le Trésor du Prieuré d'Oignies aux soeurs de Notre-Dame à Namur et l'Oeuvre du Frère Hugo* (Brussels: Editions de la Librairie Encyclopédique, 1953).

Cousins, Ewert, 'The Humanity and the Passion of Christ', in *Christian Spirituality: High Middle Ages and Reformation*, ed. by Jill Raitt (New York: Crossroad, 1987), pp. 375–91.

De Ganck, Roger, *Beatrice of Nazareth in her Context*, Cistercian Fathers Series, 3 vols (Kalamazoo: Cistercian Publications, 1991).

Degler-Spengler, Brigitta, 'Die religiöse Frauenbewegung des Mittelalters. Konversen – Nonnen – Beginen', *Rottenburger Jahrbuch* (1984), 75–88.

Dereine, Charles, 'Vita apostolica dans l'ordre canonial du IXe au XIe siècle', *Revue Mabillon*, 51 (1961), 47–53.

——, Ermites, reclus et recluses dans l'ancien diocèse de Cambrai entre Scarpe et Haine (1075–1125)', *Revue Bénédictine*, 97 (1987), 289–313.

d'Haenens, Albert, 'Femmes excédentaires et vocation religieuse dans l'ancien diocèse de Liège lors de l'essor urbain (fin du xiie–début du xiiie siècle)', in *Hommage à la Wallonie* [...], ed. by Hervé Hasquin (Brussels: Université libre de Bruxelles, 1981), pp. 217–35.

Distant Echoes, ed. by John A. Nichols and Lillian Thomas Shank (Kalamazoo: Cistercian Publications, 1984).

Dronke, Peter, *Women Writers of the Middle Ages* (Cambridge: Cambridge University Press, 1984).

Dushkes, Laura S. 'Illness and Healing in the *Viitae* of Mary of Oignies' (unpublished master's dissertation, University of Washington, 1988).

Elliott, Dyan, *Spiritual Marriage: Sexual Abstinence in Medieval Wedlock* (Princeton: Princeton University Press, 1993).

Elm, Kaspar, 'Die Stellung der Frau in Ordenswesen, Semireligiosentum und Häresie zur Zeit der heiligen Elisabeth', in *Sankt Elisabeth, Fürstin, Dienerin, Heilige* (Sigmaringen: Thorbecke, 1981), pp. 7–28.

——, 'Die Entwicklung des Franziskanerordens zwischen dem ersten und letzten Zeugnis des Jakob von Vitry', in *Vitasfratrum: Beiträge zur Geschichte der Eremiten-und Mendikantenorden des zwölften und dreizehnten Jahrhunderts: Festgabe zum 65. Geburtstag Kaspar Elm*, ed. by Dieter Berg, unter Mitwirkung des Friedrich-Meinecke-Instituts der Freien Universität Berlin (Werl: Dietrich-Coelde-Verlag, 1994), pp. 173–93.

——, '*Vita religiosa sine regula*, Bedeutung, Rechtsstellung und Selbstverständnis des mittelalterlichen und frühneuzeitlichen Semireligiosentums', in *Häresie und vorzeitige Reform im Spätmittelalter*, ed. by Frantisek Smahel (Munich: Oldenbour, 1998), pp. 239–73.

Epiney-Burgard, Georgette, 'Les béguines et l'ordre cistercien aux Pays-Bas du sud (XIIIe siècle)', in *Les Mouvances laïques des ordres religieux [...]*, ed. by Nicole Bouter (Saint-Etienne: Université Jean Monnet, 1996).

Farmer, Sharon, 'Down and Out and Female in Thirteenth-Century Paris', *American Historical Review*, 103 (1998), 345–72.

Les Fonctions des saints dans le monde occidental (IIIe–XIIIe siècle), introd. by Jean-Yves Tilliette (Rome: École française de Rome, 1991).

Forni, Alberto, 'Giacomo da Vitry, predicatore e "sociologo"', *La Cultura*, 18 (1980), 44.

——, 'Maestri predicatori, santi moderni e nuova aristocrazia del denaro tra Parigi e Oignies nella prima metà del sec. xiii', in *Culto dei santi, istitutioni e classi sociali in età preindustriale*, ed. by Sofia Boesch Gajano and Lucia Sebastiani (L'Aquila: Japadre, 1984), pp. 457–70.

Frauenmystik im Mittelalter [...], ed. by Peter Dinzelbacher and Dieter R. Bauer (Ostfildern bei Stuttgart: Schwabenverlag, 1985).

Freed, John B., 'Urban Development and the "Cura Monialium" in Thirteenth-Century Germany', *Viator*, 3 (1972), 311–27.

——, *The Friars and German Society in the Thirteenth Century* (Cambridge, MA: Mediaeval Academy of America, 1977).

Frencken, Goswin, *Die Exempla des Jacob von Vitry: ein Beitrag zur Geschichte der Erzählungsliteratur des Mittelalters,* Quellen und Untersuchungen zur lateinischen Philologie des Mittelalters, 5.1 (Munich: Beck, 1914).

Funk, P., *Jakob von Vitry: Leben und Werke,* Beiträge zur Kulturgeschichte des Mittelalters und der Renaissance, 3 (Berlin: Teubler, 1909).

Geyer, Iris, *Maria von Oignies: Eine hochmittelalterliche Mystikerin zwischen Ketzerei und Rechtgläubigkeit,* Europäische Hochschulschriften (Frankfurt am Main: Lang, 1992).

Glente, Karin, 'Mystikerinnen aus männlicher und weiblicher Sicht: Ein Vergleich zwischen Thomas von Cantimpré und Katharina von Unterlinden', in *Religiöse Frauenbewegung und mystische Frömmigkeit im Mittelalter,* ed. by Peter Dinzelbacher and Dieter R. Bauer (Cologne: Böhlau, 1988), pp. 251–64.

Goodich, Michael, *Vita Perfecta: The Ideal of Sainthood in the Thirteenth Century* (Stuttgart: Hiersemann, 1982).

——, '*Ancilla Dei*: The Servant as Saint in the Late Middle Ages', in *Women of the Medieval World: Essays in Honor of John N. Mundy,* ed. by Julius Kirshner and Suzanne F. Wemple (Oxford: Blackwell, 1985), pp. 119–36.

Grégoire, Réginald, 'L'Adage ascétique *nudus nudum Christum sequi*', *Studi storici in onore di Ottorino Bertolini,* ed. by Ottavio Banti and others (Pisa: Pacini, 1972), pp. 395–409.

Grundmann, Herbert, *Religiöse Bewegungen im Mittelalter* (Berlin: Ebering, 1935; 2nd edn, Darmstadt: Wissenschaftliche Buchgesellschaft, 1961).

——, *Religious Movements in the Middle Ages: The Historical Links Between Heresy, the Mendicant Orders, and the Women's Religious Movement in the Twelfth and Thirteenth Century,* trans. by Steven Rowan (Notre Dame: University of Notre Dame Press, 1995).

Harmless, William, *Desert Christians: An Introduction to the Literature of Early Monasticism* (Oxford: Oxford University Press, 2004).

Hinnebusch, William A., *The History of the Dominican Order,* 2 vols (New York: Alba House, 1965).

Hucq, E., 'Le sarcophage presumé de la bienheureuse Marie d'Oignies', *Annales de la Société archéologique de Namur,* 38 (1928), 231–44.

Huygens, R. B., 'Les passages des lettres de Jacques de Vitry relatifs à Saint François d'Assise et à ses premiers disciples', in *Hommages à Leon Herrmann* (Brussels: Latomus, 1960), pp. 446–53.

Images of Sainthood in Medieval Europe ed. by Renate Blumenfeld-Kosinki and Timea Szell (Ithaca: Cornell University Press, 1991).

The Invention of Saintliness, ed. by Anneke B. Mulder-Bakker (London: Routledge, 2002).

King, Margot H., 'The Sacramental Witness of Christina Mirabilis: The Mystic Growth of a Fool for Christ's Sake', in *Peace Weavers,* ed. by Lillian Thomas Shank and John A. Nichols (Kalamazoo: Cistercian Publications, 1987), pp. 145–64.

——, 'The Desert Mothers Revisited: The Mothers of the Diocese of Liège', *Vox Benedictina,* 5 (1988), 325–54.

Kleinberg, Aviad M., *Prophets in their Own Country: Living Saints and the Making of Sainthood in the Later Middle Ages* (Chicago: University of Chicago Press, 1992).

Kurtz, Patricia Deery, 'Mary of Oignies, Christine the Marvellous and Medieval Heresy', *Mystics Quarterly,* 14 (1988), 186–96.

Ladner, G. B., 'Homo Viator: Medieval Ideas on Alienation and Order', *Speculum*, 42 (1967), 233–59.

Lapanski, D., *Evangelical Perfection: An Historical Examination of the Concept in Early Franciscan Sources* (New York: Franciscan Institute, 1981).

Lauwers, Michel, 'Expérience béguinale et Récit hagiographique: a propos de la "Vita Mariae Oigniacensis" de Jacques de Vitry (vers 1215)', *Journal des savants* (1989), 61–103.

——, 'Paroles de femmes: sainteté féminine l'église du XIIIᵉ siècle face aux béguines', in *La Critique historique à l'épreuve: Liber discipulorum Jacques Paquet*, ed. by Gaston Braive and Jean-Marie Cauchies (Brussels: Publication des Facultés universitaires Saint Louis, 1989), pp. 99–116.

——, 'Entre Béguinisme et Mysticisme: La vie de Marie d'Oignies (d. 1213) de Jacques de Vitry ou la définition d'une sainteté féminine', *Ons Geestelijk Erf*, 66 (1992), 46–69.

——, '*Noli me tangere*: Marie Madeleine, Marie d'Oignies et les pénitentes de xiiiᵉ siècles', *Mélanges d'École française de Rome: Moyen Age*, 104 (1992), 209–68.

Lauwers, Michel and Walter Simons, *Béguins et béguines à Tournai au bas moyen âge: les communautés béguinales à Tournai du XIIIᵉ au XVᵉ siecle* (Tournai: Archives du chapitre Cathédral; Louvain-la-Neuve: Université Catholique de Louvain, 1988).

Leclercq, Jean, 'Jours d'ivresse', *La Vie Spirituelle*, 76 (1947), 574–91.

——, *Initiation aux auteurs monastiques du Moyen Âge: L'Amour des lettres et le Désir de Dieu*, 2nd edn. (Paris: Cerf, 1956).

——, *The Love of Learning and the Desire for God*, trans. by Catherine Misrahi (New York: Fordham University Press, 1960).

Le Goff, Jacques, *La Naissance du Purgatoire* (Paris: Gallimard, 1981).

——, *The Birth of Purgatory*, trans. by Arthur Goldhammer (Chicago: University of Chicago Press, 1984).

Lejeune, R., 'L'évêque de Toulouse: Foulquet de Marseille et la principauté de Liège', in *Mélanges Félix Rousseau: Études sur l'histoire du pays mosan au moyen-âge* (Brussels: La Renaissance du Livre, 1958), pp. 433–48.

Leyser, Henrietta, *Hermits and the New Monasticism: A Study of Religious Communities in Western Europe, 1000–1150* (London: Macmillan, 1984).

Link, E. M., 'Hugo von Oignies' (Inaugural-Dissertation, Albert-Ludwigs-Universität zu Freiburg im Breisgau, 1964).

Little, L. K., *Religious Poverty and the Profit Economy in Medieval Europe* (London: Elek, 1978).

Longère, Jean, *La Prédication médiévale* (Paris: Études augustiniennes, 1983).

——, 'Les chanoines réguliers d'après trois prédicateurs du XIIIᵉ siècle: Jacques de Vitry, Guibert de Tournai, Humbert de Romans', in *Le Monde des chanoines (XIᵉ–XIVᵉ siècle*s), ed. by Marie Humbert Vicaire (Toulouse: Edouard Privat, 1989).

Macy, Gary, *The Theologies of the Eucharist in the Early Scholastic Period: A Study of the Salvific Function of the Sacrament according to Theologians c. 1080–c. 1220* (Oxford: Clarendon Press, 1984).

Makowski, Elisabeth, '*Mulieres Religiosae*, Strictly Speaking: Some Fourteenth-Century Canonical Opinions', *Catholic Historical Review*, 85 (1999), 1–14.

Markowski, Michael, '*Crucesignatus*: Its Origins and Early Usage', *Journal of Medieval History*, 19 (1984), 157–65.

Marsolais, Miriam, 'Marie d'Oignies: Jacques de Vitry's Exemplum of an Ideal Victorine Mystic' (unpublished master's dissertation, Berkeley, Graduate Theological Union, 1988).

Matter, E. Ann., *The Voice of My Beloved: The Song of Songs in Western Medieval Christianity* (Philadelphia: University of Pennsylvania Press, 1990).

McCall, John P., 'Chaucer and the Pseudo Origen "De Maria Magdalena": A Preliminary Study', *Speculum*, 46 (1971), 491–509.

McDonnell, Ernest W., *The Beguines and Beghards in Medieval Culture, with Special Emphasis on the Belgian Scene* (New Brunswick: Rutgers University Press, 1954).

McEntire, Sandra, *The Doctrine of Compunction in Medieval England: Holy Tears* (Lewiston NY: Edwin Mellen Press, 1990).

McGuire, Brian, *Friendship and Community: The Monastic Experience, 350–1250* (Kalamazoo: Cistercian Publications, 1988).

——, 'Purgatory, the Communion of Saints, and Medieval Change', *Viator*, 20 (1989), 61–84.

McNamara, Jo Ann, 'Living Sermons: Consecrated Women and the Conversion of Gaul', in *Peace Weavers*, ed. by John A. Nichols and Lillian Thomas Shank (Kalamazoo: Cistercian Publications, 1987), pp. 19–37.

——, 'The Need to Give: Suffering and Female Sanctity in the Middle Ages', in *Images of Sainthood in Medieval Europe* ed. by Renate Blumenfeld-Kosinki and Timea Szell (Ithaca: Cornell University Press, 1991), pp. 199–221.

——, *Sisters in Arms: Catholic Nuns through Two Millennia* (Cambridge: Harvard University Press, 1996).

Mens, Alcantara, *Oorsprong en betekenis van de Nederlandse Begijnen- en Begardenbeweging: Vergelijkende studie, xii*^e*–xiii*^e *eeuw* (Antwerp: Standaard Boekhandel, 1947).

——, 'L'Ombrie italienne et l'Ombrie brabançonne: deux courants religieux parallèles d'inspiration commune', *Études Franciscaines*, 17 (1968), 44–47.

Metz, R., 'Recherches sur la condition de la femme selon Gratien', *Studia Gratiana*, 12 (1967), 377–96.

Moore, Robert I., 'Heresy, Repression, and Social Change in the Age of Gregorian Reform', in *Christendom and its Discontents: Exclusion, Persecution, and Rebellion, 1000–1500*, ed. by Scott L. Waugh and Peter D. Diehl (Cambridge: Cambridge University Press, 1996), pp. 19–46.

Monks and Nuns, Saints and Outcasts, ed. by Sharon Farmer and Barbara Rosenwein (Ithaca: Cornell University Press, 2000).

Muessig, Carolyn, 'Paradigms of Sanctity for Thirteenth-Century Women', in *Models of Holiness in Medieval Sermons*, ed. by Beverly Mayne Kienzle (Louvain-la-Neuve: Fédération Internationale des Instituts d'Études Médiévales, 1996), pp. 85–102.

——, 'Prophecy and Song: Teaching and Preaching by Medieval Women', in *Women Preachers and Prophets through Two Millennia of Christianity*, ed. by Beverly Mayne Kienzle and Pamela J. Walker (Berkeley: University of California Press, 1998), pp. 146–58.

——, 'Audience and Preacher: *Ad Status* Sermons and Social Classification', in *Preacher, Sermons and Audience in the Middle Ages*, ed. by Carolyn Muessig (Leiden: Brill, 2002), pp. 255–76.

Mulder-Bakker, Anneke B., *De Kluizenaar in de Eik: Gerlach van Houthem en zijn verering* (Hilversum: Verloren, 1995).

——, 'Yvetta of Huy: Mater et Magistra', in *Sanctity and Motherhood: Holy Mothers in the Middle Ages*, ed. by Anneke B. Mulder-Bakker (New York: Garland, 1995), pp. 225–58.

——, 'The Prime of their Lives: Women and Age, Wisdom and Religious Careers in Northern Europe', in *New Trends in Feminine Spirituality: The Holy Women of Liège and their Impact*, ed. by Juliette Dor, Lesley Johnson, and Jocelyn Wogan-Browne (Turnhout: Brepols, 1999), pp. 215–36.

——, 'Saints without a Past: Sacred Places and Intercessory Power in Saints' Lives from the Low Countries', in *The Invention of Saintliness*, ed. by Anneke B. Mulder-Bakker (London: Routledge, 2002), pp. 38–57.

Mundy, John Hine, *The Repression of Catharism at Toulouse: The Royal Diploma of 1279* (Toronto: Pontifical Institute of Mediaeval Studies, 1985).

Murray, A., 'Confession as a Historical Source in the Thirteenth Century', in *The Writing of History in the Middle Ages: Essays Presented to Richard William Southern*, ed. by R. H. Davis and J. M. Wallace-Hadrill (Oxford: Clarendon Press, 1981), pp. 275–322.

Neel, Carol, 'The Origins of the Beguines', *Signs: The Journal of Women in Culture and Society*, 14 (1989), 321–41.

New Trends in Feminine Spirituality: The Holy Women of Liège and their Impact, ed. by Juliette Dor, Lesley Johnson, and Jocelyn Wogan-Browne (Turnhout: Brepols, 1999).

Newman, Barbara, 'On the Threshold of the Dead: Purgatory, Hell, and Religious Women', in her *From Virile Woman to WomanChrist: Studies in Medieval Religion and Literature* (Philadelphia: University of Pennsylvania Press, 1995), pp. 108–36.

——, 'Possessed by the Spirit: Devout Women, Demoniacs, and the Apostolic Life in the Thirteenth Century', *Speculum*, 73 (1998), 733–70.

——, 'Devout Women and Demoniacs in the World of Thomas of Cantimpré', in *New Trends in Feminine Spirituality: The Holy Women of Liège and their Impact*, ed. by Juliette Dor, Lesley Johnson, and Jocelyn Wogan-Browne (Turnhout: Brepols, 1999), pp. 35–60.

——, 'What Did It Mean to Say "I Saw"?: The Clash Between Theory and Practice in Medieval Visionary Culture', *Speculum*, 81 (2005), 1–43.

Oliver, Judith, *Gothic Manuscript Illumination in the Diocese of Liège (c. 1250–c. 1330)* (Leuven: Peeters, 1988).

——, 'Devotional Psalters and the Study of Beguine Spirituality', in *On Pilgrimage: The Best of Vox Benedictina 1984–1993*, ed. by Elspeth Drurie and Dewey Kramer (Toronto: Peregrina, 1994), pp. 211–34.

On Pilgrimage: The Best of Vox Benedictina 1984–1993, ed. by Elspeth Drurie and Dewey Kramer (Toronto: Peregrina, 1994).

Peace Weavers, ed. by Lillian Thomas Shank and John A. Nichols (Kalamazoo: Cistercian Publications, 1987).

Petrakopoulos, Anja, 'Sanctity and Motherhood: Elizabeth of Thuringia', in *Sanctity and Motherhood: Holy Mothers in the Middle Ages*, ed. by Anneke B. Mulder-Bakker (New York: Garland, 1995), pp. 259–96.

Petroff, Elizabeth Alvida, *Medieval Women's Visionary Literature* (Oxford: Oxford University Press, 1986).

Platelle, Henri, 'La violence et ses remèdes en Flandres au XIe siècle', *Sacris erudiri*, 20 (1971), 101–73.

——, 'Le Recueil des miracles de Thomas de Cantimpré et la vie religieuse dans les Pays-Bas et le Nord de la France au XIIIe siècle', in *Actes de 97e Congrès National des Sociétés Savantes*,

Section de philologie et histoire jusqu'à 1610, Nantes, 1972 (Paris: Bibliothèque nationale, 1979), pp. 469–98.

Poncelet, Edouard, 'Chartes du Prieuré d'Oignies de l'ordre de Saint Augustin', *Annales de la Société archéologique de Namur*, 31 (1913), 1–104.

Prediche alle donne del secolo XIII: Testi di Umberto da Romans, Gilberto da Tournai, Stefano di Borbone, ed. by Carla Casagrande (Milan: Bompiani, 1978–).

Les Religieuses en France au XIIIᵉ siècle: table ronde organisée par l'Institut d'études médiévales de l'Université de Nancy II et le C.E.R.C.O.M., 25–26 juin 1983, ed. by Michel Parisse (Nancy: Presses universitaires de Nancy, 1985).

Religiöse Frauenbewegung und mystische Frömmigkeit im Mittelalter, ed. by Peter Dinzelbacher and Dieter R. Bauer (Cologne: Böhlau, 1988).

Renaissance and Renewal in the Twelfth Century, ed. by Robert L. Benson and Giles Constable (Oxford: Clarendon Press, 1982).

Ringler, Siegfried, *Viten- und Offenbarungsliteratur in Frauenklöstern des Mittelalters* (Munich: Artemis, 1980).

Roisin, Simone, 'L'efflorescence cistercienne et le courant féminin de piété au XIIIᵉ siècle', *Revue d'histoire ecclésiastique*, 39 (1945), 458–86.

——, *L'Hagiographie cistercienne dans le diocèse du Liège au xiiiᵉ siècle*, (Louvain: Bibliothèque de l'Université, 1947).

——, 'Réflexions sur la culture intellectuelle en nos abbayes cisterciennes médiévales', in *Miscellanea historica in honorem Leonis van Essen* (Brussels: Éditions Universitaires 1947), pp. 245–56.

Rubin, Miri, *Corpus Christi: The Eucharist in Late Medieval Culture* (Cambridge: Cambridge University Press, 1991).

Sanctity and Motherhood: Essays on Holy Mothers in the Middle Ages, ed. by Anneke B. Mulder-Bakker (New York: Garland, 1995).

Sandor, Monica, 'The Popular Preaching of Jacques de Vitry' (unpublished doctoral dissertation, University of Toronto, 1993).

——, 'Jacques de Vitry and the Spirituality of the *Mulieres Religiosae*', in *On Pilgrimage: The Best of Vox Benedictina 1984–1993*, ed. by Elspeth Drurie and Dewey Kramer (Toronto: Peregrina, 1994), pp. 173–89.

Schmidt, Hans J., 'Die trinitarische Spekulation in deutscher Mystik und Scholastik', *Zeitschrift für deutsche Philologie*, 72 (1953), 24–53.

Schmitt, Jean-Claude, *Mort d'un hérésie: l'église et les clercs face aux béguines et aux béghards du Rhin supérieure du XIVᵉ siècle* (Paris: Mouton, 1978).

——, *Les Revenants: les vivants et les morts dans la société médiévale* (Paris: Gallimard, 1994).

——, *Ghosts in the Middle Ages: The Living and the Dead in Medieval Society*, trans. by Teresa Lavender Fagan (Chicago: University of Chicago Press, 1998).

Schmitz, Yves, *Sainte Marie de Nivelles dite d'Oignies* (Nivelles: Les Presses de l'Imprimerie Havaux, 1963).

Schulenburg, Jane Tibbetts, 'Sexism and the Celestial Gynaeceum: From 500 to 1200', *Journal of Medieval History*, 4 (1978), 117–33.

——, 'The Heroics of Virginity: Brides of Christ and Sacrificial Mutilation', in *Women in the Middle Ages and the Renaissance: Literary and Historical Perspectives*, ed. by Mary Beth Rose (Syracuse: Syracuse University Press, 1986), pp. 29–72.

Seeing and Knowing: Women and Learning in Medieval Europe 1200–1550, ed. by Anneke B. Mulder-Bakker (Turnhout: Brepols, 2004).

Le Serpent et ses Symboles [...], ed. by Maryse Choisy, Alliance mondiale des religions, 9 (Méolans-Revel: Éditions DésIris, 1994).

Simons, Walter, 'The Beguine Movement in the Southern Low Countries: A Reassessment', *Bulletin de l'Institut historique Belge de Rome*, 54 (1989), 63–105.

——, 'Reading a Saint's Body: Rapture and Bodily Movement in the *Vitae* of Thirteenth-Century Beguines', in *Framing Medieval Bodies*, ed. by Sarah Kay and Miri Rubin (Manchester: Manchester University Press, 1994), pp. 1–23.

——, *Cities of Ladies: Beguine Communities in the Medieval Low Countries, 1200–1565* (Philadelphia: University of Pennsylvania Press, 2001).

——, 'Staining the Speech of Things Divine: The Uses of Literacy in Medieval Beguine Communities', in *The Voice of Silence: Women's Literacy in a Men's Church*, ed. by Thérèse de Hemptinne and Maria Eugenia Góngora (Turnhout: Brepols, 2004), pp. 85–110.

Southern, R. W., *Western Society and the Church in the Middle Ages* (Harmondsworth: Penguin, 1970).

Sweetman, Robert, 'Thomas of Cantimpré, *Mulieres Religiosae* and Purgational Piety: Hagiographic *Vitae* and the Beguine "Voice"', in *In a Distinct Voice: Medieval Studies in Honor of Leonard E. Boyle*, ed. by Jacqueline Brown and William P. Stoneman (Notre Dame: Notre Dame University Press, 1997), pp. 606–28.

Teetaert, Amedée, *La Confession aux laïques dans l'église latine depuis le VIIIᵉ siècle jusqu'au XIVᵉ siècle: étude de théologie positive* (Paris: Gabalda, 1926).

Thurston, Herbert, *The Physical Phenomena of Mysticism* (Chicago: Regnery, 1952).

——, *Surprising Mystics* (London: Burns and Oates, 1955).

Le Trésor d'Oignies et le Frère Hugo: Exposition, crypte de la Collégiale Sainte Gertrude 1 juin–15 juillet 1963 (Nivelles: Imprimerie Havaux, 1963).

Van der Toorn-Piebenga, Gryte A., 'De *Vita Mariae Oigniacensis* in Scandinavie', *Ons Geestelijk Erf*, 65 (1991), 13–22.

Van Ostade, Annick, 'Het Leven van de gelukzalige Maria van Oignies' (graduate paper, Katholieke Universiteit Leuven, Departement Geschiedenis, n.d.).

Vauchez, André, *La Sainteté en occident aux derniers siècles du moyen âge d'après les procès de canonisation et les documents hagiographiques* (Rome: École française de Rome, 1981).

——, *Les Laïcs au moyen âge: pratiques et expériences* (Paris: Cerf, 1987).

——, 'Prosélitisme et action antihérétique en milieu féminin au XIIIᵉ siècle: La vie de Marie d'Oignies (d. 1213) par Jacques de Vitry', in *Propagande et contre-propagande religieuses*, ed. by Jacques Marx (Brussels: Éditions de l'Université de Bruxelles, 1987), pp. 95–110.

——, *The Laity in the Middle Ages: Religious Beliefs and Devotional Practices*, trans. by Margery J. Schneider, ed. by Daniel E. Bornstein (Notre Dame: University of Notre Dame Press, 1993).

——, *The Spirituality of the Medieval West: From the Eighth to the Twelfth Century*, trans. by Colette Friedlander (Kalamazoo: Cistercian Publications, 1993).

——, *La Spiritualité du moyen âge occidental: VIIIᵉ–XIIIᵉ siècles* (Paris: Seuil, 1994).

——, *Sainthood in the Later Middle Ages*, trans. by Jean Birrell (Cambridge: Cambridge University Press, 1997).

——, 'Saints admirables et saint imitables: les fonctions de l'hagiographie ont-elles changé aux derniers siècles du moyen-âge?', in *Les Fonctions des saints dans le monde occidental (IIIe–XIIIe siècle)*, introd. by Jean-Yves Tilliette (Rome: École française de Rome, 1991), pp. 161–72.

Voluntate Dei leprosus: les lépreux entre conversion et exclusion aux XIIème siècle, ed. by Nicole Bériou and François-Olivier Touati (Spoleto: Centro italiano di studi sull'alto medioevo, 1991).

Warren, Ann K. *Anchorites and their Patrons in Medieval England* (Berkeley: University of California Press, 1985).

Wenzel, Siegfried, 'Acedia 700–1200', *Traditio*, 22 (1966), 73–102.

——, *The Sin of Sloth: Acedia in Medieval Thought and Literature* (Chapel Hill: University of North Carolina Press, 1967).

Winston-Allen, Anne, *Stories of the Rose: The Making of the Rosary in the Middle Ages* (University Park, PA: Pennsylvania State University Press, 1997).

Women Preachers and Prophets through Two Millennia of Christianity, ed. by Beverly Mayne Kienzle and Pamela J. Walker (Berkeley: University of California Press, 1998).

Ziegler, Joanna E., 'The Curtis Beguinage in the Southern Low Countries and Art Patronage: Interpretation and Historiography', *Bulletin de l'Institut historique belge de Rome*, 57 (1987), 31–70.

——, *Sculpture of Compassion: The Pietà and the Beguines in the Southern Low Countries c. 1300–c. 1600* (Brussels: Institut historique belge de Rome; Rome: Academia Belgica, 1992).

CONTRIBUTORS

Brenda M. Bolton taught history at Queen Mary and Westfield College, University of London. Her publications on beguines and religious women in the Low Countries are seminal. Her recent publications mostly concern Pope Innocent III.

Hugh Feiss is a Benedictine monk at the Monastery of the Ascension, Jerome, ID, USA. He received graduate degrees from the Catholic University of America, University of Iowa, and the Anselmianum (Rome). He has translated a number of medieval works, most recently, with Ronald Pepin, *Mary of Egypt: Three Medieval Lives in Verse* (Cistercian Publications).

Suzan Folkerts (MA) graduated in Medieval History and Medieval Studies at the University of Groningen. She co-operated in the project 'Narrative Historical Sources in the Northern Low Countries, 600–1550', at the Department of History of the University of Groningen. Since 2003 she has been working on her PhD thesis on the late-medieval transmission of thirteenth-century *Vitae* of pious laymen and women of the southern Low Countries at the same university.

Margot H. King obtained her PhD (1967) at the University of California at Berkeley in Comparative Literature. In 1982 she founded Peregrina Publishing Co., and published annotated translations of female saints' lives, with introductions and bibliographies. In 1984 she published the first issue of *Vox Benedictina*, a journal devoted to a study of the lives and writings of religious women and men. . *Vox Benedictina* ceased publication in 1994 but she continued to publish the Peregrina translations until her official retirement in 2005. Among her publications are *The Desert Mothers: A Survey of the Female Anchoretic Tradition* (1984); translations of *The Life of Christina Mirabilis*, by Thomas de Cantimpré (1985), *The Life of Marie d'Oignies,* by Jacques de Vitry (1988), *The Life of Lutgard of Aywières,* by Thomas de Cantimpré (1989), and *The Life of Margaret of Ypres*, by Thomas de Cantimpré (1990). She is currently organizing her large collection of early woodcuts for Monastic Matrix, an online scholarly resource for the study of European Christian women from 400 to 1600 CE.

Anneke B. Mulder-Bakker was trained in history and Church history as well as in medieval studies. She taught at the University of Groningen and is now Emerita at Leiden University where she is affiliated to the research project on medieval Dutch literature and learning. She has published widely on historiographical and hagiographical topics as well as gender. Among her studies published in English are *Sanctity and Motherhood* (1995), *The Invention of Saintliness* (2003), *Seeing and Knowing: Women and Learning in Medieval Europe* (2004), *The Prime of Their Lives; Wise Old Women in Pre-Industrial Europe* (2004), and *Lives of the Anchoresses: The Rise of the Urban Recluse in Medieval Europe* (2005).

MEDIEVAL WOMEN: TEXTS AND CONTEXTS

All volumes in this series are evaluated by an Editorial Board, strictly on academic grounds, based on reports prepared by referees who have been commissioned by virtue of their specialism in the appropriate field. The Board ensures that the screening is done independently and without conflicts of interest. The definitive texts supplied by authors are also subject to review by the Board before being approved for publication. Further, the volumes are copyedited to conform to the publisher's stylebook and to the best international academic standards in the field.

Titles in series

Jutta and Hildegard : The Biographical Sources, ed. by Anna Silvas (1998).

New Trends in Feminine Spirituality: The Holy Women of Liège and their Impact, ed. by Juliette Dor, Lesley Johnson and Jocelyn Wogan-Browne (1999).

Medieval Women: Texts and Contexts in Late Medieval Britain: Essays for Felicity Riddy, ed. by Jocelyn Wogan-Browne, Rosalynn Voaden, Arlyn Diamond, Ann Hutchinson, Carol Meale, and Lesley Johnson (2000).

The Knowing of Woman's Kind in Childing: A Middle English Version of Material Derived from the Trotula and other Sources, ed. by Alexandra Barratt (2001).

Seeing and Knowing: Women and Learning in Medieval Europe 1200–1550, ed. by Anneke B. Mulder-Bakker (2004).

Send Me God: The Lives of Ida the Compassionate of Nivelles, Nun of La Ramée, Arnulf, Lay Brother of Villers, and Abundus, Monk of Villers, by Goswin of Bossut, trans. by and with an introduction by Martinus Cawley OCSO and with a preface by Barbara Newman (2003).

St Katherine of Alexandria: Texts and Contexts in Western Medieval Europe, ed. by Jacqueline Jenkins and Katherine J. Lewis (2003).

Writing the Wilton Women: Goscelin's Legend of Edith and *Liber confortatorius*, ed. by Stephanie Hollis with W. R. Barnes, Rebecca Hayward, Kathleen Loncar, and Michael Wright (2004).

Household, Women, and Christianities in Late Antiquity and the Middle Ages, ed. by Anneke B. Mulder-Bakker and Jocelyn Wogan-Browne (2006)

The Writings of Julian of Norwich: 'A Vision Showed to a Devout Women' and 'A Revelation of Love', ed. by Nicholas Watson and Jacqueline Jenkins (2006)

Les Cantiques Salemon: The Song of Songs in MS Paris BNF fr. 14966, ed. by Tony Hunt (2006)

Carolyn P. Collette, *Performing Polity: Women and Agency in the Anglo-French Tradition, 1385–1620* (2006)